The North Korean Conundrum:
Balancing Human Rights and Nuclear Security

THE NORTH KOREAN CONUNDRUM: BALANCING HUMAN RIGHTS AND NUCLEAR SECURITY

Edited by Robert R. King and Gi-Wook Shin

Stanford

Walter H. Shorenstein
Asia-Pacific Research Center
Freeman Spogli Institute

THE WALTER H. SHORENSTEIN ASIA-PACIFIC RESEARCH CENTER
(Shorenstein APARC) addresses critical issues affecting the countries of Asia, their regional and global affairs, and U.S.-Asia relations. As Stanford University's hub for the interdisciplinary study of contemporary Asia, we produce policy-relevant research, provide education and training to students, scholars, and practitioners, and strengthen dialogue and cooperation between counterparts in the Asia-Pacific and the United States.

The Walter H. Shorenstein Asia-Pacific Research Center
Freeman Spogli Institute for International Studies
Stanford University
Encina Hall
Stanford, CA 94305-6055
http://aparc.fsi.stanford.edu

The North Korean Conundrum: Balancing Human Rights and Nuclear Security
may be ordered from:
Brookings Institution Press
https://www.brookings.edu/bipress/
books@brookings.edu

Walter H. Shorenstein Asia-Pacific Research Center, 2021.
Copyright © 2021 by the Board of Trustees of the Leland Stanford Junior University.

Library of Congress Control Number: 2021946422

First printing, 2021
ISBN 978-1-931368-65-0

Contents

Tables and Figures

Tables

Figures

Abbreviations

CEDAW	Convention on the Elimination of All Forms of Discrimination against Women
COI	Commission of Inquiry
CPR	civil and political rights
CRC	Convention on the Rights of the Child
CRPD	Convention of the Rights of Persons with Disabilities
DMZ	Demilitarized Zone
DPRK	Democratic People's Republic of Korea (North Korea)
EOV	explanation of vote
GA	UN General Assembly
GDR	German Democratic Republic
HRC	UN Human Rights Council
ICC	International Criminal Court
ICCPR	International Covenant on Civil and Political Rights
ICESCR	International Covenant on Economic, Social, and Cultural Rights
ICT	information and communications technology
IAEA	International Atomic Energy Agency
IMEI	international mobile equipment identity
KCNA	Korean Central News Agency (North Korea)
KCTV	Korean Central Television (North Korea)
NGO	non-governmental organization
NKHR	Citizens' Alliance for North Korean Human Rights

NKHRA	North Korean Human Rights Act
OGD	Organizational Guidance Department (North Korea)
OHCHR	Office of the High Commissioner for Human Rights (UN)
PAD	Propaganda and Agitation Department (North Korea)
PDS	public distribution system
R2P	Responsibility to Protect
ROK	Republic of Korea (South Korea)
SEZ	special economic zone
SNK	Save North Korea (ROK NGO)
SR	special rapporteur
SSD	State Security Department
UDHR	Universal Declaration of Human Rights
UNGA	UN General Assembly
UNSC	UN Security Council
UPR	Universal Periodic Review
VOA	Voice of America
WGEID	Working Group on Enforced or Involuntary Disappearances (UN HRC)

Contributors

TAE-UNG BAIK is a professor of law at the William S. Richardson School of Law and the director of the Center for Korean Studies at the University of Hawaii at Manoa. He is also serving as chair-rapporteur of the United Nations Human Rights Council Working Group on Enforced or Involuntary Disappearances, which reviews enforced disappearance cases submitted by UN member states. Baik teaches international human rights law, comparative law, and Korean law, and previously taught at the Faculty of Law, University of British Columbia. He received his first law degree from Seoul National University's College of Law, and earned his master's (LLM) and doctoral (JSD) degrees in international human rights law from Notre Dame Law School. He was admitted to the bar as an attorney-at-law in the State of New York.

Baik was a visiting scholar at the East Asian Legal Studies Program, Harvard University Law School. He worked for Human Rights Watch in New York as a research intern and consultant, and served on the 56th United Nations Sub-Commission on the Promotion and Protection of Human Rights as a legal adviser to the delegation of South Korea. Baik was engaged in the democracy movement in the Republic of Korea in the 1980s and 1990s and was incarcerated twice, with Amnesty International designating him as a prisoner of conscience. His selected publications include *Seeking the Human Rights Community in Asia* (in Korean, 2017), "Nonjudicial Punishments of Political Offenses in North Korea—With a Focus on *Kwanriso*" (*American Journal of Comparative Law*, 2016), and *Emerging Regional Human Rights Systems in Asia* (2012).

VICTOR CHA holds the D.S. Song-KF Professorship in Government and International Affairs and serves as vice dean for faculty and graduate affairs in the School of Foreign Service at Georgetown University. He is also senior vice president and the Korea Chair at the Center for Strategic and International Studies in Washington, D.C. He is a Senior Fellow in Human Freedom at the George W. Bush Institute. He was a 2019–20 Koret Fellow in the Korea Program at the Shorenstein Asia-Pacific Research Center. From 2004 to 2007 he served in the White House as director for Asian affairs at the National Security Council. In that position, he was responsible primarily for Japan, the Korean Peninsula, Australia/New Zealand, and Pacific Island nation affairs. Cha was also the deputy head of delegation for the United States at the Six-Party Talks in Beijing, and received two Outstanding Service commendations during his tenure at the National Security Council. He is the author of five books, including the award-winning *Alignment Despite Antagonism: The United States-Korea-Japan Security Triangle* (Stanford University Press, 1999), and *The Impossible State: North Korea, Past and Future* (Harper Collins Ecco, 2012), which *Foreign Affairs* named in 2012 as a "Best Book on the Asia-Pacific." His most recent book is *Powerplay: Origins of the American Alliance System in Asia* (Princeton University Press, 2016). Cha holds a BA, MIA, and PhD from Columbia University, as well as an MA from Oxford University.

THOMAS FINGAR is a Shorenstein APARC Fellow in the Freeman Spogli Institute for International Studies at Stanford University. He was the inaugural Oksenberg-Rohlen Distinguished Fellow (2010–15) and the Payne Distinguished Lecturer at Stanford in 2009. From 2005 through 2008, he served as the first deputy director of national intelligence for analysis and, concurrently, as chairman of the National Intelligence Council. Fingar served previously as assistant secretary of the State Department's Bureau of Intelligence and Research (2000–01 and 2004–05), principal deputy assistant secretary (2001–03), deputy assistant secretary for analysis (1994–2000), director of the Office of Analysis for East Asia and the Pacific (1989–94), and chief of the China Division (1986–89). Between 1975 and 1986 he held a number of positions at Stanford University, including senior research associate in the Center for International Security and Arms Control.

Fingar is a graduate of Cornell University (AB in government and history), and Stanford University (MA and PhD both in political science).

His most recent books are *Reducing Uncertainty: Intelligence Analysis and National Security* (Stanford University Press, 2011), *The New Great Game: China and South and Central Asia in the Era of Reform*, editor (Stanford University Press, 2016), *Uneasy Partnerships: China and Japan, the Koreas, and Russia in the Era of Reform* (Stanford University Press, 2017), *Fateful Decisions: Choices that Will Shape China's Future*, co-edited with Jean Oi (Stanford University Press, 2020), and *From Mandate to Blueprint: Lessons from Intelligence Reform* (Stanford University Press, 2021).

RYAN KAMINSKI was previously the policy advisor for human rights at the United Nations Foundation. Before that, he worked as a consultant and research associate with the Council on Foreign Relations' International Institutions and Global Governance Program. Kaminski was also a Fulbright English Teaching Fellow at the Education University of Hong Kong. He holds a master's in international affairs from Columbia University, and a bachelor's from the University of Chicago. Kaminski is a Council on Foreign Relations Term Member and Security Fellow with the Truman National Security Project.

MINJUNG KIM is an associate executive director at Save North Korea (SNK), a human rights NGO helping North Korean refugees, and a vice president at *Future Korea Media*, a media company that publishes a biweekly journal focusing on international and domestic issues in South Korea. She is an omni-activist whose work ranges from mid-wave radio broadcasting and the management, from planning to execution, of diverse human rights improvement projects for North Korea, to the operation of a media company that covers national defense, national security, and foreign policy. She has successfully raised an annual budget of $300,000 to support mid-wave radio broadcasting, and produces radio programs as a project director. Her work with SNK began at its birth in 1999. Since then, she has organized and presented research results at numerous seminars and events on North Korea worldwide and organized public campaigns to increase public awareness of North Korean human rights abuses and to mobilize global public opinion into action. Kim has also developed and coordinated various projects, including sending leaflet-balloons and hidden cameras into North Korea to encourage internal and civil activities, assisting the movement of North Korean refugees into South Korea via underground railroads, and aiding refugees to adjust socially and culturally. At *Future Korea Journal*, she has written, researched, and edited articles on North Korean affairs. Kim is a visiting researcher at the Walsh School of Foreign Service of Georgetown University. She was a research fellow at the Yonsei Institute for Modern Korean Studies and at the Korea Advanced Institute of Science & Technology (KAIST). Kim received an MA and a BA from Yonsei University and is a PhD candidate for international studies at the Yonsei Graduate School of International Studies.

ROBERT R. KING was the 2019–20 Koret Fellow for the fall quarter at Shorenstein Asia-Pacific Research Center. From 2009 to 2017 King served as the special envoy for North Korean human rights issues at the Department of State, an ambassadorial-ranked position. He has been senior advisor to the Korea Chair at the Center for Strategic and International Studies, a senior fellow at the Korea Economic Institute, and a board member of the Committee for Human Rights in North Korea in Washington, DC. Previously, King served for 25 years on Capitol Hill (1983–2008) as chief of staff to Congressman Tom Lantos (D-California), and staff director of the House Foreign Affairs Committee (2001–08). King is author of *Patterns of Impunity: Human Rights in North Korea and the Role of the U.S. Special Envoy* (Shorenstein Asia-Pacific Research Center, 2021). He has a PhD from the Fletcher School of Law and Diplomacy, Tufts University.

SEAN KING joined Park Strategies, a New York business advisory firm managed by former U.S. senator Alfonse M. D'Amato, in 2006. His focus is Asia, generating business and supporting clients in the region. He is also an affiliated scholar at the University of Notre Dame's Liu Institute for Asia and Asian Studies. Before joining Park Strategies, King spent five years at the U.S. Department of Commerce in Washington, DC, where he served as senior advisor for Asia in the U.S. and Foreign Commercial Service. Before joining Commerce, he was based in Singapore for both PricewaterhouseCoopers and Citibank. He also worked for the New York State Department of Economic Development, on whose behalf he led a 1997 trade mission to Taiwan. King makes regular public speaking appearances, is a frequent on-air television guest, and his opinions and quotes have appeared in numerous publications. He has authored two book chapters on Taiwan. He has an MBA from Notre Dame and an undergraduate degree from American University in Washington, DC. As part of his MBA, King did a summer internship for Citibank in Taipei. In a previous Cold War life, he visited the former East Germany four times. He is fluent in Swedish.

MICHAEL KIRBY is a former Justice of the High Court of Australia. When he retired from the High Court of Australia in 2009, Kirby was Australia's longest-serving judge. He was acting chief justice of Australia twice. He has served on three university governing bodies, being elected chancellor of Macquarie University in Sydney (1984–93). He served as a member of the World Health Organization's Global Commission on AIDS (1988–92); as president of the International Commission of Jurists, Geneva (1995–98); as UN Special Representative for Human Rights in Cambodia (1993–96); as a member of the UNESCO International Bioethics Committee (1995–2005); as a member of the High Commissioner for Human Rights' Judicial Reference Group (2007–09); and as a member of the UNAIDS Reference Group on HIV and Human Rights(2004–19). He was a commissioner of the UNDP Global Commission of HIV and the Law (2011–12). Kirby was appointed to the Advisory Council of Transparency International, based in Berlin, in 2012. In 2013–14, he was appointed chair of the UN Commission of Inquiry on Human Rights Violations in North Korea. He was a commissioner of the UNAIDS Lancet Commission on AIDS to the Right to Health (2013–14); the Global Fund's Equitable Access Panel (2015–16); the UN Secretary-General's High Level Panel on Access to Essential Medicines (2015–16); and UNAIDS/OHCHR's panel on overreach of criminal law (2017); and co-chair of the International Bar Association's Human Rights Institute (2018–present). Kirby was awarded the Australian Human Rights Medal in 1991, the Gruber Justice Prize in 2010, and has been Patron of the Kirby Institute on Blood Borne Diseases in UNSW Sydney, Australia, since 2011. In May 2017 he was invested by Japan with the insignia of the Order of the Rising Sun, Gold and Silver Star in Tokyo, with an audience with the emperor of Japan. In 2018 he was elected a Fellow of the Royal Society of New South Wales; he was named for the 2018 United Nations Honour by the United Nations Association of Australia; he was appointed a Distinguished Fellow of Australia and New Zealand School of Government in 2019; he was also named winner of the Global 100 Firm of the Year-Arbitration-Australia, and Bali International Arbitration and Mediation Centre named him one of its 2019 top ten arbitrators in the Asia/

Pacific. In 2019 Macquarie University conferred on him the honorary title of Chancellor Emeritus "as a public recognition of [his] exceptional and distinguished service to the University, and in perpetuity."

NAT KRETCHUN is the senior vice president for programs at the Open Technology Fund (OTF), a congressionally funded non-profit organization that supports the development and deployment of anti-censorship, privacy, and security technologies for populations living under repressive information censorship regimes. Kretchun oversees programmatic activities for OTF's multi-million-dollar funding portfolio. He previously served as a senior associate director at InterMedia, where he managed quantitative and qualitative research projects with a particular focus on Asia and hard-to-access populations. He has designed, fielded, and analyzed studies ranging from large-scale nationally representative surveys of China to qualitative studies examining digital communication patterns among Uyghur populations. Since 2009, he has done extensive research with North Korean refugees, defectors, and travelers, running annual surveys and conducting qualitative studies for a number of government and non-government clients focused on information access in North Korea. He is the primary author of *A Quiet Opening: North Koreans in a Changing Media Environment* and its follow-up, *Compromising Connectivity: Information Dynamics Between the State and Society in a Digitizing North Korea.*

JOON OH is a professor of United Nations studies at Kyung Hee University in Seoul, Korea. He is also the chair of Save the Children Korea and a board member of Save the Children International. Previously he was Ambassador and Permanent Representative of the Republic of Korea to the United Nations in New York from 2013 to 2016. During that time, he also served as the 71st president of the Economic and Social Council and as president of the Conference of States Parties to the Convention on the Rights of Persons with Disabilities in 2015 and 2016. Before that, he was the Korean ambassador to Singapore (2010–13) and deputy minister for multilateral and global affairs in the Ministry of Foreign Affairs and Trade in Seoul (2008–10). The Korean government twice awarded him the Order of Service Merit, in 1996 and 2006. In 2018, Oh received a Global Korea Award from Michigan State University. Rehabilitation International gave him a Global Presidential Award in 2016 in acknowledgment of his achievements as president of the Convention on the Rights of Persons with Disabilities.

He also received the 2014 Youngsan Diplomat of the Year award for his work on North Korean human rights issues. He published his first book in Korean, *For Mica, Who Contemplates Life*, in 2015. He received a master's degree in international policy studies from Stanford University in 1991.

GI-WOOK SHIN is the William J. Perry Professor of Contemporary Korea in sociology and a senior fellow at the Freeman Spogli Institute for International Studies at Stanford University. He established Stanford's Korea Program in 2001, and has been directing the Walter H. Shorenstein Asia-Pacific Research Center at Stanford since 2005. As a historical-comparative and political sociologist, his research concentrates on social movements, nationalism, development, and international relations, with focus on Korea and broader Asia. Shin is the author/editor of over twenty books and numerous articles. His books include *Shifting Gears in Innovation Policy from Asia* (2020), *Strategic, Policy and Social Innovation for a Post- Industrial Korea: Beyond the Miracle* (2018); *Divergent Memories: Opinion Leaders and the Asia-Pacific War* (2016); *Global Talent* (2015); *New Challenges for Maturing Democracies in Korea and Taiwan* (2014); and *One Alliance, Two Lenses: U.S.-Korea Relations in a New Era* (2010). Shin is currently writing a book to explain the rise of four Asia-Pacific giants (Japan, China, India, and Australia) and editing a volume on Korean democracy.

MARTYN WILLIAMS is a non-resident fellow at the Stimson Center's 38 North and founder of the "North Korea Tech" blog. A long-time watcher of North Korean technology, in 2019 he authored *Digital Trenches: North Korea's Information Counter-Offensive,* a report on the DPRK's response to digital communications, for the Committee for Human Rights in North Korea. Williams is originally from the United Kingdom and has been based in the United States since 2011, after living for sixteen years in Tokyo, Japan. He was previously a journalist for IDG News Service, a technology newswire, in both Tokyo and San Francisco and was a 2011–12 Knight Journalism Fellow at Stanford University.

PETER YEO is senior vice-president at the United Nations Foundation (UNF) and leads the foundation's strategic engagement with Congress and U.S. administrations to advance policy changes that support the

UN's work for global progress. Under Yeo's leadership, the foundation has helped ensure multi-billion-dollar payments from the U.S. government to the UN; forged a strategic alliance with the United Nations Association of the United States of America to create the largest network of UN supporters across the United States; championed U.S. law standing against child marriage with the support of Girl Up; and advanced year-over-year increases in U.S. bilateral and multilateral global health spending. Yeo joined the UNF and the Better World Campaign in 2009 with over twenty years of legislative, analytical, and management experience, including senior roles on Capitol Hill and in the State Department. Prior to arriving at UNF, Yeo served for ten years as the deputy staff director at the House Foreign Affairs Committee chaired by Rep. Tom Lantos (D-CA) and Rep. Howard Berman (D-CA). He has worked on a broad range of foreign policy and foreign aid issues. On behalf of the House Foreign Affairs Committee Democrats, he led the successful negotiations for the landmark HIV/AIDS, Tuberculosis, and Malaria Act of 2003, commonly known as PEPFAR, as well as the successful $50 billion reauthorization of the law in 2008. He also shepherded into law several measures dealing with China, Tibet, Burma, and East Timor. Prior to his work with the committee, he served as a deputy assistant secretary at the U.S. State Department during the second Clinton administration, where he led the negotiations around repayment of the U.S. arrears to the United Nations and was part of the U.S. delegation to the climate negotiations in Kyoto. Yeo holds a BA in East Asian studies from Wesleyan University as well as an MA in East Asian studies from Harvard University. He is also a member of the Council on Foreign Relations, a leading independent nonpartisan foreign policy think tank, and a board member of the U.S. Global Leadership Coalition.

Preface

Organized by the Korea Program at the Shorenstein Asia-Pacific Research Center (APARC), the Koret Workshop brings together an international panel of experts in Korean affairs to discuss contemporary Korean affairs and U.S.-Korean relations. This book is based on papers presented and discussed at a three-part conference on North Korean human rights, held on June 16–18, 2020, at Stanford University. Initially scheduled to be held on March 13, 2020, it was postponed to June and conducted virtually due to COVID-19. In close collaboration with the Center's 2019 Koret Fellow, Ambassador Robert King, a former U.S. special envoy for North Korean human rights, the conference convened leading experts and practitioners working on North Korea from the United States, South Korea, and Australia.

As is apparent, issues of human rights in North Korea are complex and involve multiple actors. They are related to matters such as North Korean living conditions, inter-Korean relations, denuclearization, information flows to the country, and international cooperation, to name a few. Likewise, they involve various actors. Besides the two governments of Korea, they include South Korean NGOs and activists, the U.S. government, the United Nations, and global human rights groups. As such, the chapters assembled in this book seek to capture the multiplicity of issues and actors related to human rights in North Korea. In particular, we focus on three interrelated issues: the UN's role (chapters 2–4), information flows (chapters 5–7), and denuclearization (chapters 8 and 9). We conclude the book with two comparative discussions (chapters 10 and 11).

Besides the chapter authors, a number of experts attended the conference to serve as paper discussants and provide valuable input. They included: Greg Scarlatoiu, executive director of the Committee for Human Rights in North Korea; Andray Abrahamian, a foreign service officer at the U.S. Department of State and a former Koret Fellow at Shorenstein APARC; Stephen Noerper, senior director for policy at the Korea Society; Keith Luse, executive director at the National Committee on North Korea; Dafna Zur, associate professor of Korean literature and culture at Stanford University; Yumi Moon, associate professor of history at Stanford University; and Annika Betancourt, visiting fellow at the Brookings Institution's Center for East Asia Policy Studies. Yong Suk Lee, deputy director of the Korea Program at Shorenstein APARC, served as a moderator.

I am grateful to the Koret Foundation for its generous support of the conference and the Koret Fellowship. I also extend my appreciation to Heather Ahn and George Krompacky at Shorenstein APARC for their valuable support in organizing the conference and preparing this volume, respectively.

Gi-Wook Shin
Director
Shorenstein APARC & the Korea Program

The North Korean Conundrum

1 North Korea: Human Rights and Nuclear Security

An Introduction

Robert R. King and Gi-Wook Shin

In June 2020, Tomás Ojea Quintana, the United Nations special rapporteur on human rights in the Democratic People's Republic of Korea (DPRK), warned that the country faced "widespread food shortages and malnutrition" since the closure of its border with China in order to prevent the spread of the COVID-19 virus. Some 90 percent of North Korea's trade comes from or through China, and the border closing created significant economic difficulties. Quintana called for North Korea to immediately release prisoners with vulnerable health conditions consistent with UN recommendations. He also called for the UN Security Council to "reconsider" sanctions on North Korea to ensure the flow of food supplies to those in need.[1]

That same day, the U.S. Department of State released its annual International Religious Freedom Report, noting U.S. sponsorship of a UN General Assembly resolution condemning North Korea's "longstanding and ongoing systematic, widespread, and gross violations of human rights." The report added that the United States had extended the designation of the North as a "Country of Particular Concern," and an improvement in human rights, including religious freedom, would be required for the full normalization of relations between the two countries.[2] While North Korea's nuclear weapons and its security

---

1 Office of the UN High Commissioner for Human Rights, "Media Statement by the UN Special Rapporteur on the Situation of Human Rights in the Democratic People's Republic of Korea," June 9, 2020, https://www.ohchr.org/en/NewsEvents/Pages/DisplayNews.aspx?NewsID=25929&LangID=E.
2 U.S. Department of State, *Democratic People's Republic of Korea (DPRK) 2019, International Religious Freedom Report* (Washington, DC: U. S. Department

threat have occupied the center stage and eclipsed other issues in recent years, human rights remain important to U.S. policy. The issue is not a luxury or an obstacle to the urgent international effort to deal with the North's threat to international security, but should be an integral part of policy toward the North.

We are not suggesting that human rights should have the highest priority in dealing with the North, but we seek to explore the role that human rights ought to play as a key element of any comprehensive policy for dealing with North Korea. There is no question that security issues are of great concern to the United States, South Korea, and the rest of the world. But there is also no question that focusing on security issues to the exclusion of other issues will not bring a resolution to the North Korean threat. The question is how we can move forward in a way that addresses the very serious security concerns while at the same time bringing human rights and humanitarian concerns into the equation. The objective is not to delegitimize or undermine the regime but rather to help North Korea to move toward becoming a positive and contributing participant in the international community.

Human Rights and U.S. Policy on the DPRK

Former president Donald Trump initially treated human rights as a stick to use against the North in order to induce Pyongyang to make progress on denuclearization. In his first United Nations speech in New York City in September 2017, he verbally attacked Kim Jong-un with derogatory epithets, including labeling him "Little Rocket Man." As part of his attack, he also publicly denounced the North's human rights record: "No one has shown more contempt for other nations and for the well-being of their own people than the depraved regime in North Korea."[3]

Just a few months later, in January 2018, in his first State of the Union Address before a joint session of the United States Congress, the president devoted one-tenth of his speech to North Korea, with

---

of State, 2019), https://www.state.gov/wp-content/uploads/2020/06/KOREA-DEM -REP-2019-INTERNATIONAL-RELIGIOUS-FREEDOM-REPORT.pdf.

3 "Remarks by President Trump to the 72nd Session of the United Nations General Assembly," September 19, 2017, Trump White House archive, https://trump whitehouse.archives.gov/briefings-statements/remarks-president-trump-72nd -session-united-nations-general-assembly/.

much of that criticism focused on its human rights record.[4] A group of North Korean defectors sat with Mrs. Trump in the gallery of the House of Representatives during the speech. Also with Mrs. Trump were the parents of American college student Otto Warmbier, who had been arrested and held in a North Korean prison for a year and a half before being returned to his family in the United States in a comatose state. He died shortly after his return. One of the iconic moments of the State of the Union Address was when the president introduced Ji Seong-ho, a refugee from North Korea who, while searching for food during the North's famine in the mid-1990s, was horribly injured in a fall from a moving train. Mr. Ji held his crutches over his head in a gesture of triumph as the U.S. Congress gave him a standing ovation.[5]

Two months after that speech, President Trump agreed to meet with North Korean leader Kim Jong-un in Singapore. The summit on June 12, 2018, was a media frenzy, producing multiple images of smiling leaders but little in terms of substantive agreement. Nine months later, in February 2019, the two leaders met again in Hanoi, Vietnam, but that session ended badly when the final round of discussions, the closing meal, and the scheduled ceremonial signing of a joint statement were all abruptly canceled. Both leaders brusquely left Hanoi without a proper farewell. The two met again briefly a few months later with South Korean president Moon Jae-in on June 30, 2019, for photographs, holding hands and chatting in the Demilitarized Zone between the two Koreas. This took place during a visit by President Trump to Seoul and the meeting did not involve substantive discussions with the North Korean leader, however.

No further progress was made during the Trump presidency. No meaningful progress was made on denuclearization, and North Korean invective against the United States resumed. Even the dialogue between North and South Korea sputtered to a halt, despite repeated calls from Seoul. In June 2020, the North carefully choreographed the perfect

---

4 "Remarks by President Trump in State of the Union Address," January 30, 2018, Trump White House archive, https://trumpwhitehouse.archives.gov/briefings-statements/remarks-president-trump-state-union-address/.

5 Mr. Ji was subsequently elected a member of the South Korea National Assembly in April 2020. Robert R. King, "Two Prominent Defectors Elected to South Korean National Assembly," *The Peninsula* (blog), Korea Economic Institute, April 17, 2020, https://keia.org/the-peninsula/two-prominent-defectors-elected-to-south-korean-national-assembly/.

symbol of its anger and frustration with the South with a massive explosion that destroyed the North-South liaison office.

Despite the failure of summit diplomacy, however, Trump did not return to using human rights as a cudgel against Kim Jong-un as he had before their first meeting. There was no criticism by Trump or senior administration officials of Pyongyang's human rights record. Not only did former president Trump refuse to publicly raise human rights issues, he did not even criticize the North for conducting missile tests—he called "short-range missiles" trials "very standard," though they are still considered to be a threat to U.S. national security. Senior-level discussions on strategic issues did not follow. North Korea showered bitter invective on the United States, Japan, South Korea, and the United Nations and claimed to have the ability to fire missiles capable of delivering a nuclear warhead against any part of the United States.

Former president Trump seemed anxious to reach an agreement with Kim Jong-un when media interest was high. Photos were taken of the two leaders holding hands and video footage showed Trump gingerly stepping across the border, making him the first sitting U.S. president to set foot in North Korea. When it became clear that progress was not going to take place without serious prolonged effort and careful strategic thought, the president shifted his focus to issues in other parts of the world. President Moon Jae-in called for a new U.S.–North Korea summit in July 2020, but the North quickly quashed that suggestion and Trump was preoccupied with the fallout from the COVID-19 pandemic in the United States and the November 2020 U.S. presidential election campaign.[6] Despite the United States carefully distancing itself from any criticism of North Korea on human rights issues, no progress at all was made on security questions.

Following the election of President Joe Biden, his new administration proceeded cautiously with North Korea. The initial focus was strengthening ties with South Korea and Japan. But it is clear that there is a greater focus on human rights.[7] Secretary of State Antony Blinken

---

6   Robert R. King, "Moon Jae-in Urges Trump-Kim Summit before U.S. Election," *The Peninsula* (blog), Korea Economic Institute, July 6, 2020, https://keia.org/the-peninsula/moon-jae-in-urges-trump-kim-summit-before-u-s-election/.

7   Following the Biden-Moon summit in Washington, D.C., a joint statement said the two leaders "agree to work together to improve the human rights situation in the DPRK and commit to continue facilitating the provision of humanitarian aid to the neediest North Koreans." See White House, "U.S.-ROK Leaders' Joint

said the United States would appoint a special envoy for North Korean human rights, as required by U.S. law, but which the Trump administration failed to do for its entire four-year tenure.[8] The United States also resumed participation at the United Nations Human Rights Council.[9] This was an about-face from the policy pursued by Trump.

Human rights are only one aspect of foreign policy and must not be the tail wagging the diplomatic dog (see chapter 11 for more discussion of this issue). Policy toward North Korea inherently involves a variety of interrelated issues that we frequently separate for analytical purposes or because they are dealt with in different ways or by different entities. But these issues are interconnected; they are not really separable. We need to look at the interrelationship of security issues (and particularly nuclear security issues), human rights and humanitarian issues, and unique inter-Korean problems. The principal focus of this book, however, is on human rights and how dealing with this problem is shaped and affected by the political issues with which it is so entwined.

Human Rights and Regime Survival

North Korea is consistently identified as one of the world's worst human rights abusers. With regard to freedom of the media and access to information, the international ranking by Reporters without Borders places North Korea dead last of 180 countries.[10] Freedom House's annual ranking on political rights and civil liberties places North Korea at 191 out of 195 countries in the world.[11] Annual reports from the UN special rapporteur on North Korean human rights and the UN

Statement," May 21, 2021, https://www.whitehouse.gov/briefing-room/statements -releases/2021/05/21/u-s-rok-leaders-joint-statement/.

8   Jeongmin Kim, "Blinken 'Feels Strongly' about Re-Appointing a North Korea Human Rights Envoy," *NK News*, March 11, 2021.

9   Antony J. Blinken, "U.S. Decision to Reengage with the UN Human Rights Council," press statement, U.S. Department of State, February 8, 2021, https:// www.state.gov/u-s-decision-to-reengage-with-the-un-human-rights-council/.

10   "2020 World Press Freedom Index," Reporters Without Borders (Rapporteurs sans Frontières), https://rsf.org/en/ranking.

11   Sarah Repucci, *Freedom in the World 2020: A Leaderless Struggle for Democracy* (Washington, DC: Freedom House, 2020), 28, https://freedomhouse.org/sites/ default/files/2020-02/FIW_2020_REPORT_BOOKLET_Final.pdf.

Commission of Inquiry (COI) on human rights in the Democratic People's Republic of Korea have detailed these abuses[12] (see chapter 2 for discussion of the commission, its findings, and the response by key stakeholders to the report). While the North's human rights abuses have been well documented, we are still in need of a robust analysis of why these abuses are integral to the nature and existence of North Korea as we know it.

The Kim regime is an unstable house of cards, in large part because of the continued existence and flourishing of the South. South Korea—with twice the population but forty times the per capita income of the North—has become a respected and engaged participant in the international community. Ban Ki Moon, a former South Korean foreign minister, was the previous secretary general of the United Nations (2007–16). South Korea has served two terms as a non-permanent member of the UN Security Council. South Korea is also a member of the Group of Twenty (G-20), the prestigious international forum of the world's leading economic powers. North Korea, by contrast, is an international outsider. It has an economy and a standard of living equivalent to a poor sub-Saharan African country. It is a frequent recipient of international humanitarian food and medical assistance. It is an international bully that uses threats of military force against its neighbors as well as against the United States. Its leaders are known for confrontational and intemperate rhetoric, accompanied by occasional outbursts of military violence primarily against South Korea. One of the most reprehensible actions was the destruction of a South Korean naval vessel, killing forty-six South Korean sailors in 2010. North Korea's leader is universally believed to have ordered the murder of his half-brother with a deadly nerve agent at the international airport in Kuala Lumpur, Malaysia, in 2017.

North Korea exists largely because the repressive Kim family dictatorship remains in power and continues to retain control. The North exists as a separate entity at great cost to the standard of living of the

---

12   See UN General Assembly, Report of the Special Rapporteur on the Situation of Human Rights in the Democratic People's Republic of Korea, A/HRC/43/58 (February 25, 2020), https://www.ohchr.org/EN/HRBodies/SP/CountriesMandates/KP/Pages/SRDPRKorea.aspx; see also UN Human Rights Council, Report of the Detailed Findings of the Commission of Inquiry on Human Rights in the Democratic People's Republic of Korea, A/HRC/25/CRP1 (February 7, 2014), https://undocs.org/A/HRC/25/CRP.1.

North Korean people. China and Russia support North Korea, but the Kim regime maintains full control over its population. The extent of Soviet control in East Germany, however, was far greater than Chinese or Russian influence in North Korea. China certainly has an interest in a North Korean buffer between its northeast provinces and South Korea and Japan, but China does not play the role in North Korea that the Soviet Union played in East Germany. China could certainly make absorption of the North by the South much more difficult, and it certainly would seek to extract a price—at a minimum, eliminating an American military and political presence in the South and probably considerably more. But Chinese influence in North Korea is more limited and less vital than Soviet influence was to the existence of East Germany (see chapter 10 for the East German–North Korean comparison).

The success and the appeal of the South, the presence of U.S. military forces in South Korea and Japan, and the Kim regime's paranoia regarding its survival have led North Korean leaders to believe that its very existence would be threatened if it does not maintain absolute control over its own people. The belief in hostile evil Americans and the myth of horrible living conditions in South Korea are considered essential by the Kim regime. Religious belief is also seen as a threat to the North's leadership. If North Koreans were allowed to accept an alternate spiritual reality, they could well be in conflict with the regime's raison d'être. This reasoning has led to the creation of brutal prison camps, a massive internal security force, major efforts to control access to information, tight restrictions on movement within the country, and prohibition of travel abroad. Pyongyang enforces these policies because it believes it must for survival.

The elite cadre essential to carry out the leader's policies and to maintain the political system is sustained in large part by rewards—access to consumer goods, automobiles, travel, and status simply not available to average North Koreans. But, to assure their loyalty, they are also subject to the same punishments as other North Korean citizens. Fear inspires compliance.

This is made clear by one example, related by the ambassador of a country that has diplomatic relations with North Korea, who had been resident in Pyongyang for several years. What he witnessed illustrated the lengths to which the regime goes to assure elite loyalty. In early December 2013, the ambassador was at dinner in one of the exclusive new restaurants in downtown Pyongyang. It was crowded and noisy, and a large new flat screen television was showing the evening news. Abruptly, an eerie silence fell over the bustling restaurant as all of the guests suddenly gave undivided attention to the television news. They watched in astonishment as the live broadcast reported that Jang Song-taek—uncle of Supreme Leader Kim Jong-un, vice chairman of the State Military Commission, and one of the most senior officials in the government and party—had been arrested by armed security officers and dragged out of a party Politburo meeting, and this was shown on television. The ambassador said that when the broadcast ended, the restaurant immediately emptied as the stunned elite diners silently but quickly left. The message was clear: no one was too important or too well connected to be beyond the absolute reach of Kim Jong-un. Jang's trial and execution was announced two days later.[13]

The Kim family believes that its precarious house of cards is held together by its ability to violate at a whim the human rights of the most important people in the regime as well as the least important worker or peasant in the most remote corner of the country. They can be incarcerated and tortured without cause and without recourse. This brutal tyranny gives the Kim regime the ability to ignore the wishes and interests of the people it rules. More of the country's resources would be devoted to food and medical care rather than nuclear weapons and the military if public sentiment played a greater role in the allocation of resources. A regime that is more responsive to the wishes of its people would devote resources to their well-being—food, healthcare, education—rather than to military and internal security controls.

This is not to suggest that pursuing regime change is a solution to either North Korea's security threat or to its denial of human rights to the North Korean people. The U.S. experience with Afghanistan and Iraq, to name only two very recent examples, has not been particularly successful. Nevertheless, progress on human rights may well be the prerequisite to meaningful improvement on security issues. A country that is willing to oppress its own people will feel even less constraint about using force against its neighbors or against distant nations. A regime that puts the welfare and well-being of its own people below its

---

13 "North Korea Images Confirm Removal of Kim Jong-un's Uncle Chang Song-thaek," BBC News, December 9, 2013, https://www.bbc.com/news/world-asia -25295312. The ambassador related his anecdote directly to co-author Robert R. King.

acquisition of nuclear weapons will not hesitate to use those nuclear weapons against others. Without improved human rights for North Korea's people, which will lead to greater internal pressure on the regime for different priorities in resource allocation, we are unlikely to see progress on the security issues that are central to U.S. and South Korean concerns with North Korea.

The United Nations' Role

The United Nations has played an important role in international efforts to manage North Korea's acquisition of nuclear weapons and advanced missile technology over the last two decades. The North is seen as a serious security threat because it has failed to show restraint or to follow accepted international practices and norms in its foreign policy, and the United Nations has been a critical voice in building international support against its nuclear ambitions. The North's closest allies, China and Russia, have joined the United States, South Korea, and many other international participants through the United Nations in opposing North Korea's nuclear and missile programs. The UN Security Council has imposed international sanctions against the North. The legitimacy and the enforcement of these Security Council actions are dependent on the support of China and Russia. As permanent members of the UN Security Council, either could veto sanctions against the North if they chose, but China and Russia have worked with the United States, Britain, France, and other countries to constrain Pyongyang.

The United Nations has also played a key role in prodding North Korea to make progress on human rights conditions. Its UN membership has been important in North Korea's effort to enhance its international legitimacy and stature, but that requires improving its reputation, including progress on human rights. Human rights is an international obligation, a moral commitment, of nations that seek international equality and full participation in the community of nations. At the same time, respect for human rights encourages countries to follow international policies that contribute to global peace, security, and domestic well-being. North Korea, as well as all other member countries of the UN, has at least nominally accepted the obligation to respect internationally recognized human rights. The UN Charter, in its first paragraph, explicitly provides that among its purposes is "promoting and encouraging respect for human rights and for fundamental freedoms for all without distinction as to race, sex, language, or religion."[14]

In an effort to gain international legitimacy and enhance the success of its bid to join the United Nations, North Korea acceded to the International Covenant on Civil and Political Rights (ICCPR) in 1981—a full decade before it was admitted to membership in the United Nations. In 1997, six years after becoming a full UN member, North Korea attempted to withdraw from its human rights obligations and from participation in the ICCPR because it had been criticized by other countries for its horrible human rights record. The UN General Assembly, however, adopted a resolution stating: "The International Covenant on Civil and Political Rights does not contain any provision regarding termination and does not provide for denunciation or withdrawal."[15] North Korea is the only country that has attempted to withdraw from the international covenant on human rights. If North Korea is to receive the international legitimacy and recognition that UN membership brings, it must live up to the obligations of membership, including those related to human rights.

The Trump administration largely turned a blind eye to North Korea's failure to observe its international human rights obligations to make progress on nuclear and security issues, but no such progress was made. One must also wonder, if North Korea does not observe the human rights obligations that all UN members accept, what assurance we have that the North will keep the international commitments it has made or may make in the future—such as agreements on denuclearization and security matters.

The North Korean regime spent millions and millions of dollars to conduct nuclear tests two days after a devastating flood impoverished and destroyed the homes and the food supply of a significant portion of its people.[16] Such a regime will have no problem taking military action against other countries, even if that action produces great suffering for

---

14 "United Nations Charter," Article 1, https://www.un.org/en/sections/un-charter/un-charter-full-text/.

15 "U.N. Blocks Rights Move by North Korea," *New York Times*, October 31, 1997.

16 Anna Fifield, "North Korea Defied World with Nuclear Test. Now It Seeks Aid for Flood Disaster," *Washington Post*, September 12, 2016.

its own people. A country that first rebuilds border fences and guard posts along its flood-ravaged frontier to prevent its citizens from traveling freely across the border to find food and seek employment in order to rebuild their homes and feed their families following a natural disaster is a regime that will give no second thought to using its military forces to intimidate and coerce its neighbors.

North Korea seeks full acceptance and recognition of the community of nations, but the leaders in Pyongyang must understand that this cannot be achieved without efforts on other issues, and in particular human rights. In fact, the international effort to raise the profile of human rights with North Korea over the last two decades has had some positive effects, even though North Korean officials quickly denounce and impute evil political motives to those who raise these issues, and even though the North has not gone nearly as far as we would like to see it go. As Michael Kirby discusses in chapter 2, the release of the Report of the Commission of Inquiry on Human Rights in the Democratic People's Republic of Korea in 2014 did have some positive effects. When the report was released, the North Korean foreign minister appeared in New York at the high-level session of the UN General Assembly for the first time in fourteen years. At that same time, senior officials of the North Korean embassy to the UN participated in a discussion of the country's human rights at the Council on Foreign Relations in New York—a first for such a discussion on this issue with the prestigious American think tank.[17]

At the UN Human Rights Council in Geneva, North Korean officials discussed their human rights record in the process of the Universal Periodic Review (UPR). The first time this review was held in 2009–10, North Korea received 147 recommendations from other UN member states. The North ignored all of these comments—a serious violation of UN practice and precedent. Five years later, in 2014, when North Korea underwent its second UPR just weeks after the COI report was released and debated, the North received 267 suggestions, and its diplomats commented on all of them. Furthermore, North Korean officials went back to the 147 recommendations they received but ignored five

---

17 "Ambassador Jang Il-hun on Human Rights in North Korea," Council on Foreign Relations, October 21, 2014, https://www.youtube.com/watch?v =iBKXTDmhFGA.

years earlier, and in 2014 they addressed a number of these earlier suggestions.

The lengthy report submitted by North Korea in response to the 2014 UPR process was largely a defense of North Korea's policies, but there were modest indications of progress.[18] In the 2009 UPR session, recommendations from other member countries (including the United States) suggested that North Korea should accede to the UN Convention on Rights of Persons with Disabilities. The North signed the convention in July 2013. It also signed the Optional Protocol on the Rights of the Child and an international anti-terrorism agreement. While changes were not major, the fact that the North took steps to improve the perception of its human rights record in these non-controversial areas is positive.[19]

Much still remains to be done, but the North has come to recognize that such progress in establishing its international legitimacy and credibility in the United Nations is important to the regime's image and its standing. Pressing the North on human rights can have a beneficial impact on moving the regime in the right direction, despite its renouncement and resistance, and UN organizations and international cooperation on the North have been helpful.

Against this backdrop, the first part of this book addresses the UN role in North Korean human rights issues. In chapter 2, Justice Michael Kirby, who chaired the UN Commission of Inquiry, recounts origins, processes, and challenges of writing the report and examines how the main stakeholders including Pyongyang, Seoul, Washington, Beijing, and Moscow have responded to the 400-page authoritative report. In chapter 3, South Korean ambassador Joon Oh, who was his country's Permanent Representative to the United Nations (2013–16), discusses the issue from a South Korean perspective, offering three approaches

---

18   UN General Assembly, Human Rights Council, Report of the Working Group on the Universal Periodic Review, Democratic People's Republic of Korea, A/HRC/27/10 (July 2, 2014), https://www.refworld.org/pdfid/53eb231d4.pdf.

19   See, for example, Katharina Zellweger, *People with Disabilities in a Changing North Korea* (Stanford: Walter H. Shorenstein Asia-Pacific Research Center, 2014), https://aparc.fsi.stanford.edu/publications/people_with_disabilities_in_a_changing_north_korea; and Robert R. King, "The 2018 PyeongChang Winter Paralympics and North Korea's Record on People with Disabilities," *The Peninsula* (blog), Korea Economic Institute, March 5, 2018, https://keia.org/the-peninsula/the-2018-pyeongchang-winter-paralympics-and-north-koreas-record-on-people-with-disabilities/.

that Seoul can take to improve the human rights situation in the North—non-political, institutional, and non-governmental approaches.

In chapter 4, Peter Yeo, president of the Better World Campaign and the senior vice president at the United Nations Foundation, and Ryan Kaminski, former senior program manager for human rights at the United Nations Foundation, discuss the U.S. government's role at the United Nations in focusing on North Korean human rights. After reviewing the lack of attention and action toward North Korean human rights violations during the Trump administration, they call for reorienting U.S. foreign policy priorities so that the United States can restore leadership in using the UN to bolster the global focus on the abysmal human rights situation in the country.

Access to Information

The North Korean leadership has shown a great ability to extract resources from the economy and from its people in order to maintain its disproportionately large military establishment and to develop costly nuclear weapons and missiles. One of the crucial elements in making these resource allocations is maintaining control over the population and, in particular, controlling information to which the North Korean people have access. The UN COI concluded that

> citizens are denied the right to have access to information from independent sources; State-controlled media are the only permitted source of information. . . . [A]ll media content is heavily censored and must adhere to directives issued by the Workers' Party of Korea. Telephone calls are monitored and mostly confined to domestic connections for citizens. Citizens are punished for watching and listening to foreign broadcasts, including foreign films and soap operas.[20]

Even if individuals have access to external information not controlled by the government, there are limits to what they can do. There is no freedom of expression, assembly, association, or religious belief. Political opposition, independent media, and civil society are not permitted to exist.

---

20   UN General Assembly, Human Rights Council, Report of the Commission of Inquiry on Human Rights in the Democratic People's Republic of Korea, A/HRC/25/63, ¶26–31 (February 7, 2014), https://www.ohchr.org/EN/HRBodies/HRC/CoIDPRK/Pages/CommissionInquiryonHRinDPRK.aspx.

Access to online media is even more stringently controlled. The international internet is not unavailable in the North. The only option that is available is a government-controlled *intra*net, on which content is very carefully managed. Cell phone conversations and text messages are constantly and rigorously monitored. Most North Koreans personally know someone who has been imprisoned or punished for attempting to access unauthorized information. It is illegal to own a radio or a television set that has the capability to be tuned to a station other than officially approved domestic channels. It is illegal to watch or listen to foreign radio or television broadcasts.

Although accessing information not censored by the government is difficult and dangerous, North Koreans do receive external information, principally on radio and with USB (thumb) drives. They clandestinely follow South Korean soap operas and watch or listen to other foreign information and entertainment that give at least some in the North a picture of life beyond the 38th parallel. South Korean radio broadcasts, including news and entertainment, reach the North, and in border areas television transmissions from neighboring countries are received. This information is also spread from person to person, although the risk of being caught remains significant.[21] In addition, Korean language news and information programming from the U.S. government's Voice of America and Radio Free Asia reach North Korea. Broadcasts in the Korean language from China, where a significant Korean-speaking population lives just across the border, are also heard in the North. Although this broadcasting is directed at Korean-speaking Chinese citizens, it has strong listenership in North Korean areas along the border with China. The Chinese-controlled media gives more information than what is available on the even more tightly controlled North Korean media. The British Broadcasting Corporation (BBC) has a modest program in Korean, and refugee or defector groups and religious organizations also transmit radio programming aimed at North Korea.

Digital entertainment, including some news programming, reaches the North through channels from China on USB drives. South Korean soap operas ("dramas") and K-pop are reportedly very popular in the

---

21 Robert R. King, "North Koreans Want External Information, but Kim Jong-un Seeks to Limit Access," Center for Strategic and International Studies, May 15, 2019, https://www.csis.org/analysis/north-koreans-want-external -information-kim-jong-un-seeks-limit-access.

North. Such content is not legally available in the North, and possession of this prohibited material carries a significant risk of severe punishment. Although such programs are chiefly seen and heard in the North primarily for entertainment, the material provides insight into life in South Korea and elsewhere. Greater knowledge about actual conditions in South Korea and elsewhere would make the average North Korean far less enthusiastic about making sacrifices for their leader's military programs. Access to information makes it more difficult for official propaganda to successfully circulate lies and untruths.

Unsurprisingly, the Kim regime is very sensitive to the flow of external information into the country. Kim Yo-jong, sister of the Supreme Leader, Kim Jong-un, harshly criticized Seoul for continuing to allow non-government organizations (NGOs) in South Korea to send anti-regime leaflets via balloon into the North. She denounced the balloons as a "provocation graver than gun and artillery fire."[22] The North then cut off recently established channels of government-to-government communication between the two Koreas and destroyed in a "terrific blast" the joint liaison office where both Koreas had briefly maintained contact offices in Kaesong on the North Korean side of the North-South border. The North's official Korean Central News Agency (KCNA) called the explosion the action of "enraged people" retaliating against "human scum," referring to North Korean defectors living in the South. Seoul expressed "severe regret" for the North's provocative move. Kim You-geun, first deputy chief of the South Korean National Security Council, expressed regret that this action "betrayed the hopes of peace on the Korean peninsula."[23]

Three of the chapters below (5, 6, and 7) discuss various efforts of supplying outside information and media into the North and the regime's ways of dealing with such efforts. Minjung Kim, director of the South Korean human rights NGO Save North Korea (SNK), discusses South Korean NGOs' efforts to reach North Korea in chapter 5. This has added relevance and urgency as Seoul is restricting activities

---

22 "Kim Yo-jong Rebukes S. Korean Authorities for Conniving at Anti-DPRK Hostile Act of 'Defectors from North,'" *Rodong Sinmun* (English), June 4, 2020, https://kcnawatch.org/newstream/1591257669-272137200/kim-yo-jong-rebukes-s-korean-authorities-for-conniving-at-anti-dprk-hostile-act-of-defectors-from-north/.

23 Min Joo Kim, "North Korea Blows Up Joint Liaison Office, Dramatically Raising Tensions with South," *Washington Post*, June 16, 2020.

of those NGOs working on North Korean human rights issues in response to protests from Pyongyang.

Nat Kretchun, deputy director of the Open Technology Fund, which is a non-profit corporation encouraging global internet freedom technologies, discusses North Korea's changing information environment in chapter 6. He argues that the United States and its allies need a new information strategy to counter the regime by creating alternative information infrastructures and undermining government control over state networks.

Martyn Williams, a North Korea media and tech specialist and the author/editor of the website North Korea Tech, discusses how the North Korean regime has responded to foreign information in chapter 7. In his view, the regime is far from giving up control over what people watch and listen to and has been adept at countering foreign information flow into the country through new techniques and software such as "Red Flag," "Trace Viewer," file watermarking, and digital signatures. He calls for "continuing development and innovation" to stay a step ahead of the regime in disseminating information to the North Korean people.

Integrating Human Rights, Humanitarian, and Security Issues

Human rights received little attention not only from the Trump administration, but also the Moon Jae-in administration in South Korea. The United States' North Korea Human Rights Act mandates the appointment of a special envoy for North Korean human rights. The envoy's role is to participate in the making of U.S. policy toward North Korea at senior levels in the Department of State to assure that human rights are integrated into that policy. The position remained unfilled for the entire four years of the Trump administration. At the same time, the South Korean government has also paid scant attention to human right issues, giving high priority to inter-Korean collaboration. Like Washington, Seoul has not filled the position of ambassador for North Korean human rights. Rather than seeing human rights as an obstacle to resolving the very serious security issues with North Korea or to promoting inter-Korean cooperation, Washington and Seoul should see progress on human rights as integral to a broader engagement strategy with the North.

Engagement with North Korea on a broad range of issues would help establish a more wide-ranging relationship that could improve the atmosphere for dealing with security challenges. The standard template seems to call for resolution of the nuclear and security issues with the presumption that all other aspects of the relationship will then fall into place. The argument can be made—though it has never been tried—that dealing with the North on humanitarian, human rights, and other aspects of engagement in order to build confidence and establish relationships could have a positive impact in resolving the more complex security issues.

Negotiation with the North is difficult. North Korean envoys must satisfy an autocratic dictator, who has a hostile attitude toward the United States, and those who fail to please the leader risk losing not only their government position and perquisites, but conceivably their lives and the well-being of their families as well. If the only engagement with North Korea is on the most difficult and sensitive issues for both sides, there is little opportunity to build confidence that could help in facing these issues. It would be easier to work on confidence-building measures if the issues also include less sensitive issues than nuclear security, in order to build a broader relationship.

There is no question that sanctions against North Korea are appropriate in order to limit its security threat to South Korea, Japan, the United States, and other countries. But such action does not preclude humanitarian and other types of engagement that do not increase North Korea's military capabilities. Medical assistance with COVID-19, multi-drug-resistant tuberculosis, and other significant health problems in North Korea, which are not focused on the Pyongyang elite, can be monitored and their proper delivery assured. U.S. sanctions and travel restrictions, however, have made humanitarian as well as educational and cultural engagement with North Korea difficult if not impossible. The reason for limiting travel was supposedly concern for the welfare of American citizens, but the restrictions were later strengthened because humanitarian aid was determined not to be in the U.S. "national interest."[24] There exists a belief by some that limiting American citizen travel to the North would put additional pressure on Pyongyang, but there has been little evidence of this.

---

24   Robert R. King, "Why U.S. Moves to Block NGO Travel to N. Korea Are Counterproductive—and Wrong," *NKNews*, October 14, 2018, https://www .nknews.org/2018/10/why-u-s-moves-to-block-ngo-travel-to-n-korea-are-counter productive-and-wrong/.

One of the weaknesses of the U.S. focus on nuclear security is that Washington is asking the North to give up a major military capability, but only negative incentives are used—import sanctions and monetary controls—with a promise to lift sanctions after there is progress on denuclearization and other security concerns. We need to provide positive incentives up front on issues that are not necessarily related to security, areas where beneficial cooperation is possible that do not enhance the North's military capabilities. The challenge is how to move North Korea toward becoming a positive and contributing participant in the international community, and how to achieve this in a way that balances both security and human rights considerations.

This tricky relationship between human rights and security is discussed in two chapters. In chapter 8, Tae-Ung Baik, professor of law at the University of Hawaii and director of the university's Center for Korean Studies, discusses the interrelationship between pushing North Korea on human rights and denuclearization. He argues that bringing up human rights to North Korea would not necessarily deter the regime from diplomatic negotiations but human rights improvement is required to seek permanent peace and stable relationships on the Korean Peninsula. Victor Cha, D. S. Song–Korea Foundation Chair in Government and International Affairs at Georgetown University as well as Korea Chair at the Center for Strategic and International Studies, refutes zero-sum thinking about human rights and denuclearization in chapter 9. In his view, it is simply inconceivable for the United States to achieve political normalization in its relationship with the DPRK without addressing human rights. He argues that "integrating human rights into our strategy is not choice, but a necessity."

We conclude this book with two chapters on comparative experiences. In chapter 10, Sean King, senior advisor at Park Strategies and former senior advisor for Asia at the U.S. and Foreign Commercial Service, broadens our approach toward North Korean human rights by exploring East German lessons. Based on his expertise and experience with Asian and German affairs, he argues that if South Korea wants to replicate what happened in Germany three decades ago, it should prioritize North Koreans' rights and their contact with the outside world.

In chapter 11, Thomas Fingar, former U.S. deputy director of National Intelligence for Analysis and currently a fellow at Shorenstein APARC, discusses the interrelationship between human rights and foreign policy. He argues that any proposals seeking to integrate negotiations and tradeoffs on human rights into broader foreign policies must first clarify whether the goal is to work with or against the regime. Otherwise, it will be very difficult to marshal the support needed to make human rights part of the overall policy package, and Pyongyang will simply assume that any initiative from South Korea, the United States, or elsewhere is intended to weaken the regime.

We believe that North Korean human rights should not be ignored or overlooked in our engagement with the regime based on the false premise that bringing them up would undermine our efforts to move the North toward denuclearization. Instead, we need to reignite a lost momentum in addressing this important issue in a broad engagement with North Korea. It is expected that the Biden administration will pay more attention to human rights in dealing with the North. We hope that this book can be useful as the United Nations, the United States, and South Korea as well as non-governmental organizations seek to address human rights conditions in the North.

I. The Role of the United Nations

2 The COI Report on Human Rights in North Korea

Origins, Necessities, Obstacles, and Prospects

Michael Kirby

The origins of the Commission of Inquiry (COI) of the UN Human Rights Council (HRC) on North Korea can be traced back to the end of the Second World War. This saw the creation of the United Nations following the adoption of the UN Charter.[1] In its opening paragraphs, the Charter identified the UN's key commitments. These were to save future generations from "the scourge of war" and to reaffirm "faith in fundamental human rights, in the dignity and worth of the human person, [and] in the equal rights of men and women in nations large and small." Also envisaged was the establishment of conditions "under which . . . international law might be maintained; so that social progress and better standards of life in larger freedom" might be attained.[2] The Charter defined the UN's purposes and principles.[3] It provided for its membership.[4] It also identified its principal organs.[5]

Although priority was given to protection of "fundamental human rights," no definition of that concept was provided. Nor was an effective enforcement mechanism established. The task of giving meaning to the ideal expression was assigned to a committee chaired by Eleanor Roosevelt, widow of the wartime leader of the United States. The

---

1   Charter of the United Nations, adopted June 26, 1945; entered into force October 24, 1945.
2   Charter of the United Nations, Preamble.
3   Charter of the United Nations, chapter 1.
4   Charter of the United Nations, chapter 2.
5   Charter of the United Nations, chapter 3.

drafters recommended the adoption of the Universal Declaration of Human Rights (UDHR). The draft of that document was duly accepted by the General Assembly of the United Nations, meeting in Paris, on December 10, 1948.[6]

The UDHR was a declaration of the UN General Assembly. It was not a treaty that nations could subscribe to or reject. It became a cornerstone of the UN's commitment to international human rights. By joining the UN, as the two Korean states did in 1991, they were taken to accept this principled basis of the UN system. No court or similar mechanism was created to enforce the UDHR. However, in the years after 1945, important UN treaties, binding on the States Parties that ratified them, were adopted. Agencies were created to monitor observance of the UDHR and subsequent UN treaty law. "Special procedures" were later established to follow up individual complaints about abuses of human rights. These "special procedures" eventually included the appointment of "special rapporteurs" and "commissions of inquiry." The latter procedure represented a step toward a more detailed and formal investigation and report of alleged abuses of human rights.[7]

The creation of a COI by the HRC invariably contemplated a more solemn, better-resourced, multi-member investigation when compared to that by a special rapporteur or other officeholder. Ordinarily, it addressed more serious and sensitive issues of fact-finding, judgment, and recommendations. Commonly, it was viewed as a more substantial political step. Invariably, a proposal to create a COI of the HRC led to a vote upon which, typically, the HRC was sharply divided. Opponents or abstainers were usually countries that were opposed in principle to the creation of HRCs because of the risk that they presented of political division. Other opponents or skeptics typically included allies or regional associates of the country concerned. Still others included states that were inferentially mindful of the risk that they might themselves face being subjected to similar detailed investigation, leading to condemnation. Yet, in the establishment of the COI on the DPRK, uniquely, there was no call in the council for a vote. The case of the DPRK was, from the start, different.

---

6   UN General Assembly, Resolution 217A, Universal Declaration of Human Rights (adopted December 10, 1948).

7   Christian Henderson, ed., *Commissions of Inquiry: Problems and Prospects* (Oxford: Hart Publishing, 2017), 11–14.

Mandate of the UN COI on the DPRK

The Korean Peninsula was annexed by Imperial Japan in 1910 and ruled as an undivided territory until 1945. As the Second World War edged toward its conclusion, the Allied Powers agreed in Cairo that, after the war, Korea would be divided between spheres of influence respectively of the United States of America and the Soviet Union. This division resulted in the creation of two states: the Republic of Korea (ROK) in the South and the Democratic People's Republic of Korea (DPRK) in the North. Each of these states vied to become the legitimate government of the entire Korean landmass. There was no act of self-determination to justify the separation between the two, which neither side accepted. Eventually, in 1950, the stalemate was broken, leading to the Korean War that was ended by an armistice in 1953. Effectively, this divided Korea at a point proximate to the geographical midpoint, near where the war had begun.

The Demilitarized Zone (DMZ) that now divides the Korean Peninsula is the most heavily militarized international border in the world. The legacy of the Korean War remains unresolved. The wounds are still deeply felt in both Korean states. There has never been a peace treaty or a formal end to the Korean War.

After the armistice, each of the Korean states continued to exhibit features of autocratic rule. However, by the 1990s, the ROK had emerged as a viable democracy. It changed its government at regular elections. It generally conformed to the rule of law. It established powerful courts that even removed presidents when they were held to have defaulted in their duties. It established a strong and inventive economy, growing to be one of the top ten in the world. The DPRK, on the other hand, suffered long-term economic difficulties, recurring famines, and increasingly disturbing reports of human rights violations. Nonetheless, each of the Korean states was admitted on its own application for membership in the United Nations on the same day, September 17, 1991. The DPRK, like the ROK, had ratified a number of human rights treaties sponsored by the United Nations, including the International Covenant on Civil and Political Rights. When the DPRK later asked how it could terminate the irksome obligations it had assumed under the covenant, it was told that there was no facility for withdrawal. This was a position that the DPRK apparently never challenged.

In 2004, the HRC established a mandate for a special rapporteur (SR) on human rights in the DPRK to respond to the growing number of reports of serious abuses of human rights occurring in that country. The original SR (Professor Vitit Muntarbhorn, Thailand) endeavored to fulfill his mandate. However, despite the resolutions of the HRC calling for cooperation on the part of the DPRK, this was not forthcoming. Professor Muntarbhorn was succeeded as SR in 2013 by Marzuki Darusman of Indonesia. His efforts suffered the same fate. There was no cooperation. Admission to the country was repeatedly denied. The DPRK condemned the mandate for the SR. It denounced the creation of the mandate as a hostile act. Faced with increasing numbers of refugees ("defectors") passing from the DPRK, usually through China to the ROK and because of persisting complaints of serious wrongs in the DPRK, Darusman urged the HRC to establish a COI.[8] His report as SR argued for the need for "an international, independent, and impartial inquiry mechanism with adequate resources to investigate, and more fully document, the grave, systematic, and widespread violations of human rights in the DPRK."[9]

As a result of this recommendation, in January 2013, High Commissioner for Human Rights Navi Pillay considered the proposal for a COI. She reported to the HRC on the extended record of complaints over decades and the added seriousness of the fact that the DPRK was by that stage apparently possessed of nuclear weapons as demonstrated by reports based on seismic tests. The high commissioner's proposal was conveyed to the then president of the HRC (Ambassador Hertzel, Poland). A COI was established without a vote. Such was the widespread concern about the human rights situation reportedly emerging from available information on the DPRK and the refusal of the DPRK to cooperate in any way with the UN special procedures. The same uncooperative attitude had been exhibited in 2009 when the DPRK underwent its first cycle of Universal Periodic Review. It participated in the process. However, it did not agree to a single recommendation that was addressed to it for the improvement of human rights in the country. This was a unique stance on the part of a member state. At last, the United Nations

---

8   United Nations General Assembly, Human Rights Council, Report of the Detailed Findings of the Commission of Inquiry on Human Rights in the Democratic People's Republic of Korea, A/HRC/25/CRP.1, 5, ¶7 (February 7, 2014).

9   A/HRC/25/CRP.1, 5, ¶7.

had run out of patience. The COI was established. Darusman, as SR, Sonja Biserko (Serbia) were named as members. I was designated as the third member and chair of the COI.[10]

The mandate of the COI on the DPRK required it to investigate and report, with relevant recommendations, on nine substantive areas of concern. These included reported violations of the right to food, violations involving prison camps, torture and inhuman treatment, violations involving arbitrary arrest and detention, discrimination, and the systemic denial and violation of basic human rights and fundamental freedoms, violations of freedom of expression, violations of the right to life, violations of the freedom of individual movement, and enforced disappearances, including the abductions of nationals of other states, notably Japan.

The COI's Methodology

The COI promptly went to work, holding its first meeting in Geneva on July 1, 2013. At that meeting, a methodology was agreed upon by the members, including regarding outreach to the DPRK and other countries most affected, the conduct of public hearings, and engagement with the international media. The COI addressed invitations for engagement to relevant diplomatic missions in Geneva, including those of the DPRK, the ROK, Japan, China, the Russian Federation, the European Union, France, the United Kingdom, and the United States of America. Full cooperation was afforded by the ROK, Japan, the European Union, France, the United Kingdom, and the United States. The DPRK ignored the COI's approach completely.

Russia and China agreed to receive visits from the members of the COI. So eventually did the Lao People's Democratic Republic, Thailand, and other neighboring states. From the start, there was a distinction between the respective responses of the Russian Federation and of China. The Russian mission received the COI and its secretariat with courtesy and at the level of its ambassador to the United Nations in Geneva. China agreed to a meeting but assigned a medium-level official to the Geneva mission. Inferentially, this was to signify its disapproval of the mandate, its unwillingness to cooperate, and its unwillingness to permit the COI to visit border territories adjoining the DPRK or to meet Chinese officials or experts in Beijing, as requested by the COI.

---

10   A/HRC/25/CRP.1, 5, ¶3.

The Russian ambassador approached his several interactions with the COI in a candid and realistic way. He explained that the Soviet Union, up until its post-1989 disintegration, had been a major financial supporter of the DPRK. It viewed some reports of human rights abuses in the DPRK as a probable leftover from a form of government that Russia itself had by now discarded, but understood from the history it had shared with the DPRK. The Russian ambassador encouraged the COI, where any reports of improvements in the human rights situation in the DPRK came to notice, to acknowledge these and to express praise and encouragement. The COI accepted this advice as, for example, when the DPRK ratified the Convention on the Rights of Persons with Disabilities (2007). Later in New York, when an Arria briefing[11] was conducted with invited members of the UN office, the Russian ambassador to the Security Council in New York sent the deputy head of mission to apologize for his "unavoidable" absence. She insisted that no disrespect toward the COI was intended.

No such courtesy was exhibited by the People's Republic of China or its representatives at any level either in Geneva or New York. From the start, China's attitude was hostile, antagonistic, and basically disrespectful. The members of the COI were simply performing functions assigned to them by a mandate adopted by the UN HRC. The members of the COI understood the position adopted by China, given that it was repeated emphatically many times. The Russian diplomats were more professional. The Chinese diplomats, by way of contrast, appeared petulant and unprofessional. Perhaps this was because they were generally junior in rank, itself an apparently deliberate snub of the COI.

The methodology adopted by the COI on the DPRK proved persuasive and effective within the United Nations and beyond. A large body of oral testimony was received in public hearings. These were conducted after the model of the Anglo-American tradition for the conduct of public inquiries. The testimony, substantially organized by the COI's secretariat, addressed the nine subjects in the COI's mandate. The hearings were recorded on film, uploaded to the internet, and supplemented by transcripts produced from the original oral testimony and provided, as appropriate, in the English, Korean, and Japanese languages. The

---

11   Michael D. Kirby, "The United Nations Report on North Korea and the Security Council: Interface of Security and Human Rights," *Australian Law Journal* 89 (2015): 724.

testimony was thus available to the United Nations and the international community, in particular in the ROK and Japan. It was not generally available in the DPRK. That country established an intranet, but permits access to the internet only to elite supporters or beneficiaries of the regime. To contentions that the testimony was unreliable, the COI responded repeatedly by offering to correct any established errors, continuously requesting access to the country but without avail. The COI even invited the DPRK to arrange for representatives to present their evidence and arguments at the public hearings in Seoul. This was awkward for various legal reasons for the ROK. However, the ROK was persuaded to permit it in case the DPRK requested it. All such approaches were ignored by the DPRK.

At the conclusion of its hearings and deliberations, the COI provided an advance copy of the manuscript of its draft report to the DPRK by way of its diplomatic representatives in Geneva. Again, this was ignored. However, the draft report included, as an annexure to the text, a copy of the letter earlier sent by the COI chair, on its behalf, to Kim Jong-un, Supreme Leader of the DPRK.[12] UN officials questioned the sending of such a letter, saying that it was not ordinary UN practice. However, as the report contained allegations that had not been placed before, or answered by, the state concerned, the requirements of due process obliged the COI to provide the details of such allegations to those immediately affected, including the Supreme Leader of the DPRK himself.

Specifically, the letter to Kim Jong-un contained a warning about the findings of violations of human rights made by the COI, including findings of crimes against humanity. This included an express warning about the "command" principle in international law. By that principle, a person in command of the actions of others, who knew, or should have known, that such grave crimes were being committed yet failed to take all necessary and reasonable measures to prevent or redress their occurrence, could be rendered personally liable for the breach [". . . including possibly yourself"].[13] A warning was also given of the recommendation in the COI report drawing the situation in the DPRK

12   The letter to the Supreme Leader is dated January 20, 2014. See UN Human Rights Council, Report of the Commission of Inquiry on Human Rights in the Democratic People's Republic of Korea, A/HRC/25/63, 23–25 (February 7, 2014)

13   A/HRC/25/63, 25.

to the attention of the International Criminal Court (ICC). To this letter and the draft report attached, the COI received no direct reply. Later it received insults and criticism, both published and stated orally before the HRC and the General Assembly both in Geneva and New York when the report was tabled or referred to. However, the opportunity to engage directly with the COI was rejected.

In response to particular inquiries addressed to the mission of China in Geneva, the COI received a letter concerning the treatment of persons claiming refugee status in China. China is a party to the Refugees Convention and Protocol of the United Nations. The letter from China in response to the COI's inquiries came from the Chargé d'Affaires a.i. and Ambassador in the Permanent Mission of China to the United Nations in Geneva, Wu Haitao.[14] Its expressed position was that DPRK citizens who had entered China illegally "do it for economic reasons. Therefore they are not refugees."[15] The letter also stated:

> . . . I wish to reiterate that China does not support the establishment of the Commission of Inquiry on Human Rights in the Democratic People's Republic of Korea by the Human Rights Council. China's position remains unchanged. . . . China hopes that the Commission of Inquiry on Human Rights in the DPRK can function in an objective and impartial manner, and not be misled by unproved information. China requests this letter to be included in the Commission's report to the Human Rights Council.

China (and other countries) repeatedly objected to the COI as a matter of principle. It asserted that the creation of the COI was divisive and not the way to advance human rights through the United Nations. The careful process of the COI to determine the proof and reliability of evidence was "unproved" in the eyes of China because, in advance, China had decided so. This is not the way contested evidence is to be assessed in an independent inquiry. It did not convince the COI.

Findings of Human Rights Abuses and Crimes Against Humanity

It is worth noting at this point that the COI report rejected a number of the complaints made to it concerning alleged human rights violations

---

14 A/HRC/25/63, 33.
15 A/HRC/25/63, 33–36.

on the part of the DPRK. These included allegations that the testimony established proof of the international crime of genocide. The COI's conclusion in this respect was based on the lack of proof of an intentional effort to completely or partly destroy a group of the population based on its nationality, ethnicity, race, or religion.[16] Specifically, the COI concluded that the evidence of the radical reduction of the Christian population of North Korea might have an innocent explanation falling short of genocide.[17] The COI also rejected as unproved allegations of the presence and use of chemical weapons in the DPRK. It specifically accepted that there had been some improvements in the DPRK's treatment of persons with disabilities. However, otherwise, the COI accepted much of the testimony received by it from witnesses concerning human rights violations, many of them rising to the level of "crimes against humanity." The COI concluded:

> Systematic, widespread and gross human rights violations have been, and are being, committed by the [DPRK], its institutions, and officials. In many instances, the violations of human rights found by the Commission constitute crimes against humanity. These are not mere excesses of the state. They are essential components of a political system that has moved far from the ideals on which it claims to be founded. The gravity, scale, and nature of these violations reveal a state that does not have any parallel in the contemporary world. Political scientists of the 20th century characterised this type of political organization as a totalitarian state: a state that does not content itself with ensuring the authoritarian rule of a small group of people, but seeks to dominate every aspect of its citizens' lives and terrorizes them from within.[18]

Crimes against international human rights law were found in respect of each of the nine specific substantive areas included in the mandate given to the COI by the HRC. The conclusions of the COI contained specific findings, where possible, about the persons or institutions responsible, in international or local law, for proven offenses.[19]

The conclusions in the COI report also contained a number of findings and recommendations that were specifically addressed to the DPRK, calling for immediate improvements in the human rights situation at

---

16   A/HRC/25/CRP.1, 350, ¶1156.
17   A/HRC/25/CRP.1, 351, ¶1159.
18   A/HRC/25/CRP.1, 365, ¶1211.
19   A/HRC/25/63, 16–18, ¶89, esp. (m), (n), (o), (p), (q), (r), (s).

home and in outreach to the United Nations, its neighbors, and, in particular, the ROK. Recommendations were also addressed to China, urging it to "respect the principle of non-refoulment," which forbids repatriating persons to the DPRK unless that action is verified by international human rights monitors.[20] China was urged to provide the Office of the High Commissioner for Refugees with full and unimpeded access to the DPRK and to persons seeking contact with it. China was also encouraged to request technical assistance from the UN to help it meet its obligations under international refugee law. Specific proposals were made for the regularization of the status of women and men from the DPRK who marry or have a child with a Chinese citizen who are denied civic equality and to prevent agents of the DPRK from abducting their alleged nationals from Chinese territory.[21]

So far as the international community was concerned, the COI recommended that the Security Council should refer the situation of the DPRK to the International Criminal Court and adopt targeted sanctions concerning those who appear to be most responsible for the crimes against humanity.[22] The High Commissioner for Human Rights, with the support of the HRC and General Assembly, was urged to establish a regional structure to ensure continuing accountability for human rights violations on the part of DPRK, following the end of the COI's mandate. Such a structure was subsequently established in Seoul. It continues to operate.[23] In a sense, it continues the fact-finding work of the COI. It interviews persons who have escaped from the DPRK and are willing to offer testimony about the human rights abuses they had experienced or witnessed.

Many recommendations arising out of the COI's findings were addressed to the leadership, government, and institutions of the DPRK. Some were addressed to states that historically enjoyed friendly ties with DPRK. Donors and others were urged to form human rights contact groups to raise concerns and provide support for initiatives to improve the human rights situation in the DPRK.[24] The need for humanitarian aid and for its provision in the DPRK was called to notice.[25] A call

---

20 A/HRC/25/63, 19, ¶90 (d).
21 A/HRC/25/63, 19, ¶90 (e) and (f).
22 A/HRC/25/63, 20, ¶94 (a).
23 A/HRC/25/63, 20, ¶94 (c).
24 A/HRC/25/63, 21, ¶94 (h).
25 A/HRC/25/63, 21, ¶94 (i).

was also made for convening a conference to consider, and if agreed to ratify, a "final peaceful settlement of the [Korean] war [consistent with] the principles of the Charter of the United Nations, including respect for human rights and fundamental freedoms."[26]

The report of the COI was delivered in accordance with its mandate. It was on time, unanimous, and within budget. It was first published by the COI on February 7, 2014. A month later, it was presented by the COI to a plenary meeting of the HRC in Geneva. At the end of March 2014 the report was endorsed by a strong vote of the HRC, on a resolution proposed by the European Union and Japan.[27]

In accordance with the recommendation of the COI, the HRC sent the COI's report to the General Assembly of the United Nations in New York. It was there assigned, in the normal way, to the General Assembly's Third Committee. A strong resolution was prepared for the consideration of the Third Committee by the same co-sponsors. It included the proposal for referral to the ICC. This would involve the invocation of an exceptional source of jurisdiction in the ICC arising from referral of a matter to it by the Security Council in the case of a state party of the UN that has not ratified the Rome Treaty establishing the ICC. DPRK is not a party to that treaty. However, it is a member of the United Nations.[28] It is therefore subject to this exceptional non-consensual jurisdiction.

Within the General Assembly, a large majority was assembled to support the recommendations of the COI. However, Cuba moved a procedural amendment proposing delay in the light of what it said was the "new spirit of cooperation" evident, so it claimed, by the participation of the DPRK in UPR.[29] Cuba therefore urged the General Assembly to delay in the substantive resolution on the part of the Assembly. Eventually, this procedural amendment was defeated in the Third Committee. In the final decision in the plenary session of the General Assembly, the vote for the resolution, supporting the COI report, was

---

26   A/HRC/25/63, 21, ¶94 (j).

27   The HRC vote was adopted on a resolution presented in draft on February 17, 2014, 30 pro, 6 con, 11 abstentions.

28   A referral may be made by vote of the Security Council. The Rome Statute was adopted on July 17, 1998: 2187 UNTS 90. There had earlier been two such referrals by the Security Council in the cases of Darfur and Libya.

29   Hanna Song, *A Second Chance: North Korea's Implementations of Its Recommendations during Its Second Universal Periodic Review* [in Korean] (Seoul: Database Center for North Korean Human Rights, 2019).

116 pro, 20 con, and 55 abstentions.[30] Given the strong findings and recommendations of the COI report and the seductive arguments for postponement and delay offered by the Cuban proposal, the outcome was a powerful endorsement of the COI report on the DPRK. It was a rebuff to the DPRK and its dwindling but familiar band of supporters, generally led by China and the Russian Federation.

Change in the composition of the Security Council was approaching at the time of the foregoing votes in the General Assembly, including the departure of Australia as a non-permanent member of the UN Security Council. It was at this stage, therefore, that the Arria Briefing of interested members of the Security Council was convened on the initiative of the French Republic, the United States of America (Permanent Five members), and Australia. They proposed that the UNSC should place the matter of the DPRK on its agenda, to remain there until removed by vote of the Council.

In the result, eleven members of the Security Council supported this resolution. Two members (China and the Russian Federation) opposed it. Two members (Chad and Nigeria) abstained. The result was that the requisite majority was found for a "procedural motion" of the Security Council, namely more than ten of the fifteen Council members present and voting.[31] China and Russia did not press to a vote their contention that the step asked of the Security Council was not correctly classified as procedural.[32] In consequence, the matter of the DPRK (and thus the issues presented by the COI report) was added to the UNSC's agenda for consideration. Effectively, this was to result in a recurrent opportunity for a debate in each successive year.

In subsequent Decembers, the UN Security Council returned to consider the DPRK, including any progress on its human rights record.

---

30   UN General Assembly, Resolution Adopted by the General Assembly on 18 December 2014, A/RES/69/188 (January 21, 2015).

31   Kirby, "United Nations Report," 725–26.

32   The three non-permanent members of the UNSC that did not sign the letter requesting that the Council take up the issue were lobbied by China and Russia to oppose the procedural vote. Of those three, Argentina ultimately joined in voting for the resolution and the other two (Chad and Nigeria) abstained. China then lobbied energetically against the resolution on the merits. It argued first on camera and then in open session. However, on December 22, 2014, the UNSC voted to add the matter of the DPRK to the Security Council's agenda. The votes were 11 pro, 2 con (China and Russia), and 2 abstentions (Chad and Nigeria).

However, in December 2019, for the first time, the United States of America abstained on taking up the procedural resolution once again. It did so under instructions from the Trump administration.[33] Some further changes in that administration's response to the COI report must now be described, for they constituted a significant shift in the approach to universal human rights generally and to the COI report on the DPRK, in particular.

Change and the Trump Administration

The election of the Trump administration coincided with an escalation in the development and testing by the DPRK of nuclear weapons and long-range missiles. On August 8, 2017, President Trump stated that such initiatives would be met with "fire, fury and frankly power, the likes of which the world has never seen before."[34] Without mentioning it by name, President Trump also chastised China for continuing to support the DPRK.[35] This was to become a recurring theme.

Nevertheless, the United States then moved to arrange meetings between President Trump and the DPRK Supreme Leader, Kim Jong-un. On June 12, 2018, in Singapore, President Trump and Chairman Kim conducted their first summit. Its stated object was the building of a "lasting and robust peace regime on the Korean Peninsula." During the course of the meeting, President Trump committed to providing the DPRK with security guarantees. Chairman Kim reaffirmed the

---

33 Colum Lynch, "Desperate to Save Diplomacy, White House Blocks U.N. Meeting on North Korean Atrocities," *Foreign Policy*, December 2, 2019, https:// foreignpolicy.com/2019/12/09/white-house-blocks-un-meeting-north-korea -atrocities-trump-kim/.

34 Peter Baker and Choe Sang-Hun, "Trump Threatens 'Fire and Fury' Against North Korea if It Endangers U.S.," *New York Times*, August 8, 2017, https://www .nytimes.com/2017/08/08/world/asia/north-korea-un-sanctions-nuclear-missile -united-nations.html.

35 In his speech before the UN General Assembly, Trump said, "It is an outrage that some nations would not only trade with such a regime, but would arm, supply, and financially support a country that imperils the world with nuclear conflict." See "Remarks by President Trump to the 72nd Session of the United Nations General Assembly," September 19, 2017, Trump White House archive, https:// trumpwhitehouse.archives.gov/briefings-statements/remarks-president-trump -72nd-session-united-nations-general-assembly/.

"unwavering commitment" of the DPRK to complete the denuclearization of the Korean Peninsula."[36]

On February 27–28, 2019, a second summit meeting took place between the two leaders. It convened in Hanoi, Vietnam. Following a
dinner on the first day, the summit broke up abruptly on the second
morning, without agreement or the issuance of a closing statement.

A third meeting between the two leaders took place briefly on
June 30, 2019, at the DMZ, Panmunjom. For the first time in the case
of a U.S. president in office, Mr. Trump entered the DPRK territory.
During intervals between these meetings, Chairman Kim had three en-
counters with President Xi of China and also a meeting with President
Putin of the Russian Federation, held in Vladivostok.

At the close of 2019, the Chinese and Russian governments un-
veiled a proposal of their own at the UN Security Council stated to be
based on "humanitarian grounds"[37] to provide the DPRK with wide-
ranging relief from the sanctions imposed by the UNSC since 2006.
The United States, however, rejected the Chinese and Russian move
to relax North Korean sanctions, calling it "premature." A Security
Council diplomat declared that the "UN Security Council cannot support a resolution that subsidizes the DPRK's ongoing development
of weapons of mass destruction by sanctions relief."[38] In the resulting North Korea Human Rights 2019 resolution in the UN General
Assembly, adopted for the fifteenth year in succession, there was one
significant change in late 2019. The ROK, together with the United
States, was missing from the liberal democratic nations that normally
sponsored it. This led to a statement issued by Tomás Quintana, the
United Nations SR on the DPRK. He stated that the absence of the

---

36   "Joint Statement of President Donald J. Trump of the United States of America and Chairman Kim Jong Un of the Democratic People's Republic of Korea
at the Singapore Summit," White House, June 12, 2018, https://trumpwhitehouse
.archives.gov/briefings-statements/joint-statement-president-donald-j-trump
-united-states-america-chairman-kim-jong-un-democratic-peoples-republic-korea
-singapore-summit/.

37   "China and Russia to Hold More UN Talks on Lifting Sanctions; Pitch for
N. Korea—Proposal Would See DPRK Receive Relief from Sanction Measures Related to the Livelihood of the Civilian Population," NK News, January 5, 2020.

38   The official spoke on the condition of anonymity. See Michelle Nichols, "Russia, China to Hold More U.N. Talks on Lifting North Korea Sanctions: Diplomats," Reuters, December 29, 2019, https://www.reuters.com/article/us-northkorea
-usa-un/russia-china-to-hold-more-u-n-talks-on-lifting-north-korea-sanctions
-diplomats-idUSKBN1YX0LD.

ROK from the resolution "sends a message that implies that human rights, the importance of respecting and protecting the human rights of the people in North Korea, is something that comes second in [the ROK's] effort to build a relationship with [the DPRK]."[39] However, although 60 countries co-sponsored the UNGA resolution, the ROK for the first time since 2008 declined to do so. As a result, a joint letter was addressed by 22 countries, as well as 76 non-governmental bodies, urging President Moon Jae-in of South Korea to maintain his support for human rights in the DPRK.[40] This representation did not draw a response from the ROK.

How did this situation come about? Is it an indication of a new, less insistent approach on the part of the ROK toward human rights in the DPRK? Does the ROK withdrawal from the statement of global concern about human rights in the DPRK, together with the U.S. withdrawal in December 2019 from support for a debate on the DPRK in the Security Council, indicate an acceptance by the ROK and the United States of the DPRK's often repeated assertion that references to human rights concerns are "political" and bound to be "counter-productive"?

The ROK's Ambivalent Stand on Human Rights

After the division of the Korean Peninsula, the ROK government was often a mixture of military rule or dominance by conservative political parties with deep hostility toward the ruling elite in the DPRK, particularly the successive members of the family of Kim Il-sung. However, an exception was the Kim Dae-jung administration (1998–2003). President Kim introduced the "Sunshine Policy." This favored a measure of détente in the relations between the ROK and the DPRK. Kim Dae-jung was lauded by progressives in and out of Korea as a genuine human rights activist and hero. He had made his name during the authoritarian era of the ROK, which lasted up to the late 1980s, immediately prior to his election. President Kim was succeed by Roh Moo-hyun, who

---

39 "UN Human Rights Expert: Seoul Sent Wrong Message to Pyongyang," *New Delhi Times*, December 20, 2019, www.newdelhitimes.com/un-human-rights -expert-seoul-sent-wrong-message-to-pyongyang/.

40 "Letter to President Moon Jae-in, South Korea on Human Rights in North Korea," Human Rights Watch, December 16, 2019. President Moon also refused to receive a visit from the parents of Otto Warmbier, a young U.S. citizen, who died after his expulsion from the DPRK, following his imprisonment and alleged mistreatment in North Korea.

served 2003–08. Both Kim and Roh reached out to, and visited, the DPRK. Both presidents laid great emphasis on the priority of achieving the reunification of the Korean Peninsula. Each shared a belief that the DPRK would ultimately embrace at least minimal changes so far as human rights were concerned. Both Kim and Roh were disinclined to raise civil and political rights (CPR) issues for fear that doing this would derail further inter-Korean relations and engagement without achieving any significant gains for security, national reunification, or human rights.

The response to the Sunshine Policy from the DPRK was, however, disappointing, including for its advocates and defenders in the ROK. The "conservative" opposition to presidents Kim and Roh in the ROK relied on the ongoing evidence of abuse of human rights in the DPRK to maintain the necessity of keeping a distance between the two states. As a result, in late 2007, Lee Myung-bak was elected as the president of the ROK in succession to President Roh. President Lee brought back to office the "conservative" approach and policies (2007–13). He was accused of hostility to public demonstrations and of dismantling the Sunshine Policy. His term was followed by that of President Park Geun-hye (2013–17).

Each of the "conservative" administrations drew a sharp distinction between their government and the preceding "progressive" decade. The resumed emphasis on CPR in the DPRK became a dominating force in ROK national politics. It made it difficult to effectively pursue the achievement of significant progress in inter-Korean relations. It possibly weakened the aspiration that China might agree to act as an intermediary for eliciting changes in the DPRK and facilitating improvement in the plight of refugees leaving the DPRK via China. China had its own internal reasons for resisting emphasis on CPR in the case of the DPRK. Any such emphasis would have had obvious implications for international attention to the state of human rights (especially CPR) in China.

Because I had enjoyed the honor of hosting Kim Dae-jung when he visited Australia shortly before his election as president, I followed closely his policies and "Sunshine" approach. Upon my appointment to the chair of the COI in 2013, long after the presidency and subsequent death of Kim Dae-jung, I visited the Peace Center established in his honor in Seoul to celebrate his life and service. I took the opportunity to meet and pay respects to his widow, Lee Hee-ho. During the conduct of the COI, I repeatedly indicated my desire to enlarge contacts with the then opposition parties in the ROK, reputedly followers of the policies of Kim Dae-jung. They were largely absent from the many South Korean bodies engaging with the COI.

By way of contrast, during her service as president of the ROK, which coincided with the visits of the COI, President Park Geun-hye repeatedly engaged with the COI. We met her twice at the Blue House. She insisted that the ambition closest to her heart was the achievement of the reunification of North and South Korea. However, she advocated the objective of reunification on a basis of freedom, human rights, and prosperity.[41] She also sought to strengthen ties between the ROK and China and the ROK and the Russian Federation. She took advantage of a state visit to Germany, soon after her narrow election win as president of the ROK, to urge practical steps and joint projects to the benefit of both sides of the Korean divide.[42]

In December 2016, President Park Geun-hye was impeached by decision of the National Assembly of the ROK for allegedly having been engaged in influence peddling. Her impeachment was unanimously upheld, and given force, by order of the Constitutional Court of the ROK on March 10, 2017. In consequence, she was removed from office. A presidential election was held immediately. It resulted in the return of a "progressive" candidate, Moon Jae-in, who assumed office as president of the ROK in May 2017. President Moon immediately reestablished several policies of presidents Kim and Roh. Specifically, he arranged inter-Korean summit meetings with the DPRK Supreme Leader Kim Jong-un in April, May, and September 2018. He was also present at the brief yet symbolic meeting of President Trump with Kim Jong-un at the DMZ on June 30, 2019.

Like presidents Kim and Roh, both of whom he admired, President Moon, following his election in May 2017, took immediate steps to attempt an improvement of relations with the DPRK. In July 2017, President Moon, like his predecessor, also chose Berlin as the venue at which to proclaim his commitment to the peaceful reunification of the two Korean states as a long-term project. His policies have not emphasized (or for the most part even mentioned) the human rights of the people of North Korea, certainly not in terms

---

41 "South Korea's President Park Geun-hye's North Korean Strategy," Heritage Foundation, accessed October 16, 2015.

42 Kim Tae-gyu, "Park Offers NK Massive Aid," *Korea Times*, March 28, 2014, http://www.koreatimes.co.kr/www/nation/2014/03/113_154283.html.

of CPR. His primary emphasis has been on reducing the dangers of armed conflict, reducing maximum hours of work, increasing minimum wages, and other policies of a labor leader. He has also been successful in confronting COVID-19. But he has been criticized for his policies on the rights of refugees from the DPRK and of those who want to distribute by balloon, across the DMZ, leaflets critical of the DPRK.[43]

It has to be acknowledged that the hard-line policies on human rights, especially on CPR, evident during the decade that preceded the election of President Moon's administration, did not achieve any substantial progress in the DPRK, either on the issue of respect for the human rights of the people of the DPRK (especially CPR) or of denuclearization and security. The one new element that does appear to have had an impact on the DPRK has been the strengthening of the UN sanctions that remain solidly in place under successive UNSC resolutions.

A chief reason for the trial and execution of the uncle by marriage of Kim Jong-un, Jang Song-thaek, soon after the installation of Kim Jong-un as Supreme Leader was, reportedly, the latter's concern that Jang had aspirations to lead the DPRK down a reformist Chinese path.[44] His execution and later the murder of the Supreme Leader's half-brother, Kim Jong-nam, at Kuala Lumpur Airport in February 2017, demonstrated vividly the destructive feature of the political governance of the DPRK described in detail in the COI report.[45] So far as the DPRK is concerned, lawlessness, like human rights violations, is tolerable because it is effective and ordered by the Kim leadership. This happens because such conduct in the DPRK is unaccountable. It is effectively beyond legal restraints at home. Seemingly, it is also immune from effective responses outside its own borders. The latest

---

43 "Regarding Fighters for a Free North Korea and Keunsaem," North Korea Freedom Coalition, July 15, 2020, www.nkfreedom.org/2020/07/15/regarding -fighters-for-a-free-north-korea-and-keunsaem/.

44 The execution of Jang Song-thaek in December 2013 is noted in the COI report, A/HRC/25/CRP.1, 43, ¶57.

45 Subsequently, Malaysia suspended diplomatic relations with DPRK. However, these were quietly restored and the Malaysian embassy in the DPRK was reopened in January 2020. See Prashanth Parameswaran, "What's Behind Malaysia's North Korea Embassy Reopening Announcement?" *The Diplomat*, January 7, 2020, https://thediplomat.com/2020/01/whats-behind-malaysias-north-korea-embassy -reopening-announcement/.

illustration of this feature of the DPRK is the destruction by explosives of the joint liaison office in Kaesong on the order of the Supreme Leader's sister, Kim Yo-jong. Such petulant destructive conduct is also a feature of the conduct of leaders who do not feel restrained by ordinary rules and constraints.

The only response to the actions of critics that the DPRK acknowledges is the series of sanctions imposed by the UNSC. Unused to constraints of the rule of law and human rights, the DPRK repeatedly and vehemently demands the repeal of the UN sanctions. Admittedly, some humanitarian burdens flow from the UN sanctions. But with no apparent progress at home in terms of the human rights of the people of the DPRK and increasing risks and dangers in terms of its expanding nuclear arsenal and missile capacity, it is hard to conclude that the sanctions against the DPRK can be safely released at this time.

Where Principle and Realism Meet

The 2014 COI report on the DPRK was an evidence-based and closely reasoned examination of testimony, publicly received, that was overwhelming and convincing. That testimony was considered by experienced decision-makers on the COI who published their report and presented it to the international community at the highest levels.

When, at the conclusion of the Second World War, the international community established the United Nations, it did so at a critical moment in human history. It was conscious that the failures of the League of Nations[46] had led to a second brutal conflict of global proportions within fewer than twenty years. That conflict eventually occasioned even more terrible sufferings on the part of civilians, members of the military, and especially minorities. By its end, that conflict and its outcome yielded up evidence of genocide and the Holocaust. It gave birth to international treaty law governing genocide and to the new international war crimes and "crimes against humanity." Such crimes amount to acts of violence on the part of states and individuals that "shock the conscience of humanity."[47]

---

46   Sir Frederick Pollock, *League of Nations* (London: Stevens and Sons, 1920).
47   Philippe Sands, *East West Street: On the Origins of Genocide and Crimes Against Humanity* (New York: Vintage Books, 2016).

It was in the aftermath of the discovery and response to such crimes that the international community began the long journey toward providing remedies and redress to those who had suffered and for their families haunted by the memories of the victims—and for communities and nations for whom the enormous wrongs were part of haunting grievances that called out for redress. Eventually, tribunals were created, including the International Military Tribunals and the International Criminal Court and other like tribunals. These bodies were created to ensure that such grave crimes would not go unconsidered and unpunished, as they had in the past, and that humanity would not turn its back, as it had done in the 1930s and the 1940s. It would respond. Humanity would investigate. It would consider serious findings. And it would act upon proven evidence and follow up on appropriate recommendations.

In due course, the international community went beyond the creation of laws, national criminal courts, and international tribunals. It endorsed the concept of the "responsibility to protect," which captures a simple and powerful idea.[48] The "responsibility to protect" was unanimously adopted by the UN General Assembly at the 2005 World Summit. It is not acceptable simply to wring our hands and cry "never again." Action must be taken, however difficult and even dangerous the path of pursuing such action can sometimes be.

Of course, there are major problems facing the international community, in providing the urgent attention and action that is essential to reducing and eliminating the dangers of nuclear weapons and intercontinental missiles that could deliver them.

To acquiesce meekly in assertions that findings of such crimes are the result of "hostility" and that they did not, and could not, occur (while denying access to the world to inspect and evaluate such denials for itself) is also a reaction lacking in persuasiveness or rationality. To refuse action on the footing that findings of the need for action amount to "political" prejudice and evidence of hatred and hostility is also not a rational response to the demand for action. When the Charter of the

---

48 Gareth Evans, *The Responsibility to Protect: Ending Mass Atrocity Crimes Once and for All* (Washington, DC: Brookings Institution Press, 2008). See also UN General Assembly "2005 World Summit Outcome," A/Res/60/1 (October 24, 2005), https://www.un.org/en/development/desa/population/migration/generalassembly/docs/globalcompact/A_RES_60_1.pdf.

United Nations was adopted and the UDHR and UN treaty law on human rights was formulated and brought into effect, the world moved beyond acquiescence and frozen incapacity.

There is no convincing (or even optimistic) evidence that the alternative strategies advocated by the "progressives" or "conservatives" in the ROK, or the wider world, will hasten change in the DPRK. Charm and sunshine have not worked. Isolation and hectoring have failed. Threats seem hollow in light of the dangers of retaliation. The only strategy that appears to cause real pressure upon the DPRK is that of the economic sanctions, imposed by votes of the UN Security Council in which DPRK's partial allies, China and Russia, earlier took an affirming part—and repeated insistence upon the persuasive power of evidence-based reports such as that of the COI.

Doing nothing and praying for change is not an acceptable strategy in the case of the DPRK. This is so given the urgency occasioned by the ongoing suffering of the people of the DPRK and the dangers of a conflict where accidents and mistakes might occur in highly populated places and emotionally charged circumstances.

Military confrontation of the DPRK is far too risky. Reviving the Six-Party Talks and mixing economic temptations with blunt and honest communications seem the best way forward at this time. The Marshall Plan that followed the Second World War rescued many countries from the dangerous cycle of competing ideologies. The one truly imaginative image advanced by President Trump in his negotiations with the DPRK was probably that of Trump hotels, golf clubs, resorts, economic advancement, and tourism. If that were to happen, the DPRK might begin the journey that Cambodia commenced after 1991, for all the faults and limitations of the Hun Sen regime. The prospect of foreign universities and English-language institutions might tempt the Supreme Leader, who grew up in a Western society (Switzerland) and who knows the endless attractions they offer to young people.

The continuation of the present approach is full of danger. Silence about human rights is intolerable. Within the ROK, there is a large population of refugees from the North. They should be engaged and consulted. They will have much knowledge and experience concerning what is needed and what might work. Dreaming about reunification will not make it happen. Imagination and new strategies are sorely needed. But releasing the pressure of sanctions without assured dividends in the observance of human rights, dismantling of weaponry, and achievement of security is not the way to go.

Rational thought and a knowledge of history suggest that change will come in the DPRK. For the sake of Korea and the world, a greater sense of urgency and realism are required to help change have a chance. Otherwise, we are sleepwalking once again toward substantial dangers.

3 Encouraging Progress on Human Rights in North Korea

The Role of the United Nations and South Korea

Joon Oh

H aving gone through the atrocities of the two world wars in the twentieth century, the international community bestowed on the United Nations, as a matter of top priority, the responsibility to protect and promote human rights of all people in the world.[1] However, the Universal Declaration of Human Rights adopted by the General Assembly in 1948, despite its historic significance as the UN's first human rights instrument, was not an international treaty binding on states. Through a long process of negotiations, two general treaties on human rights were adopted in 1966. These are the Covenant on Civil and Political Rights and the Covenant on Economic, Social, and Cultural Rights.

The decision to have two international covenants, instead of a single one, reflects the political considerations linked to the different ideologies of socialist and Western countries. Economic, social, and cultural rights were more strongly advocated by the Soviet bloc as they were intertwined with communist beliefs. Western countries considered that civil and political rights were more important and focused their efforts in protecting them. Even today, it is commonly believed that economic, social, and cultural rights require more public resources to achieve, while civil and political rights are realized under more robust democratic governance. In any case, both are based on the premise that it is the states that are responsible for protecting human rights.

---

1 For more detailed information on how the United Nations was created on the basis of three pillars including human rights, see chapter 2 in this volume.

In addition to these two, there are seven other human rights conventions that have been adopted by the UN over the last seventy-five years.[2] Most of them concern the human rights of social minorities and vulnerable groups in society, including women, children, racial minorities, migrant workers, and persons with disabilities. As such, one can say that the UN's efforts for human rights have been undertaken in two important ways: protecting human rights of citizens against violations by states and promoting the human rights of social minorities.

How Has the UN Addressed the North Korean Human Rights Issue So Far?

When it comes to protecting human rights from state violations, there are at least three levels of measures the UN can take in today's world: (1) engaging the government in question through human rights dialogue and technical cooperation, (2) naming and shaming—for example, by adopting country-specific human rights resolutions—and (3) taking new and more coercive approaches such as a citation of the responsibility to protect (R2P) and a referral to the International Criminal Court (ICC). Let us see how these measures have been applied to the case of the DPRK.[3]

Even though earlier there had been sporadic reports by advocacy groups on human rights abuses in North Korea,[4] due to the country's extreme seclusion, its human rights situation came to light only in the 1990s. Thousands of North Koreans fled their country in desperation as a result of severe food shortages that hit the country in 1994. The vast majority of them came to South Korea via China, enduring great

---

2   They all together constitute nine core international human rights instruments as defined by the Office of the UN High Commissioner for Human Rights (OHCHR). See Office of the High Commissioner, "The Core International Human Rights Instruments and Their Monitoring Bodies," https://www.ohchr.org/EN/ProfessionalInterest/Pages/CoreInstruments.aspx.

3   In this chapter, common names—South Korea and North Korea—are used together with the official country names of the two Koreas, the Democratic People's Republic of Korea (DPRK) and Republic of Korea (ROK).

4   Amnesty International began to issue some basic reports on the DPRK in 1977. For example, see *Amnesty International Report 1977* (London, England: Amnesty International Publications, 1977), https://www.amnesty.org/download/Documents/POL100061977ENGLISH.PDF.

hardships. The North Korean defectors testified before South Korean and international audiences on what they had experienced in the North. Such newly revealed information triggered debates on the regime's human rights abuses, not only among civil society but in intergovernmental institutions. The UN Commission on Human Rights and the General Assembly began deliberating DPRK's human rights conditions as part of their agenda from 2003 and 2005, respectively.

Human rights dialogue

There has been only one case of bilateral human rights dialogue with Pyongyang that is worth mentioning. It was the EU-DPRK human rights dialogue that took place in 2001 and 2002. At the dialogues, the EU reportedly raised human rights concerns, including the existence of prison camps, the use of torture, and the lack of freedom of expression and other political freedoms. North Korea broke off the talks in 2003 after the Europeans introduced a resolution on DPRK's human rights at the UN Commission on Human Rights.[5]

A more multilateral form of dialogue has been conducted in the context of the Universal Periodic Review (UPR) by the Human Rights Council. The UN Commission on Human Rights was replaced by the Human Rights Council in 2006, with a view to making the human rights discussions more effective. An important component of the Human Rights Council is the UPR, which has introduced a regular assessment of the human rights records of all UN member states. As a member state of the United Nations, the DPRK received the UPR three times during the ten years from 2009 to 2019.

The DPRK has shown relatively positive recognition of this peer review mechanism. At the latest UPR in 2019, 262 recommendations were put forward by participating peer member states.[6] North Korea accepted 132 of them, declined 74, and took note of 56. They accepted recommendations, for example, to consider acceding to the human rights conventions to which they have yet to become party. They

---

5   See UN Commission on Human Rights, Resolution 2003/10, Situation of Human Rights in the Democratic People's Republic of Korea (April 16, 2003), https:// ap.ohchr.org/documents/sdpage_e.aspx?b=1&c=50&t=11.

6   UN Human Rights Council, "Universal Periodic Review—Democratic People's Republic of Korea," https://www.ohchr.org/EN/HRBodies/UPR/Pages/KPindex .aspx.

rejected recommendations such as the one calling for the shutdown of the North's political prison camps.[7]

Human rights dialogue is also conducted through the work of expert committees established by the nine core human rights instruments. These committees, commonly called treaty bodies, review periodic reports from States Parties on the measures they have taken to carry out their obligations under each treaty. After considering the reports, treaty bodies make recommendations about how the State Party can improve its compliance with its treaty obligations.[8]

North Korea has so far ratified five human rights treaties—the Convention on the Rights of the Child (CRC), the Convention on the Elimination of All Forms of Discrimination against Women (CEDAW), the Convention of the Rights of Persons with Disabilities (CRPD), the International Covenant on Civil and Political Rights (ICCPR), and the International Covenant on Economic, Social, and Cultural Rights (ICESCR)—though in some cases, such as ICCPR and ICESCR, the DPRK's state reports are more than a decade overdue.

Naming and shaming

Article 2 (7) of the UN Charter states that the United Nations has no authority to "intervene in matters which are essentially within the domestic jurisdiction of any State," while this principle "shall not prejudice the application of enforcement measures under Chapter VII" of the charter. To put it in layman's terms, the so-called principle of non-intervention is applied to all issues except Chapter Seven enforcement for collective security. As such, what the UN can do vis-à-vis human rights violations by states has long been limited to "naming and shaming," mostly in the form of country-specific resolutions adopted by the General Assembly or the Human Rights Council.

Opinion is divided as to how effective naming and shaming has been in promoting human rights internationally. Still, the bottom line is that gathering and promulgating information on a country's human rights

---

7   The international community has for years urged DPRK to close the camps and release an estimated 80,000 to 120,000 political prisoners detained in them. But Pyongyang has so far denied the existence of such camps, dismissing such claims as "false propaganda."

8   When Treaty Bodies assess reports from States Parties they may also consider information contained in "shadow reports," which are submitted by civil society organizations and national human rights institutions.

abuses does make a difference, as no government can afford to be indifferent to its reputation. Even the most abusive governments, under certain circumstances, feel that they must take into account international public opinion. More often than not, the government's awareness that its human rights violations will necessarily have an impact on its international standing is probably the most important factor limiting the extent and the severity of those abuses.[9]

In the case of the DPRK, the UN's naming and shaming, which started in 2003, has probably been less successful compared to other cases, given Pyongyang's total rejection of outside criticisms as a uniquely sheltered society. That kind of attitude changed in 2014, a significant year for human rights in North Korea. In February that year, the UN Commission of Inquiry (COI) on Human Rights in the DPRK published a report, which concluded that the human rights violations in North Korea constituted crimes against humanity.[10]

Based on this report, the UN General Assembly adopted a new resolution in December 2014. It encouraged the Security Council to take appropriate action to ensure accountability, including through consideration of referral of the situation to the International Criminal Court and of targeted sanctions against those appearing most responsible for crimes against humanity. The DPRK government, which had shown disregard for previous UN resolutions, changed course and tried to influence the General Assembly resolution, but to no avail. Marzuki Darusman, a member of the COI, later testified that North Korea was so worried that Kim Jong-un would be personally named in the ICC referral that they offered him an opportunity to visit Pyongyang if the leader's name were to be left out of the resolution. This was North Korea's first such invitation, but Darusman did not accept the offer.[11] As recommended by the General Assembly, the Security Council put

---

9   According to studies on the "naming and shaming" approaches by the Human Rights Council, the shaming of one physical integrity violation is jointly associated with decreases in that violation and increases in other violations of human rights.

10   UN Human Rights Council, "Commission of Inquiry on Human Rights in the Democratic People's Republic of Korea," https://www.ohchr.org/EN/HRBodies/HRC/CoIDPRK/Pages/CommissionInquiryonHRinDPRK.aspx.

11   Refer to the *Washington Post* news report of January 23, 2015, titled "UN Point Man on North Korea Urges Continued Focus on Kim Jong-un," https://www.washingtonpost.com/world/asia_pacific/un-point-man-on-north-korea-urges-continued-focus-on-kim-jong-un/2015/01/23/dc922c32-cc5d-471a-8986-7f613392479b_story.html.

the issue on its agenda and held an official meeting to discuss it on December 22, 2014.

Since then, the international community has continued to press the DPRK government to engage with UN human rights mechanisms and to accept and act on the findings of the 2014 COI report. In 2018, a Human Rights Council resolution emphasized the need for advancing mechanisms to ensure that North Korean officials responsible for crimes against humanity are held to account. Pyongyang, however, has continued to refuse cooperation with UN special rapporteurs, including incumbent Tomás Ojea Quintana. Last October, Quintana said he had seen no improvement in North Korea's human rights situation during his three years as special rapporteur.[12] Another disappointing development was that the Security Council, after its annual discussion of the North Korea human rights issue for four consecutive years since 2014, was not able to put it on the agenda in 2018 and 2019. This was probably due to the unfavorable composition of the council membership for those years and to the Trump administration's political considerations to keep Pyongyang engaged in dialogue with the United States.

Responsibility to Protect and the ICC

During the last two decades, there have been new efforts by the international community in addressing serious human rights violations, beyond the traditional naming and shaming approach. These new tools include the Responsibility to Protect (R2P), the International Criminal Court (ICC), and an emerging, though controversial, concept of humanitarian intervention.

Responsibility to Protect (R2P). The Responsibility to Protect is an international commitment endorsed by the UN at the 2005 World Summit to address four key concerns of genocide, war crimes, ethnic cleansing, and crimes against humanity.[13] The R2P calls on the international community to take responsibility to protect citizens of a country that fails to safeguard its people from those four kinds of atrocities.

---

12   "UN Investigator: 11 Million North Koreans Are Undernourished," *Al Jazeera*, October 23, 2019, https://www.aljazeera.com/news/2019/10/investigator-11 -million-north-koreans-undernourished-191023005305009.html.

13   See UN General Assembly, 2005 World Summit Outcome, A/RES/60/1, ¶138– 40 (October 24, 2005), https://www.un.org/en/development/desa/population/ migration/generalassembly/docs/globalcompact/A_RES_60_1.pdf.

If there is a need to use force under the R2P, an authorization should come solely from the Security Council.[14]

The human rights situation in the DPRK technically warrants an application of the R2P, as several UN resolutions have already confirmed the existence of "crimes against humanity" being committed there, which constitutes one of the four atrocities addressed by the R2P. In reality, however, it would be extremely difficult, if not impossible, for outsiders to interfere with atrocity crimes in North Korea. Above all, using force to change the North's human rights behavior does not seem realistic, considering the position of China and Russia in the Security Council and the risks stemming from a military confrontation with nuclear-armed North Korea.

The International Criminal Court (ICC). The International Criminal Court began functioning in 2002 at its seat in The Hague, Netherlands. The ICC has jurisdiction to prosecute individuals for the international crimes of genocide, crimes against humanity, war crimes, and the crime of aggression. It is intended to complement existing national judicial systems and therefore may exercise its jurisdiction only when certain conditions are met, such as when the Security Council or individual states refer a situation to the court. In fact, there have already been several cases, in different parts of the world, in which high-level officials including heads of state were held accountable by the court for severe abuses of human rights. DPRK is not yet a member state of the ICC and therefore its case may only be referred to the court by a decision of the Security Council. That explains why Pyongyang reacted so seriously when the 2014 General Assembly resolution first recommended the Security Council to consider a referral to the ICC, in accordance with the COI report.

Humanitarian intervention. Humanitarian intervention usually refers to an unauthorized use of force by a third party to halt human rights abuses in a certain country. Proponents of humanitarian intervention argue that the world's most powerful countries have a responsibility to protect innocent civilians around the world. But opponents view military intervention as an act of thinly veiled Western dominance and an assault on state sovereignty. As such, humanitarian intervention

---

14 For instance, the council cited the R2P when it sanctioned the Libyan intervention in 2011.

is still an evolving concept at best. But, as we know, international customs are a legitimate source of international law. Thus, if more widely accepted and practiced, humanitarian intervention could have long-term and far-reaching implications for human rights in the world, including in North Korea.

How Has South Korea Dealt with the North Korean Human Rights Issue in the UN?

The ROK government began to pay attention to the North Korean human rights issue in the mid-1990s, when it emerged with the testimonies of defectors from the North. Even before that time, observers of North Korea in the South must have known how the dictatorship in Pyongyang had oppressed its citizens to stay in power. But because South Korea itself had been sometimes criticized for human rights violations, Seoul was most likely not interested in raising the issue internationally or bilaterally until its democratization in the late 1980s.

The ROK administration of President Kim Young-sam (1993–98) started to express concern over the human rights situation in the DPRK. In 1995, Minister of Foreign Affairs Gong Ro-Myung mentioned the North Korean human rights problem for the first time in his speech to the UN General Assembly. However, due to the strained inter-Korean relations at that time, such activities were often considered to be the South's North Korea bashing rather than human rights advocacy. President Kim Dae-jung, who succeeded Kim Young Sam, introduced the "Sunshine Policy," which promoted engagement with North Korea. Under the policy, his administration was reluctant to publicly pressure Pyongyang on human rights. This was not particularly conspicuous yet, as the North Korean rights issue was still off any international agenda.

But it soon became a thorny issue in 2003 when the UN Commission on Human Rights first addressed it officially. This timing coincided with the inauguration of President Roh Moo-hyun in South Korea, who represented another progressive political party. The Roh administration's stance on human rights in North Korea was somewhat more forthcoming than the previous one's, promising to convey the international community's concerns to Pyongyang through inter-Korean dialogue and to improve human rights conditions through technical cooperation. It was also argued that human rights could only be discussed in an environment where basic subsistence needs had been met, justifying the provision of humanitarian aid, including rice and fertilizer, to North Korea.

On the UN resolutions on DPRK human rights, the Roh administration did not participate in the voting (2003), abstained (2004 and 2005), voted in favor (2006), and abstained again (2007).[15] When the ROK abstained, its representative cited special inter-Korean relations as an explanation of vote, while expressing that Seoul shared the international community's concerns regarding the human rights violations in DPRK. South Korea's inconsistency in dealing with the North Korean human rights resolutions ended when it started to vote in favor of them from 2008 onward.

Under the conservative administrations of presidents Lee Myung-bak and Park Geun-hye in 2008–16, the North Korean human rights issue was given more attention and support. This period coincided with the heightened tensions surrounding North Korea's nuclear weapons program, which warranted harsher criticism against human rights abuses in the North, both in South Korea and internationally. The Park administration, parallel to the Obama administration in the United States, was active in raising global awareness on the issue. These efforts were given new momentum by the 2014 report of the UN COI on human rights in the DPRK. Domestically, the Park administration was able to pass the North Korean Human Rights Act in 2016, which had been hanging in the National Assembly for nearly ten years.[16]

When the DPRK human rights issue came to the Security Council for the first time in 2014, I myself represented the Republic of Korea, which was a non-permanent member of the Security Council at the time. In the historic meeting on December 22, 2014, I made a statement for eight minutes, and its video recording for the last three minutes (as in the text below) was widely watched and received positive public response in South Korea.[17]

---

15   In 2003 and 2004, the resolutions were adopted in the Commission on Human Rights, while those in 2005–07 were in the General Assembly.

16   For the English text, see "North Korean Human Rights Act," Korean Law Information Center, https://www.law.go.kr/eng/engLsSc.do?menuId=2&query=NORTH%20KOREAN%20HUMAN%20RIGHTS%20ACT#liBgcolor1.

17   For the whole text, see UN Security Council, The Situation in the Democratic People's Republic of Korea, S/PV.7353 (December 22, 2014), https://undocs.org/en/S/PV.7353.

Mr. President,

Speaking at this meeting is probably my last duty in the Council. When we first arrived in the Council two years ago, one of the first issues we tackled was the Democratic People's Republic of Korea's missile and nuclear issues. In the Council, my country has dealt with many issues to which we have not been party, with a view to contributing to the work of the Council. Yet, somehow, our term in the Council started, and is ending, with the North Korean issue.

It must be just a coincidence, but I say that with a heavy heart, because, for South Koreans, the people of North Korea are not just anyone. Millions of South Koreans still have family members living in the North, even though we never hear from them and even though, by now, the pain of separation has become a cold fact of life. We know that they are there, just a few hundred kilometers away from where we live. We cannot read the descriptions in the commission of inquiry report without it breaking our hearts. We cannot watch video clips from North Korea without flinching at every scene. We cannot listen to the stories of North Korean defectors without sharing their tears, without feeling as if we are there with them experiencing the tragedies.

As we leave the Council with the debate on the human rights situation in the Democratic People's Republic of Korea, we do so with an ardent wish. The ardent wish is for the situation to improve for the people of North Korea, our innocent sisters and brothers, who are on the street, in the countryside, in the prison camps, who are suffering for no reason. We only hope that one day in the future, when we look back on what we have done today, we will be able to say that we did the right thing for the people of North Korea, for the life of every man and woman, boy and girl, who has the same human rights as the rest of us. Thank you.

The new progressive administration under President Moon Jae-in, which came to power in 2017, has returned to a policy with priority on peace building and engagement with North Korea. The Moon administration is keen on improving human rights in North Korea, more through economic cooperation and humanitarian assistance than enhancing advocacy or seeking accountability. Somehow, such a low-key approach seemed to be shared by the Trump administration in the United States, which was not particularly enthusiastic about international naming and shaming when it came to human rights issues.

What Can South Korea Do for Human Rights in North Korea?

The present situation of human rights in North Korea is a great concern for the international community. Sitting on the other side of the divided Korean Peninsula, South Korea should have even greater concern. This is not only because the suffering of the North Korean people is felt more personally, but also because without protection for human rights in the North, peace and security on the peninsula will always remain fragile. Since 2018, there has been some progress in relations between the two Koreas. The Moon administration, eager to make peace more durable, seems to believe that raising the human rights issue with North Korea might risk spoiling this hard-won breakthrough.

Given these ongoing efforts to keep engaging North Korea and to avoid confronting Pyongyang, I would like to suggest that the ROK government can take at least three approaches to improve the human rights situation in the DPRK: they are (1) a non-political approach, (2) an institutional approach, and (3) a non-governmental approach.

Non-political approach

Issues related to human rights, which have a great deal to do with democratic governance, cannot avoid being regarded as political. North Korea's human rights issue, in particular, has long been subject to political debate in South Korea. However, efforts can be focused on making the issue as non-political and technical as possible. At the risk of oversimplification, one can say that using human rights issues for the purpose of bashing the Kim Jong-un regime is equally as political as turning a blind eye to these issues for fear of upsetting the regime.

Even from the perspective of an authoritarian government, while political and civil rights are necessarily linked to democratization, economic and social rights can be promoted without drastic political consequences. Therefore, until a meaningful process of democratization starts in North Korea, we can still help the North Korean people realize more economic and social rights through technical cooperation and humanitarian assistance. Needless to say, such cooperation and assistance should be conducted within the boundary of the international sanctions imposed on the DPRK due to its weapons of mass destruction programs, which effectively narrows down the option to assistance of a humanitarian nature.

At the same time, however, South Korea should continue to play its role in international naming and shaming on North Korea's human rights issue. In 2019, the ROK government stopped co-sponsoring the UN General Assembly resolution on the situation of human rights in the DPRK. This change of stance by South Korea was criticized by human rights groups in a December 2019 joint letter.[18] The ROK Ministry of Foreign Affairs explained that the decision was made "in comprehensive consideration of the overall circumstances, such as the current situation on the Korean peninsula."[19] However, this kind of political approach is not desirable, as it will only weaken South Korea's principled position on the issue internationally and vis-à-vis North Korea, thus limiting its leeway in pursuing non-political and human rights–based assistance programs in North Korea as well.

Institutional and legal approach

The North Korean Human Rights Act (NKHRA), enacted in South Korea in 2016, set guidelines for the protection and advancement of human rights for North Korean citizens in accordance with the Universal Declaration of Human Rights. It also requires Seoul to implement the recommendations of the COI report, assist North Koreans who have escaped their country, and research and publish status reports on human rights conditions in North Korea. The adoption of the NKHRA was agreed upon by both ruling and opposition parties and welcomed by civil society in South Korea. According to the NKHRA, four bodies were to be established in order to ensure proper implementation of the legislation: (1) North Korean Human Rights Advisory Committee, (2) Center for North Korean Human Rights Records at the Ministry of Unification, (3) North Korean Human Rights Documentation Office, and (4) North Korean Human Rights Foundation. All of them, with

---

18   "Letter to President Moon Jae-in Re: ROK's Stance on Human Rights in North Korea," Human Rights Watch, December 16, 2019, https://www.hrw.org/news/2019/12/16/letter-president-moon-jae-re-roks-stance-human-rights-north-korea.
19   Ministry of Foreign Affairs, Republic of Korea, "Third Committee of UN General Assembly Adopts Resolution on Situation of Human Rights in DPRK," press release, November 15, 2019, https://www.mofa.go.kr/eng/brd/m_5676/view.do?seq=320829.

the exception of the North Korean Human Rights Foundation, have become functional in varying degrees since 2017. The foundation has yet to be officially established as required by the NKHRA. There are criticisms about this lack of action, coming from both domestic and international observers. The U.S. State Department's report on human rights practices called out Seoul for being slow to establish the North Korean Human Rights Foundation, potentially due to lack of political will.[20] Special Rapporteur Quintana also called for the prompt establishment of the foundation in order to support civil society organizations working on North Korean human rights.[21]

To address these concerns without undermining inter-Korean talks, the ROK government can take measures that are specifically provided in the NKHRA and utilize the institutions established by the act. By doing so, in the face of possible pushback from North Korea, Seoul could respond by explaining its obligation to implement national legislations and enforce the rule of law. Such an approach would give more legitimacy to the ROK government's actions. The government could also reconsolidate the consensus reached among political forces on NKHRA and renew its longstanding advocacy of human rights and democracy.

Non-governmental approach

When government-level exchanges are geared more at rapprochement, it is true that raising uncomfortable issues such as human rights is not easy at inter-Korean talks. In South Korea, there are a number of civil society organizations devoted to raising awareness of and promoting human rights in North Korea. These organizations can supplement the ROK government's role in dealing with human rights issues. The government, for its part, can support these organizations' activities as an indirect way of promoting human rights in North Korea. The aforementioned December 2019 joint letter sent by a coalition of human rights groups claimed that "the only way to ensure long-term improvements

---

20 U.S. Department of State, "2019 Country Reports on Human Rights Practices: Republic of Korea," https://www.state.gov/reports/2019-country-reports-on-human-rights-practices/south-korea/.

21 Tomás Ojea Quintana, "Statement by the Special Rapporteur on the Situation on Human Rights in the Democratic People's Republic of Korea, Tomás Ojea Quintana on His Mission to the Republic of Korea, from 17 to 21 June 2019," UN Human Rights (June 21, 2019), https://www.ohchr.org/EN/NewsEvents/Pages/DisplayNews.aspx?NewsID=24718&LangID=E.

is if the North Korean government continuously hears the same message about the need for change—the message that the international community will never fully welcome North Korea unless it commits to and implements human rights reforms."[22]

Final Thoughts

All current issues involving North Korea, including its human rights situation, have to be considered in connection with the prospects of North Korea's nuclear issue. This long-standing dilemma, together with the consequent international sanctions imposed on North Korea, pose a serious hurdle to any positive change North Korea might seek, not least to the betterment of people's lives there. Under the circumstances, it is also difficult for the ROK government, no matter how willing it is, to pursue meaningful dialogue and cooperation with North Korea. Seoul might be able to continue a certain level of engagement with Pyongyang, especially on people-to-people exchanges and humanitarian assistance. But possibilities for more substantial economic cooperation, such as a reopening of the Kaesong Industrial Complex, are blocked by the UN sanctions put in place since 2017. This is why the North Korean nuclear issue constitutes the toughest stumbling block, which needs to be overcome first, in order for the two Koreas to get back on the road to cooperation and future reunification.

North Korea is at a critical juncture for its future. Nuclear bombs do not give Kim Jong-un the security he desires. What he and his ruling regime need now in order to remain in power are not weapons but food, clothes, cars, and smartphones for people on the streets and their freedom to enjoy those things. It would be in the interest of the regime itself to seek change, rather than waiting to be changed. Hopefully, Pyongyang can make the right choice and embark on a truly new beginning to change the course of the country. That would probably be the best way to eventually guide the North Korean people to life with human dignity and rights.

---

22   "Letter to President Moon Jae-in," Human Rights Watch.

4 DPRK Human Rights on the UN Stage

U.S. Leadership Is Essential

Peter Yeo and Ryan Kaminski

From its inception seventy-six years ago in San Francisco, a core tenet of the mandate of the United Nations has been to promote human rights. The UN Charter, signed on the stage of the San Francisco War Memorial on June 26, 1945, obliges all member nations to promote "universal respect for, and observance of, human rights" and to take "joint and separate action" to that end. Similarly, the Universal Declaration of Rights, adopted by the UN General Assembly with no dissenting votes in 1948, proclaims "all human beings are born free and equal in human rights." While the actions and politics of UN member states have often limited the ability of key UN bodies to fully live up to their potential to promote human rights globally and in nations with challenging human rights situations, UN coalition building—often pushed by the United States in both Republican and Democratic administrations—can still produce meaningful global action in support of internationally recognized human rights.

The sole intergovernmental body at the global level focused on human rights, the UN Human Rights Council (HRC) has been a key platform for both shining a spotlight on and seeking accountability for human rights violations. Actions taken by the HRC on the Democratic People's Republic of Korea, including the creation of a Commission of Inquiry (COI) on Human Rights in the DPRK, are strongly emblematic of the ability of particular UN member states to mobilize UN bodies to promote political, civil, economic, and social rights in countries with often horrendous human rights records.

The ability to achieve human rights "wins" in the UN context, however, is often dependent upon the leadership of the U.S. government.

Through its powerful role in the UN Security Council, its international diplomatic heft, and traditionally strong commitment to promoting human rights, the United States can uniquely rally other countries—often behind the scenes—to support meaningful action.[1] Other UN member states may care deeply about human rights issues, including in North Korea, but lack the U.S. commitment to actively pursuing these issues in all forums and the resources and mission to assemble effective global coalitions. This American role in human rights was on full display with the passage of the resolution establishing the mandate for the DPRK COI in the HRC in 2013. However, Washington's role as a diplomatic enabler and force multiplier for human rights was threatened by the unwillingness of the Trump administration to use every possible tool in its diplomatic toolbox at the UN to promote human rights in the DPRK. For those who care deeply about fundamental freedoms in the DPRK—including a complementary objective of addressing the broader range of nuclear, missile and other political matters in the country—it is imperative that American leadership on human rights in the UN context be restored.

The Record of American Leadership

The willingness of Republican and Democratic administrations to prioritize human rights in the DPRK, particularly in the UN context, is related to several factors. First and foremost, the American view of North Korea as a pariah state—isolated from most of the world and engaging in destabilizing behavior—allows for more forceful attention on all aspects of DPRK domestic and international policy, including human rights. The normal inhibitor that commercial and bilateral diplomatic relations play in constraining frank discussion on human rights has often been absent from the U.S.-DPRK relationship, except in periods of intense diplomatic discussions around North Korea's nuclear program. Further, the passage of the North Korean Human Rights Act in 2004 marked the DPRK human rights situation as a U.S. foreign policy priority. The legislation specifically indicates that "the United Nations has a significant role to play in promoting and improving human rights in North Korea" and creates a special envoy on human rights in North

---

1   For example, see Mark P. Lagon and Ryan Kaminski, *Bolstering the UN Human Rights Council's Effectiveness*, Council on Foreign Relations, January 3, 2017, https://www.cfr.org/report/bolstering-un-human-rights-councils-effectiveness.

Korea to highlight global attention in both bilateral and multilateral contexts.[2] The creation of a country-specific envoy focused solely on that country's human rights situation is highly unusual, if not unprecedented, in the U.S. government context. Furthermore, it enshrines into law that the United States intends to pursue improvements in the DPRK human rights situation at the same time as it seeks to reduce the threat posed by North Korea's nuclear and missile programs.

In the context of UN human rights mechanisms, particularly the HRC, which replaced the troubled UN Commission on Human Rights in 2006, U.S. diplomatic leadership can play a vital role in producing more meaningful human rights outcomes, including on the DPRK. Following a U.S. policy of generally boycotting the HRC during the George W. Bush administration, the council was reportedly nearing "rock bottom," consumed by anti-Israel bias and rigid regional voting blocs.[3] But this began to observably shift during the Obama administration after the United States reversed course and sought membership in the body.

Broadly speaking, two studies by the Council on Foreign Relations in 2012 and 2017 found U.S. membership in the HRC improved the body's performance in several ways. Over two successive three-year terms of membership and one year of hiatus off the council due to term limits, the U.S. record of leadership at the HRC included strengthening the council's commitment to country-level action, fortifying norms that underpin fundamental freedoms and assist at-risk populations, engaging in coalition-building across tired geopolitical lines, and building momentum for the defense of civil society seeking to engage the HRC.[4]

The United States and the EU partnered at the former UN Commission on Human Rights to establish the first mandate for a UN special rapporteur on the DRPK in 2004.[5] That mandate was ultimately

---

2   North Korean Human Rights Act of 2004, Pub. L. No. 108–333, 118 Stat. 1287 (2004), https://www.congress.gov/108/plaws/publ333/PLAW-108publ333.pdf.

3   See Suzanne Nossel, "Advancing Human Rights in the UN System," Council on Foreign Relations, May 2012, https://cdn.cfr.org/sites/default/files/pdf/2012/05/IIGG_WorkingPaper8.pdf.

4   Nossel, "Advancing Human Rights."

5   See Roberta Cohen, "The High Commissioner for Human Rights and North Korea," in *The United Nations High Commissioner for Human Rights, Conscience for the World*, ed. Felice Gaer and Christen Broecker (Boston: Martinus Nijhoff

transferred to the HRC at its inception. The effort to secure a COI on DPRK in 2013 represented a substantial escalation of the organ's track record of scrutinizing the country's overall rights record. While the EU and Japan held the pen on the draft resolution establishing the COI, Eileen Donahoe, the first U.S. ambassador to the HRC, has cited the effort as a classic case of successful U.S.-led burden sharing. During the negotiations and the run-up to the vote, the United States was able to reassure its allies at the HRC it could be counted on to provide senior-level diplomatic backing for the COI effort. The results of this level of backing could not have been starker. In a surprise to many, the HRC adopted the resolution establishing the COI by consensus, even with China sitting as a member.

In the case of establishing the COI on the DPRK, it is clear that American political and diplomatic leadership was necessary, although not sufficient, to navigate the mandate to approval amid the enticing alternative among some of its key allies of simply keeping to the status quo on the DPRK. Other member states on the council, whose support was essential to the creation of the COI, were encouraged not only by the United States, but also by activists, rights defenders, and survivors of the regime's brutality who generated global awareness, scrutiny, and accountability on human rights in the DPRK. This included a domino effect of momentum—accelerated with U.S. backing—of UN action specific to human rights in the DPRK.

U.S. leadership in scrutinizing the human rights record of the DPRK, particularly in the creation of the COI at the council, can be transformative. The countries that neighbor the DPRK—which other UN member states look to for guidance and counsel when North Korean matters arise—have reason to avoid unnecessary confrontation and, at times, urge moderation on contentious human rights issues. The Japanese government has emphasized human rights abuses in the DPRK, particularly related to the abduction of Japanese citizens and the DPRK's unwillingness to return them. However, Japanese policy toward the DPRK has traditionally been focused on normalization of relations, the long-term potential for economic relations, and the reduction of the security threat to Japanese citizens posed by North Korea's repeated nuclear and missile tests. Both the previous and current South Korean government have also taken actions to put a spotlight on human rights

Publishers, 2014), 293–310, https://www.brookings.edu/wp-content/uploads/2016/06/UNHCR-and-North-Korea-RCohen.pdf.

in the DPRK, including by aiding North Korean escapees, pushing for the implementation of COI recommendations, and detailing the DPRK human rights situation in publications. But the Moon Jae-in administration focused on improving inter-Korean cooperation, and reducing tension through dialogue and discussion, in the hopes of promoting denuclearization of the peninsula and peace between the North and South. China has, at times, not stood in the way of high-profile discussions of the DPRK human rights situation, but is unwilling to be an active champion given its complex and extensive economic and political relationship with Pyongyang. The United States, devoid of these "neighborhood considerations" and with a longstanding, bipartisan commitment to promoting human rights, has been uniquely positioned to rally other UN member states and to push the envelope on pursuing DPRK human rights.

Other UN member states not in the vicinity of the DPRK have also prioritized the discussion of human rights in North Korea and been willing to speak up in multilateral forums. Diplomats from EU nations, Australia, New Zealand, and other countries have used their platforms to speak up for DPRK human rights in multilateral forums, including the HRC, General Assembly, and the Security Council, and to vote for appropriate measures. The progress that has been achieved in highlighting the DPRK human rights situation in the UN context would not have been possible without their active support. The role of the United States in assembling this diplomatic coalition on North Korean human rights, however, cannot be understated. With a staffed ambassador-level diplomat dedicated solely to raising these issues with key partners, large diplomatic missions in New York and Geneva, and a firm commitment to advance DPRK human rights, the United States plays an outsized, important role in convincing other countries to "take the leap" to support measures that may draw the ire of Pyongyang and that may not enjoy the full-throated endorsement and commitment of the countries that neighbor the DPRK. The United States plays this role through quiet but forceful hallway diplomacy, focused diplomatic outreach to world capitals, behind-the-scenes convenings to demonstrate strength in numbers, and high-profile statements on DPRK human rights issues at opportune moments.

American Leadership After the COI

The resulting establishment of the COI and the impact of its nearly 400-page report, based on more than 200 interviews on the overall human rights situation in the DPRK, sent shockwaves through the international human rights community and caught the attention of global media outlets. Perhaps the most significant outcome of the COI report occurred in the UN Security Council in December 2014. With strong U.S. backing and diplomatic maneuvering, a discussion of the human rights situation in the DPRK was procedurally added to the UN Security Council's agenda over objections from Russia and China for the first time in history. Once more, the vote in favor was anything but assured, with a minimum nine votes necessary to add the issue to the council's agenda. In the final vote tally, the measure was added to the council's agenda with two votes above the minimum threshold.[6]

During the UN Security Council meeting, U.S. ambassador to the UN Samantha Power took North Korea's human rights abuses head on. Calling life in the DPRK a "living nightmare" she asserted, "We are methodically documenting your abuses and your impunity will not last forever. When the day comes that you are publicly held accountable, we will be ready."[7] The UN's assistant secretary general for human rights, Ivan Šimonović, also lauded the work of the COI on DPRK, claiming, "Rarely has such an extensive charge-sheet of international crimes been brought to this council's attention."[8] China and Russia predictably opposed convening the meeting at all, but were clearly on the defensive.

In 2016, the HRC took further action on the DPRK. In addition to renewing the special rapporteur mandate on the DPRK, it established a highly exceptional new panel of experts to examine pipelines and opportunities for accountability for crimes against humanity in the DPRK. Once again, the United States was a member of the HRC and supported both measures. The report of the HRC–mandated "Group of Independent Experts on Accountability" was later presented to the HRC in March 2017.[9]

---

6   United Nations, "Security Council, in Divided Vote, Puts Democratic People's Republic of Korea's Situation on Agenda Following Findings of Unspeakable Human Rights Abuses," SC/11720, December 22, 2014, https://www.un.org/press/en/2014/sc11720.doc.htm.

7   Michelle Nichols, "UN Council Meets on North Korea Human Rights Despite China Opposition," Reuters, December 9, 2016, https://www.reuters.com/article/us-northkorea-rights-un-idUSKBN13Y2BH.

8   United Nations, "Security Council, in Divided Vote."

9   Office of the UN High Commissioner for Human Rights, "Group of Independent Experts on Accountability Pursuant to Human Rights Council Resolution 31/18

FIGURE 4.1 Three cycles of UPR recommendations made to the DPRK

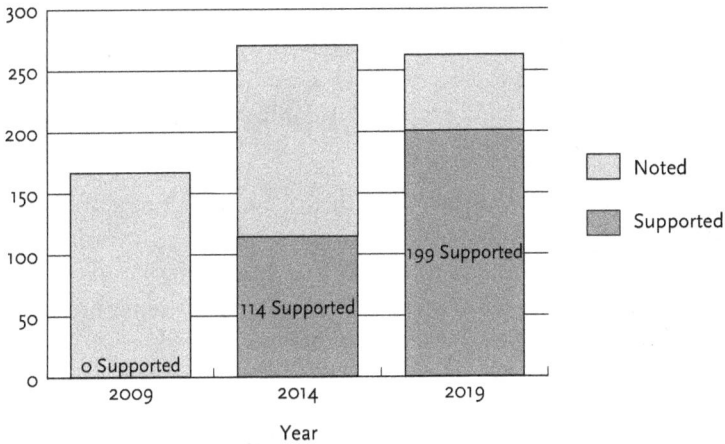

NOTE: UPR = Universal Periodic Review.
SOURCE: Author.

While the focus of this chapter is on the impact of targeted U.S. leadership at the UN to advance human rights in the DPRK, it is worth observing that this pressure has elicited at least some response from the country's leadership in regard to its engagement on human rights at the most fundamental of levels. This includes the DPRK accepting a growing number of recommendations from other UN member states during its quadrennial Universal Periodic Review (UPR) at the UN Human Rights Council. During its initial review in 2009, the DPRK accepted zero recommendations. Yet, during the second and third UPR cycles in 2014 and 2019, its acceptance rate of UPR recommendations increased, covering a wide basket of issues in the country. Accepting and implementing recommendations are not the same, but accepted UPR recommendations provide a platform in further UPR cycles as well as for other UN human rights and development mechanisms.

In 2017, DPRK permitted a first-ever official visit by a UN independent expert to the country with a focus on the human rights of persons with disabilities. Once more, these measures representing the

on the Situation of Human Rights in the Democratic People's Republic of Korea," March 13, 2017, https://www.ohchr.org/en/hrbodies/sp/countriesmandates/kp/pages/groupofindependentexpertsonaccountability.aspx.

bare absolute minimum on the spectrum of human rights engagement should not be equated with the tangible improvement of rights on the ground.

That same year, the UN Security Council again met on human rights in the DPRK. During the meeting, U.S. ambassador to the UN Nikki Haley continued the U.S. practice of calling out the Kim regime for gross violations of rights:

> We must tell and retell their [North Korean people's] stories until the world knows what's going on in the black box that is North Korea. We must tell and retell their stories, so that leaders inside and outside of this Council cannot plead ignorance. We have no excuse not to act. . . . The crisis in North Korea is one of human rights and peace and security. History will judge us on how we respond.[10]

Progress at Risk

Despite this track record, there was evident diminishment in U.S. leadership at the UN on the DPRK from the Trump administration, threatening hard-won gains relevant to pressuring Pyongyang on its abysmal track record on human rights. In light of the Trump administration's overall approach to global human rights issues, this should not have come as a surprise. From separating migrant children at the U.S. border from their families to launching the Commission on Unalienable Rights, designed to significantly narrow and politicize the American focus on human rights, the administration showed an unwillingness to promote and abide by recognized human rights, including those enshrined in the Universal Declaration of Human Rights. The administration further diminished its global credibility on human rights through its unwillingness to acknowledge and tackle endemic racism in the United States, and the concomitant need for far-reaching police reform. That said, during the Trump administration other UN member states recognized that the fundamentals of U.S. leadership on global human rights—from the annual Country Report on the Global Human Rights Practices and the International Religious Freedom Report to the daily

---

10 United States Mission to the United Nations, "Ambassador Haley Delivers Remarks to the UN Security Council on the Human Rights Situation in North Korea," December 11, 2017, https://usun.usmission.gov/ambassador-haley-delivers -remarks-to-the-un-security-council-on-the-human-rights-situation-in-north -korea/.

work of U.S. embassies and diplomats to advance human rights issues and the periodic use of certain multilateral forums to advance these matters—continued without significant modification. Under such circumstances, while U.S. credibility was diminished under Trump, it was far better to have the United States continue to use its platform to advance the cause of human rights in North Korea than to have removed the United States from the global scene.

That is why it was so unfortunate that, in December 2018, human rights in the DPRK fell off the UN Security Council's agenda, with the United States failing to secure the nine minimum votes to procedurally advance the meeting forward.[11] At the time, one U.S. official said, "If we are unable to hold this important discussion this month, we hope to revisit holding this meeting in the new year. . . . The U.S. remains deeply concerned with the human rights situation in North Korea"[12] While Ambassador Robert King, senior advisor at the Center for Strategic and International Studies as well as the former U.S. special envoy for North Korea human rights issues at the State Department, has noted that the United States tried its hand again in the new year when the UN Security Council would have had membership more favorable to convening a meeting on the human rights record of the DPRK, he asserts, "there were no signs of any U.S. effort to raise the issue in the Security Council in 2019."[13] That year saw not only a repeat of the human rights situation in DPRK falling off the UN Security Council agenda, but also apparent confusion and ultimately a flip-flop of the U.S. position on the matter.

In December 2019, while the United States held the presidency of the UN Security Council, the U.S. position on pushing for a human rights meeting focused on the DPRK took a conspicuous shift. Over the course of two weeks, the U.S. overall position evolved to three distinct

---

11   Robert King details in a number of reasons for this, including unfavorable UN Security Council membership at the time. He also cites the capacity issues and the DPRK nuclear negotiations. For more background, see his commentary "New U.S. Ambassador to the UN Should Press for Security Council Discussion of North Korean Human Rights," CSIS, September 5, 2019, https://www.csis.org/analysis/new-us-ambassador-un-should-press-security-council-discussion-north-korean-human-rights.

12   As quoted in Michelle Nichols, "U.S. Drops Bid for December UN Meeting on North Korea Abuses: Diplomats," Reuters, December 7, 2018, https://www.reuters.com/article/us-northkorea-rights-un/us-drops-bid-for-december-un-meeting-on-north-korea-abuses-diplomats-idUSKBN1O6281.

13   King, "New U.S. Ambassador."

positions. This included encouraging a trusted non-permanent member on the Security Council to gather signatures for a proposed UN Security Council meeting on the human rights record of the DPRK,[14] a transition to ambivalence on the proposed meeting, to a final position of withdrawing U.S. support for such a meeting. In late 2019, a top DPRK diplomat at the UN issued a letter to permanent and non-permanent members of the UN Security Council denouncing the potential discussion as a "serious provocation" and a "hostile policy."[15] Six days later, on International Human Rights Day, U.S. ambassador to the UN Kelly Craft hedged following a question from a journalist on potential plans for a human rights–focused meeting on the DPRK at the Security Council. "As the U.S. UN ambassador, as an American, I'm very concerned about human rights all over the world. We have not made a decision on whether or not there's a December 10 meeting," Craft responded.[16]

Later, reports emerged that eight of the fifteen council members had signed a letter supporting the UN Security Council meeting on the DPRK, but the letter fell one signature short of the minimum number necessary to move forward with procedural steps to officially put the meeting on the UN Security Council's agenda. With the United States withholding its own signature, it had effectively sunk what had been a marquee American initiative at the UN Security Council that had transcended two administrations and built political pressure on non-permanent and permanent members alike to keep North Korea's human rights record on the body's agenda. When the United States moved to reconstitute the UN Security Council meeting that same month to focus on nonproliferation issues in the DPRK, Ambassador Craft's oral remarks during the meeting did not directly mention human rights in

---

14   Colum Lynch and Robbie Gramer, "Desperate to Save Diplomacy, White House Blocks UN Meeting on North Korean Atrocities," *Foreign Policy*, December 9, 2019, https://foreignpolicy.com/2019/12/09/white-house-blocks-un-meeting-north-korea-atrocities-trump-kim/.

15   As quoted in Michelle Nichols, "North Korea Warns UN Security Council Against Discussing Country's Human Rights," Reuters, December 4, 2019, https://www.reuters.com/article/us-northkorea-usa-un/north-korea-warns-u-n-security-council-against-discussing-countrys-human-rights-idUSKBN1Y82PV.

16   U.S. Mission to the UN, "Remarks by Ambassador Kelly Craft at a UN Press Conference on the U.S. Program of Work for the December Security Council Presidency," December 6, 2019, https://usun.usmission.gov/remarks-by-ambassador-kelly-craft-at-a-un-press-conference-on-the-u-s-program-of-work-for-the-december-security-council-presidency/.

the DPRK.[17] According to reporting from Colum Lynch, writing for *Foreign Policy*, the directive for the United States to withhold support for the meeting came from the White House due to concerns the meeting would interfere with the Trump administration's negotiations with Kim Jong-un on North Korea's nuclear weapons program.[18]

It is important to understand the unique significance of human rights in the DPRK coming up at the UN Security Council. According to Robert King,

> The Security Council clearly is the UN body which receives the highest attention and holds the greatest clout, and it is also quite apparent that the North Koreans pay a particular attention to its actions. North Korea has been attentive and outspoken in defending its policies when the Security Council is involved, and the modest improvements in its human rights record (for example, in treatment of people with disabilities) indicates the importance of pressing North Korea for progress.[19]

Reactions to the meeting again falling off the UN Security Council's agenda in the mainstream human rights community were harsh and spotlighted the potentially problematic precedent the United States had set by effectively canceling the meeting. According to Louis Charbonneau, UN director at Human Rights Watch, "Kim Jong-un and other senior North Korean officials will undoubtedly be elated they can duck U.S. criticism of their human rights record once again this year."[20]

Beyond the high-stakes politicking of the UN Security Council, the downward trajectory of U.S. leadership on North Korea was felt in other arenas. At the UN Human Rights Council, where the United States voluntarily withdrew itself as a member in June 2018, the record is mixed. On the positive side, the United States continued to engage the UPR mechanism. During the review of the DPRK in 2019, the United States made three strong recommendations to Pyongyang, including the need to revise criminal laws to respect religious freedom, shut down all of its political prisoner camps, and permit the unhindered access of

---

17   U.S. Mission to the UN, "Remarks at a UN Security Council Briefing on Nonproliferation and the DPRK," December 11, 2019, https://usun.usmission.gov/remarks-at-a-un-security-council-briefing-on-nonproliferation-and-the-dprk/.

18   Lynch and Gramer, "Desperate to Save Diplomacy."

19   King, "New U.S. Ambassador."

20   Louis Charbonneau, "Who Cares about North Korea's Human Rights Abuses?" Human Rights Watch, December 10, 2019, https://www.hrw.org/news/2019/12/10/who-cares-about-north-koreas-human-rights-abuses#.

humanitarian assistance providers.[21] While no U.S. recommendations were accepted by Pyongyang, the UPR process was helpful in forcing an on-the-record, written response from the regime as well as keeping these issues in the spotlight.

Yet with the U.S. seat empty in the main HRC chamber, Washington's ability to holistically use its full voice and moral authority at the globe's highest intergovernmental human rights body was muffled at best. Conversely, adversaries and alignments of member states that seek to lessen the HRC's ability to conduct robust country-specific scrutiny are working to fill in the gaps, exploit periods when Washington is absent, and build momentum for unhelpful precedents that are unlikely to evaporate in the short term.[22]

As the delicate diplomatic and political effort to muster support for the COI on DPRK underscores, it is both a missed opportunity as well as damaging if the United States is not in the room "signaling" its support to other delegations on efforts pertaining to the DPRK. Relatedly, when votes are taken in the HRC to renew the mandate for the special rapporteur on DPRK or discuss the expert's findings on the country, the U.S. boycott of the council meant it was not expressing support for the mandate or helping bring international attention to key findings in that forum. The United States, however, did continue to engage and support action on human rights in the DPRK in the General Assembly Third Committee in New York, which passes a resolution on the topic on an annual basis.

Another area of concern is the status and disbursement of U.S. funding for the UN, including for agencies and mechanisms that play a role in supporting basic economic rights and dignity in the DPRK. The Trump administration's budget proposal in 2019 attempted to zero out funding for the Office of the UN High Commissioner for Human Rights, UNICEF, and UN Development Program, and called for across-the-board cuts to U.S. funding for the United Nations. The approach, however, was handily rejected by Congress on an overwhelmingly bipartisan basis. In response, the Trump administration moved to slow the disbursement of funds—already approved by Congress and signed

---

21   U.S. Mission to International Organizations in Geneva, "U.S. Statement at the Universal Periodic Review of North Korea," May 9, 2019, https://geneva.usmission .gov/2019/05/09/u-s-statement-at-the-universal-periodic-review-of-north-korea/.

22   See Geoffrey Roberts, "How the US Enabled Aggressions by China and Russia at the UN," PassBlue, February 24, 2020, https://www.passblue.com/2020/02/24/ how-the-us-enabled-aggressions-by-china-and-russia-at-the-un/.

into law—to the Office of the UN High Commissioner for Human Rights Office, and to unilaterally withhold certain funds to the High Commissioner on policy grounds. Due to the late and incomplete payment of dues by the United States and other multiple member states in 2019, UN High Commissioner for Human Rights Michelle Bachelet issued a rare warning on severe liquidity challenges facing the office. Despite this series of events, the Office of the UN High Commissioner for Human Rights published *The Price is Rights: The Violation of the Right to an Adequate Standard of Living in the Democratic People's Republic of Korea*, based on 214 interviews with North Korean survivors in 2017–18.[23]

Conclusion and Recommendations for the Biden Administration

The United Nations remains essential to bolstering the global focus on the abysmal human rights situation in the DPRK, but only if the United States and other nations are willing to use the UN for that purpose. Under the Obama administration and the first year of the Trump administration, the UN played a vital role in ensuring that a generation of world political leaders, human rights activists, foreign policy-minded global citizens, and the media fully understood the severe restrictions on civil and political liberties placed by the DPRK on its citizens and the fact that the DPRK remains one of the most repressive regimes in the world. The unwillingness of the Trump administration to continue to actively pursue DPRK human rights issues on the global stage, including at the UN, created a vacuum that only benefitted the government in Pyongyang. Beginning with the creation of the COI in 2013, U.S. leadership on the DPRK human rights situation in the UN has been a driving force in ensuring that the issue remained on the agenda in a variety of UN forums, including the UN Security Council and the UN Human Rights Council, and restoration of this leadership must be an important goal. The importance of American leadership does not take away from the enormous diplomatic resources devoted to the

---

23   United Nations High Commissioner for Human Rights, *The Price Is Rights: The Violation of the Right to an Adequate Standard of Living in the Democratic People's Republic of Korea* (Seoul, Korea: Office of the UN High Commissioner for Human Rights, May 2019), https://www.ohchr.org/Documents/Countries/KP/ThePriceIsRights_EN.pdf.

DPRK human rights issues by other UN member states, including those in Europe and Asia who continue to make it a priority. That said, getting the DPRK human rights situation back on the UN front burner will certainly be greatly facilitated by a reorientation of U.S. foreign policy priorities related to the DPRK.

The Biden administration has an opportunity to right the ship by renewing U.S. leadership at the UN on DPRK human rights issues. The administration's expeditious decision to end the policy of boycotting the UN Human Rights Council and secure membership on the organ is a crucial first step. The United States should also pursue the appointment of an effective and credible U.S. special envoy for North Korea human rights issues who can restore internal interagency focus as well as lead diplomatic efforts to restore the pre-existing DPRK human rights coalition in the UN context. Finally, the United States should actively exercise leadership with its allies and partners at the UN Security Council to force regular debates on the human rights situation in North Korea.

Human rights advocates need to convince the State Department and the National Security Council that human rights issues should not be deprioritized to advance negotiations to limit the DPRK's pursuit of nuclear and missile issues, as they were under the Trump administration. Despite the enactment of the North Korea Human Rights Act and a bipartisan consensus in Washington to advance DPRK human rights matters, both Democratic and Republican policymakers need to be reminded that human rights are not a "secondary issue" to be addressed once security matters are tackled effectively. In fact, creating channels for dialogue between the United States, other countries, and the DPRK on political, religious and social freedom, including through bolstered people-to-people exchanges, can play an important role in filling the gaps of trust and understanding that have undermined security negotiations and the implementation of past agreements. Progress on North Korean human rights issues will create an atmosphere that will facilitate the hard choices that need to be made to establish a fully normal relationship between UN member states and the DPRK, including the reduction of security concerns posed by the DPRK's pursuit of nuclear and missile programs.

II. The Role of Information

5 Efforts to Reach North Koreans by South Korean NGOs

Then, Now, and Challenges

Minjung Kim

The North Korean regime stands resilient. Its inability to feed its people has threatened their survival, but not that of the regime. Several factors provide explanations, but one prominent reason the regime continues to survive is the repression of its people. A regime's survival can be threatened in essentially two ways: externally or internally. In the case of North Korea, the internal threat has been effectively suppressed by repression, especially via censorship. The system of censorship in North Korea is without equal in the modern age. In particular, the censorship aims to block the inflow of outside information. And, here, the role of non-governmental organizations (NGOs) comes to the fore.

A wide range of agents can provide outside information. Broadly speaking, there are government entities and NGOs. In the case of North Korea's human rights, South Korean NGOs have been playing an essential, leading, complex, and challenging role. That is why the role of South Korean NGOs in policy on human rights in North Korea must be understood correctly. Such understanding can lay the groundwork for more effective policy decisions and practical outcomes. This chapter thus examines the role of South Korean NGOs

The author would like to thank Gi-Wook Shin, Robert King, Yumi Moon, Yong Suk Lee, George Krompacky, Heather Ahn, Victor Cha, Keith Luse, Jung Hoon Lee, Joon Oh, Greg Scarlatoiu, Nat Kretchun, Martyn Williams, Tae-Ung Baik, Sean King, Sandra Fahy, and Bumsoo Kim for feedback and comments that helped to improve this chapter.

concerning human rights issues in North Korea. In order to add specificity to the discussion, South Korean NGOs are examined via their role in penetrating North Korea with an influx of outside information. This is an especially fruitful approach because, regardless of personal and socioeconomic status, all North Korean defectors have expressed the opinion that outside information was crucial to their decisions to seek refuge, according to the survey that will be discussed below. Especially in light of the heightened challenges that human rights activities for North Koreans have faced, the survey result provides concrete evidence that supports the importance of the activities conducted by South Korean NGOs.

As such, this chapter first discusses the information influx, followed by the past, present, and future of South Korean NGOs working on human rights issues in North Korea. The chapter concludes by suggesting measures to move one step closer to solving the problem of North Korean human rights.

South Korean NGOs and Human Rights in North Korea

Through the early 1990s, only one organization in South Korea had engaged in North Korean human rights activities.[1] The first generation of such groups emerged in the late 1990s, including NGOs that have contributed to introducing the reality of North Korea to South Koreans. Ironically, this timing coincided with the presidency of Kim Dae-jung, who found the public debate on North Korean human rights issues rather embarrassing in the face of his attempts to engage with the regime.

In this beginning era there were a number of representative NGOs whose activities have played an essential role. One of those is the Citizens' Alliance for North Korean Human Rights (NKHR), established in 1996. NKHR is the first South Korean organization focusing on the protection and status of North Koreans. NKHR "initiated the transnationalization of the North Korea human rights issue."[2] The founder

---

1   The name of the organization is not disclosed here for security reasons.
2   Joanna Hosaniak, "NGOs as Discursive Catalysts at the UN and the Beyond," in *North Korean Human Rights*, ed. Andrew Yeo (Cambridge: Cambridge University Press, 2019), 131–53.

of NKHR, the late Yoon Hyun, had been involved in human rights activism since 1969 in various roles, including working as chairman of Amnesty International in South Korea and as a vice-chairman of South Korea's Civil Rights Struggle Committee. Yoon said the turning point in his work on human rights activism was when "the situation changed after South Korea democratized and significantly advanced the human rights situation in 1990."[3] NKHR has pursued the advancement of human rights in North Korea by organizing international conferences worldwide and by partnering with media and artists to increase the awareness of human rights violations in North Korea, thereby establishing an international network of NGOs that can influence government policymakers and the United Nations.[4]

Save North Korea (SNK) is another pioneering North Korean human rights NGO, originally established in March 1999 as the Commission to Help North Korea Refugees (CNKR). CNKR was founded by the late Kim Sang-chul, former mayor of Seoul and a prominent human rights lawyer. SNK collected 11,800,495 petition signatures for the protection of North Korean refugees from 1999 to 2001 and submitted them to the UN and other international organizations and governments, which resulted in the enactment of the UN Resolution on the Situation of Human Rights in the DPRK in 2003. This provided great momentum in increasing the awareness among South Koreans of the tragedy of North Koreans. The petition campaign also garnered international attention for the issue of human rights in North Korea; it was introduced to the U.S. House of Representatives and Senate and, eventually, led to the passing of resolutions on North Korean human rights in 2002.

SNK is the only NGO engaged in producing and sending messages to North Korea through mid-wave AM radio broadcasting. Since its establishment, SNK has also aided the rescue of North Korean refugees and helped them settle in South Korea by hosting various forums and organizing diverse cultural, arts, and education projects. When an unprecedented airlift to pick up 468 North Korean defectors was organized in Vietnam in 2004, SNK played a leading role in securing the safe route of refugees and lobbying the South Korean

---

3   Hosaniak, "NGOs as Discursive Catalysts," 133.
4   Citizens' Alliance for North Korean Human Rights, http://eng.nkhumanrights.or.kr/eng/info/about.php.

administration as well as its Vietnamese counterpart.[5] To produce and share more professional content to be sent to North Korea, in 2002 Kim Sang-chul established a newspaper company, Future Korean Media, which focuses on North Korean human rights issues and politics, supporting democracy, and the rule of law.

The period of evolution

It was in the early 2000s that North Korean defector-activists emerged. NK Watch was established in 2003 by Ahn Myeong-cheol, who was a prison guard in a North Korean political prison in Hoeryong until he fled the country in 1994. In addition, Kang Chol-hwan, a former prisoner at Yodok concentration camp in North Korea, has served as president of the North Korean Strategy Center since 2007. There are also several young North Korean defectors living in South Korea who have produced and shared their videos, comparing their lives in both Koreas. These new efforts are in a one-person media format, which has recently worked for many of the biggest YouTube stars and is increasingly gaining popularity, especially among young people.

Various South Korean NGOs have worked to promote the human rights and freedom of North Koreans. Until the late 1990s, NGOs devoted to North Korean causes mostly proliferated in the areas of specialized services like famine relief, public health, and medical aid in the DPRK.[6] In 1999, although there were 31 humanitarian NGOs working toward general relief, agricultural recovery, and public health and medical assistance for North Korea[7] that were registered at the Ministry of Unification, not a single one was human rights–focused. But by 2020, the number of South Korean NGOs working on North Korea human rights dramatically increased to 34 out of 430 North Korea–related NGOs as shown in table 5.1.[8]

---

5   This marked the largest number of North Korean refugees ever to be mass evacuated and arrive safely at their destination. While the Vietnamese government requested that this daring rescue airlift be a secret operation, it was unfortunately leaked out at the last minute and widely covered in media.

6   Hyuk-Rae Kim, *State-centric to Contested Social Governance in South Korea: Shifting Power* (Abingdon: Routledge, 2013), 149.

7   Kim, *State-centric to Contested Social Governance in South Korea*, 148.

8   Several NGOs in appendix table A.1, including the Helping Hands Korea and the organization "A," have also pursued humanitarian projects.

TABLE 5.1 NGOs on North Korea issues registered at the Ministry of Unification (as of January 2020)

Category		Number of NGOs	
Humanitarian organizations	Development aid/cooperation	4	
	Humanitarian aid	25	
	Kaesong Industrial Region	3	163
	Social and cultural cooperation	43	
	Supporting separated families	5	
Human rights organizations	Refugee settlement	12	
	Aid to abductees	3	34
	Improving North Korea human rights	19	
Unspecified	Analysis of current affairs	1	
	Unification culture	1	
	Unification education	12	
	Academic research	43	233
	Unification activities	103	
	Unclassified	74	
Total		430	

SOURCE: Ministry of Unification website.

Types of South Korean NGOs

In his study of South Korean NGOs, Hyuk-Rae Kim categorizes North Korean human rights NGOs into three groups. The first group of organizations is politically neutral, focusing primarily on the advocacy of human rights and humanitarian issues. Second, there are religious or faith-based organizations. The third group of organizations consists of former student activists who once admired *Juche* ideology in the 1980s but were then disillusioned by the reality of North Korea.[9] This is an accurate categorization, but it should be noted that the three categories are not mutually exclusive, nor collectively exhaustive. For instance, SNK was founded as an affiliation of the Christian Council of Korea by the late Kim Sang-chul, based on his religious motivation. While he was an iconic leader of the democratization movement, he was anti-communist in his entire life and was by no means a follower of *Juche* ideology. Kim consistently emphasized the importance of law, order, and human rights. Most of the leaders in the then progressive democratization movement who were not "baptized" with Juche ideology (and

---

9　Kim, *State-centric to Contested Social Governance in South Korea*, 149–50.

thus "innocent" of engaging in pro–North Korean activities) have continued to advocate, support, or follow Kim's legacy.

It is a common perception that the North Korean human rights community has been led by politically conservative groups. This perception has resulted—intentionally or not—in the distortion and/or alienation of North Korean human rights organizations and the related community, and also fails to reflect reality. Although generally speaking conservatives are more active in North Korean human rights activities, a variety of South Korean groups, regardless of their status as conservative or progressive, participate in such activities. For the submission of SNK's 11.8 million signatures to UN headquarters and the U.S. Congress in 2001, for example, Representative Hwang Woo-yea of the Conservative Party and Kim Young-jin of the Liberal Party joined the representative petitioner group. More than 11 million South Koreans, almost 25 percent of the population, participated in this petition movement. The signature campaign brought together members of parliament of various nations, which led to the formation of the International Parliamentarians' Coalition for North Korean Refugees and Human Rights. While it is true that this coalition is somewhat conservative-centered, lawmakers of both the ruling and opposition parties have voluntarily participated in the coalition for sixteen years, and Democrats have always been present in its annual meetings overseas.

This shows that human rights issues in North Korea are not exclusively reserved for the politically conservative—or for those who have converted to conservativism—in South Korea. Healthy liberals with sound liberal ideas who are not subject to political factionalism have been actively involved in North Korean human rights issues.

Activities of South Korean NGOs on North Korea's Human Rights Issues

North Korea's human rights movement has involved a variety of activities including information influx, defection support, and pressure on the international community. Table A.1 in the appendix provides a bird's-eye view of the key NGOs on North Korea's human rights issues and their activities, which can be boiled down to advocating change in North Korea and pushing for the freedom of its citizens. Terms like "change" and "freedom" call for further elaboration, of course. For the most part, the idea is to help North Korean citizens escape lives of poverty and scarcity so they can have an opportunity to enjoy economic, social, and cultural rights. However, for many of these NGOs and activists, there is less stress on the economic part; marketization in the form of the *jangmadang*, the "free markets,"[10] has played a critical role in enhancing the economic, social, and cultural rights of North Koreans, but it has been accompanied by negative social side effects. After more than two decades of the *jangmadang*, materialism is becoming more prevalent in North Korean society. Economic abundance is not the ultimate goal of North Korea human rights activists, many of whom are North Korean defectors. Activists have an interest in the *jangmadang* because they are effective avenues for information inflow. The most prominent factor in their decision to escape North Korea was the yearning for freedom, as attested by the survey results presented here. Accordingly, human rights activists who engage information influx activities into North Korea put more weight on the enhancement of civil and political rights than economic abundance. These activities naturally elicit criticism by the North Korean regime because these can encourage both regime change and defection.

Most of the high-ranking defectors—including Thae Yong-ho, formerly a North Korean diplomat in the United Kingdom—believe that the foreign culture and ideology entering the North via information influx will be one of the most effective determinants in changing the country. The information wall that the regime has constructed around the country is strong and comparatively easy for it to protect and maintain. The only way it can be surmounted is through continued efforts to transmit information from outside North Korea into the country. The information barricade is unaffected by U.S. government sanctions and pressure on the regime from the international community; while sanctions are an important policy tool, the regime can survive without difficulties under them as long as they can pay to satisfy the needs of the elites.

While the Kim regime has long been devoted to satisfying the needs of privileged elites, the amount of money that Pyongyang budgets to

---

10   "Free" here has limited meaning, as *jangmadang* are black markets, although implicitly recognized by the regime. Even Kim Il-sung once said, "Although *Jangmadang* is a place that should not exist in principle, in reality, not all things can be provided by the regime and thus *Jangmadang* may have some advantages." "North Korean Farmers Markets" [in Korean], 21st Century Political Science Dictionary, https://terms.naver.com/entry.nhn?docId=727483&cid=42140&category Id=42140.

secure the basic rights of its citizens is among the lowest in the world; for the most part, little or no official benefits are allocated to the public except for the ostensibly free education and healthcare systems.

Non-elite North Koreans essentially must fend for themselves; their continued loyalty to the regime is a consequence of their forced ignorance, rather than any tangible benefits provided to them. If information were allowed to freely enter the country, the absurdity and inequity of their lives under the regime would be laid bare. That is why blocking the influx of ideology and culture is one of the top priorities for maintaining the regime and its totalitarian system. The North Korean regime produces diverse media content in order to proactively limit the influx of external information by "developing their ideology and culture."[11] The North Korean regime, which has survived based on fear politics, propaganda, and agitation, devotes an enormous amount of resources—human, technological, and monetary—to block outside information. That is why the international community should recognize the weight of the information blockage issue, in addition to other dimensions of human rights issues.

South Korean NGO activities

South Korean NGOs use various approaches to help North Koreans understand the reality of their political and social situations, as well as the importance of democratic ideals. Supporting both those suffering under tyranny and those who have fortunately escaped requires multifaceted efforts, from smuggling USBs and aiding the rescue of refugees to the education of young defectors.

Numerous methods have been devised for reaching North Koreans, including DVDs, tablets, thumb drives, mobile phones, radio broadcasts, and even messages in rice bottles. By some rough estimates, 10 percent of North Korean households have a computer at home, and up to half of urban households own a Notel, a portable media player made in China.[12] Among other means of information transfer, flash memory is rising as a both effective and favored medium among

---

11   Joo-yeon Park, "Minister Tae Young-ho: 'Vietnamese-style Reform and Opening-Up of North Korea Is Impossible," *Future Korea*, October 26, 2018, http://www.futurekorea.co.kr/news/articleView.html?idxno=111955.

12   Uri Friedman, "Coming of Age in North Korea," *The Atlantic*, August 26, 2016.

the younger generation because the majority of North Koreans watch foreign content via DVD player with direct USB inputs.[13] The ease of removing and concealing flash memory devices is likely to have increased their popularity among North Koreans who want to watch foreign content. Some NGOs take a rather low-tech approach and fill trash bags with leaflets or USB drives, which are then attached to hydrogen balloons and flown into North Korea when the wind is blowing north. This tactic has a long history that goes back to divided Germany. Among the various physical ways of delivering information into North Korea, the sending of leaflets has been most harshly denounced by the North Korean regime in recent years.

Taking another approach, some South Korean NGOs support and empower North Korean defectors. NGOs have provided virtual asylum to North Koreans, mostly in the border towns in northeast China, by supplying food and shelter and helping them travel to South Korea. Numerous NGOs have also provided North Korean defectors with a diverse array of programs, including ones for education, self-support assistance, legal advice, and settlement. Although their activities are limited, some NGOs conduct programs to support and empower people living in North Korea, such as training religious leaders in North Korea. These "steps from inside" may be slower and more subtle than other approaches, but will not be easily reversible if they succeed.

Other NGOs pursue activities that attempt to enhance the international community's understanding of the plight of North Koreans, in an effort to pressure the North Korean regime to accept democratic ideas and values. Some NGOs publish human rights violation casebooks based on stories of North Korean defectors. For instance, the Database Center for North Korean Human Rights has published casebooks that show the extreme grip that Pyongyang has on the North Korean people. Unbeknownst to the outside world, the regime repeatedly violates the rights of North Koreans who are forced to work at nuclear facilities. Under a tightly closed regime that does not tolerate any criticism, nuclear weapons are made with the free labor of detainees from various gulags; their bodies cruelly exposed to radiation, these

---

13   Jeremy Hsu, "How the USB Taught North Korea to Love K-Pop," *Discover*, April 6, 2018, https://www.discovermagazine.com/technology/how-the-usb-taught -north-korea-to-love-k-pop.

weapons are being made at the cost of their lives.[14] Nowhere else on earth is nuclear development carried out in such a grim environment.

Among various methods of information influx, radio is still one of the most important sources North Koreans access for outside information, as attested in the survey below. The type and strength of radio signals are critical for reaching an audience within the North. Medium-wave (AM) radio programs are heard much more clearly than short-wave programs. In theory, at least a 100 kW output power transmitter is necessary for promising reception.[15] Unlike shortwave (3–30 MHz), which is difficult to listen to in North Korea, mid-wave (300–3000 kHz) provides a strong output for transmission, easily audible in North Korea, resulting in a significantly high level of listener ratings. Because of the relatively poor signals, shortwave radio broadcasting does not reach a large North Korean audience.[16]

The significance of media such as DVDs, USBs, and Notel is also increasing (as mentioned in chapters 6 and 7 of this volume). The U.S. government extended the North Korean Human Rights Act for five years until 2022 (North Korean Human Rights Reauthorization Act of 2017, H.R. 2061) and included provisions for diversifying the contents and tools of information influx into North Korea to encompass external media (DVDs and USBs) and digital formats, reflecting advances in technology.

One advantage of information influx via USBs is that it gives a way to gauge the information consumers' needs and interests. In the North Korean "free" markets, the *jangmadang*, goods, services, and information are traded according to the law of supply and demand. This gives us a way to gauge what kinds of content are most popular. This sort of "market research" is possible for radio broadcasters, to some extent—North Korean defectors who are hosts on these shows can surreptitiously benefit from feedback from their relatives and friends still living in the North.

---

14   Database Center for North Korean Human Rights press conference, Korea Press Center, May 24, 2018.

15   Ga-young Kim, "Radio Broadcasting Propaganda Using AM Will Attract One Million North Korean Listeners, Which Will Bring About Collapse of the North Korean Regime" [in Korean], Daily NK, September 14, 2015, http://www.dailynk .com/korean/read.php?num=106988&cataId=nk01500.

16   Other than SNK, mid-wave broadcasting is not available for NGOs because it is difficult to form a business partnership with mid-wave radio providers, and also because the South Korean government assigns no mid-wave frequencies to NGOs.

Pyongyang reacts more strongly to the influx of leaflets, cell phones, and foreign radio broadcasts than the presence of *jangmadang*, because the regime perceives the two groups of activities differently. It is more about the regime's will than its ability to control. Leaflets, cell phones, and foreign radio broadcasting are more threatening because these directly feed the people's hunger to enhance civil and political rights, something that could only hurt the regime. On the other hand, while *jangmadang* provide a path for information influx (such as USB drives), the markets also provide the regime with economic benefits that cannot be ignored. *Jangmadang* reduce the burden of feeding the people and allows officials a venue for considerable bribery. As such, *jangmadang* allows the regime to pay inadequate salaries to public servants and yet avoid most of their complaints. This is one plausible reason why the regime is more sensitive toward information influx via cell phone/radio/leaflets than via *jangmadang*. Another contributing factor is, of course, the costs and realities of blocking information influx other than *jangmadang*. The regime cannot totally jam radio signals due to the cost and electricity shortages. When Pyongyang expresses outrage at NGOs attempting to send leaflets to North Korea, it is because of the regime's limited ability to control such information—its only recourse is to complain to and pressure Seoul.

Effectiveness of information inflow: A survey

To evaluate the effectiveness of various NGO activities on North Korean human rights issues, we conducted a survey of North Korean defectors.[17] The respondents were North Korean defectors who came from a variety of backgrounds, including Pyongyang residents, former diplomats, Labor Party and other administrative officials, and artists, and who settled in and outside South Korea. In the interest of diversifying the respondent pool, we endeavored to represent the general defector population well by choosing among members of various domestic and overseas North Korean defector associations; by surveying defectors whose hometowns were both inside and outside Pyongyang; and by choosing respondents who defected at different points in time and who ultimately settled in a variety of locations.[18] Gender ratio was

---

17   The survey had 115 respondents and was conducted online from December 2019 to January 2020.
18   In order to minimize any bias caused by personal familiarity, most of the defectors with whom I have a personal relationship were excluded.

FIGURE 5.1 Year of defection

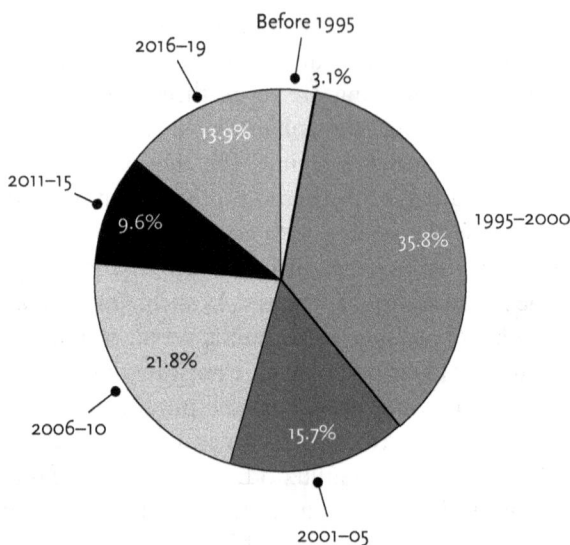

NOTE: Defectors were asked "When did you escape from North Korea?"
SOURCE: Author.

also taken into account; 72 percent of North Korean defectors entering South Korea are female, so to maximize the diversity of views, males made up 46.1 percent of the survey respondents.

Below I present descriptive statistics rather than drawing any conclusions about the population under consideration using inferential statistics. Detailed analysis of the information inflow effects on various demographical groups based on social class, region, and age is thus omitted. Rather than evaluating the effects of information inflow, I focus here on introducing human rights activities in North Korea, analyzing the role of the South Korean government, as well describing the ecosystem South Korean NGOs work in and the dilemmas they face. The survey is intended to advance our understating of North Korean human rights activities, not to derive conclusions about the defector population.

As shown in figure 5.1, about a quarter (23.5 percent) of all respondents defected after 2011, confirming the data's suitability for identifying recent trends in North Korea. As noted above, this study focused on minimizing the selection bias caused by a majority (72 percent) of female defectors; as such, the survey results were somewhat different from existing surveys. For instance, existing surveys have found that desire for freedom had a less direct effect on defection than a presence of immediate threats such as punishment or persecution. However, as shown in figure 5.2, this survey shows a majority (52.2 percent) of defectors responded they had fled "in search of freedom, or freedom from tyranny." These results indicate that a critical view of the North Korean regime was a greater determinant in escaping the country than a longing for the systems and cultures of other countries, including South Korea. In contrast to those searching for freedom, 33 percent responded they had fled "due to economic difficulty, or for a better life." Similar to various other survey results, a majority of respondents (54.8 percent) were ordinary citizens with a monthly income of less than US $10, as shown in figure 5.3.

The survey results in figures 5.4, 5.5, and 5.6 indicate a significant difference in the ripple effect according to the distribution method of information. There is clear evidence that North Koreans are tuning into radio broadcasts more. The majority of the audience (51.2 percent) shared the contents with one or two (32.2 percent) or three or more acquaintances (19.1 percent) (figure 5.4). Also, even nine defectors who are not regular listeners of radio broadcasting responded that radio is the most effective means of changing North Korea.

Table 5.2 clearly shows that radio is the favored medium for accessing outside information, and the one believed to be most effective (nine

FIGURE 5.2 Reason for defection

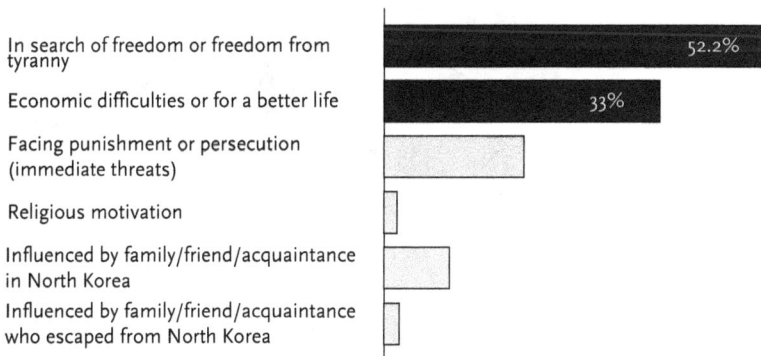

NOTE: Defectors were asked "Why did you escape from North Korea?"
SOURCE: Author.

FIGURE 5.3 Defectors' social class and income in North Korea

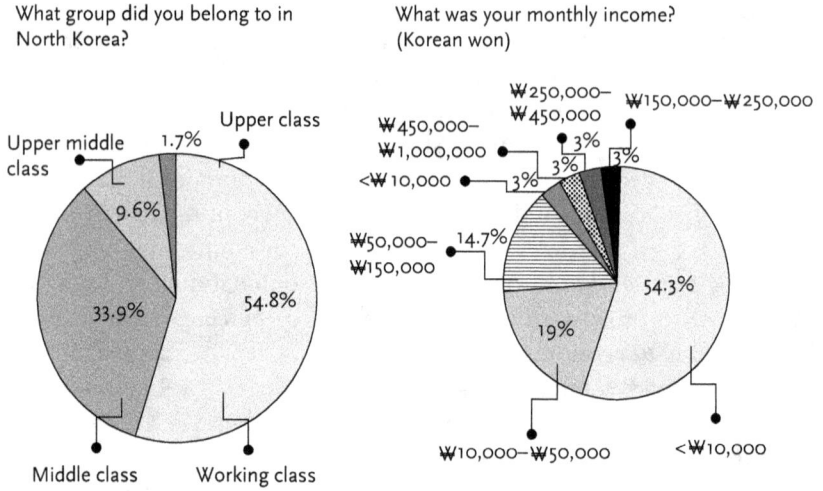

What group did you belong to in
North Korea?

Upper class
Upper middle class   1.7%
9.6%
33.9%   54.8%

Middle class   Working class

What was your monthly income?
(Korean won)

₩250,000–
₩450,000   ₩150,000–₩250,000
₩450,000–
₩1,000,000   3%   3%
<₩10,000   3%
3%
₩50,000–   14.7%
₩150,000
19%   54.3%

₩10,000–₩50,000   <₩10,000

SOURCE: AUTHOR.

FIGURE 5.4 Ripple effect

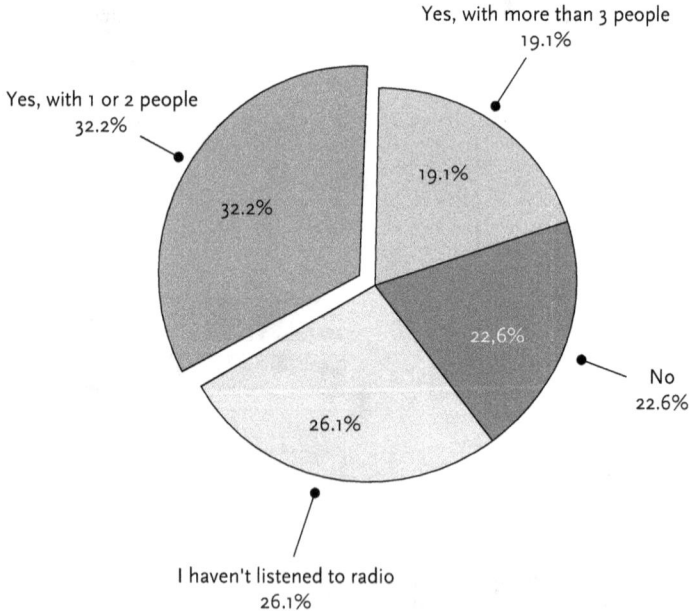

Yes, with more than 3 people
19.1%

Yes, with 1 or 2 people
32.2%

32.2%   19.1%

22,6%

26.1%   No
22.6%

I haven't listened to radio
26.1%

NOTE: Defectors were asked "Have you shared the contents of radio programs with your
friends or family?"
SOURCE: Author.

TABLE 5.2 Method of information inflow

	How did you access outside information? (multiple choice)	Which method do you think is most effective? (choose two)
Television	30.4	36.5
DVD	28.7	29.6
MP3/MP4	5.2	13.9
Radio	**43.5**	**51.3**
Mobile phone (NK network)	0.9	5.2
Mobile phone (Chinese network)	11.3	25.2
Notel or similar player	3.6	15.7
Computer or tablet	2.6	13.9
Leaflets	30.4	38.3
All methods equally important	—	28.7
Did not access outside information	20.0	—

SOURCE: Author.

of the defectors who thought radio most effective did not even listen regularly); furthermore, most (51.2 percent) of those who listen to radio share information about the broadcasts with others, with nearly 20 percent of listeners sharing with more than three other people (see figure 5.4), which likely indicates radio broadcasts have a significant ripple effect.

After the influence of family or friends (48.7 percent), 34.8 percent of respondents indicated that information from radio broadcasts had the greatest weight on their decision to defect (see figure 5.5). Due to the difficulty of connecting to the internet or satellite television networks, North Koreans are much more dependent on radio, and despite scrutiny by the government, radio listeners are increasing in numbers.[19]

A key factor deciding which broadcasts North Koreans listen to is whether the radio signal is able to reach them. As shown in figure 5.6, the stations with the lowest number of listeners—the BBC, Unification Radio, Open North Korea Radio, Free Chosun, and North Korea Reform Radio—all broadcast only by shortwave. The United States' Radio Free Asia (RFA) and Voice of America (VOA),[20] as well as the

---

19   Lee Jae-Jun, "Japan's Radio for North Korea, 'Shiokaje,' Suspends Broadcasting in May" [in Korean], Newsis, October 4, 2018, http://www.newsis.com/view/?id=NISX20181004_0000434177&cID=10101&pID=10100.

20   VOA and RFA are affiliated with the U.S. Agency for Global Media (formerly the Broadcasting Board of Governors, or BBG) under the U.S. Department of State's oversight and both have conducted medium-wave broadcasts to North

FIGURE 5.5 Influences on the decision to defect

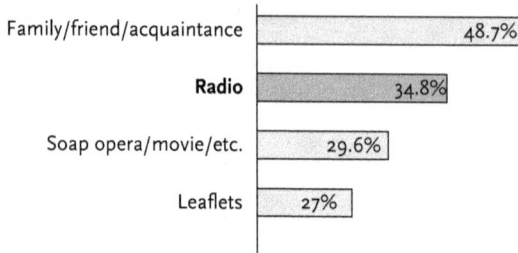

Family/friend/acquaintance	48.7%
Radio	34.8%
Soap opera/movie/etc.	29.6%
Leaflets	27%

NOTE: Defectors were asked to choose two influences on their decision to leave the country. SOURCE: AUTHOR.

FIGURE 5.6 Medium-wave vs. shortwave broadcasting

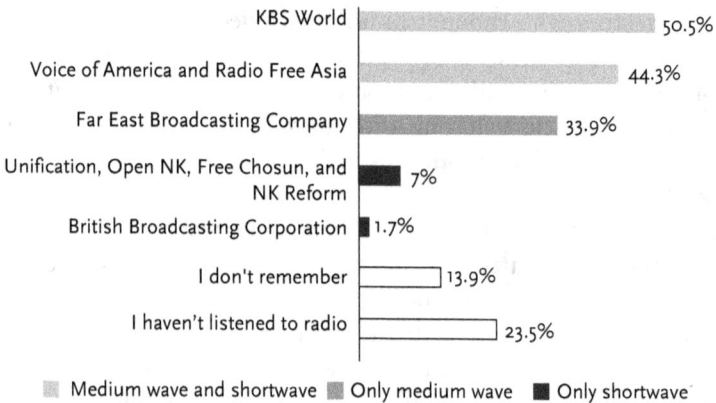

KBS World	50.5%
Voice of America and Radio Free Asia	44.3%
Far East Broadcasting Company	33.9%
Unification, Open NK, Free Chosun, and NK Reform	7%
British Broadcasting Corporation	1.7%
I don't remember	13.9%
I haven't listened to radio	23.5%

▨ Medium wave and shortwave ▨ Only medium wave ■ Only shortwave

NOTE: Defectors were asked to choose which radio stations they listened to (multiple choice). SOURCE: Author.

Far East Broadcasting Company and South Korea's KBS World, are all broadcast either by medium wave or by both medium and short-wave. Save North Korea has also been producing medium-wave radio

---

Korea. VOA is a national broadcaster established in 1942 during World War II, and RFA is an international broadcaster established in 1996 under international broadcasting law legislated by the U.S. Congress.

FIGURE 5.7 Most effective information content

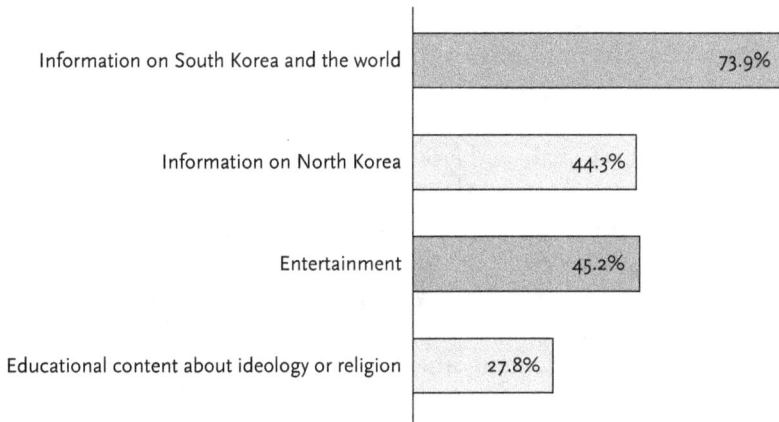

Information on South Korea and the world — 73.9%

Information on North Korea — 44.3%

Entertainment — 45.2%

Educational content about ideology or religion — 27.8%

NOTE: Defectors were asked to choose which kinds of information content were most effective in inducing changing in North Korea (they could choose two).
SOURCE: AUTHOR.

programs based on a business partnership with an existing medium-wave radio broadcaster.[21]

The majority of the North Korean radio audience listens to programming between twelve midnight and six o'clock in the morning to avoid surveillance by the authorities. Favorite content of the North Korean audience includes news briefs, particularly news involving the Korean Peninsula, interviews with North Korean defectors, and international commentary on events happening inside North Korea.[22] Presumably this is because such content helps North Koreans realize a true picture of their lives and the regime, seeing beyond the fabricated and falsified information spoon-fed to them. Survey results on information content (figure 5.7) support this assumption—defectors responded that news or real-life information

---

21 All other NGOs including Unification Media Group and Free NK Radio, in addition to Sound from Wilderness (CMI), Voice of the Martyrs Korea (VOM), Trans World Radio (TWR) Korea, and Advent World Radio (AWR) broadcast via shortwave radio from Central Asia and other places.

22 Broadcasting Board of Governors, "Fiscal Year 2008 Budget Request: Executive Summary," n.d., https://www.usagm.gov/wp-content/media/2011/12/bbg_fy08_budget_request.pdf.

about the outside world (73.9 percent) is more critical to changing North Korea than entertainment such as movies or popular dramas (soap operas) (45.2 percent).

In addition, the author's own direct and personal discussions with North Korean defectors over many years have uncovered further details on the demographic characteristics of radio listeners. It is true that radio listeners are likely to be older than those who use USB and Notel—this demographic characteristic is not limited to the North Korean audience. Nonetheless, the majority of radio listeners in their twenties and thirties have noted that radio programming is addictive, turning many of them into long-term loyal listeners. Also, because the content is tailored to delivering information related to North Korean realities, radio is more attractive than other mediums in influencing and mobilizing North Korean youths and elites.

Younger audiences in their twenties and thirties prefer lighter content in general. Many defectors have stated that they listened to the radio for music. However, radio broadcasts also have content that appeals to young male listeners. There was, for instance, a male North Korean defector who escaped North Korea in his late twenties after listening to a medium-wave radio program. He was a "listening agent" (*bangcheong yowon*), meaning that he was responsible for listening solely to foreign radio and reporting the contents to the North Korean authorities. Of course, this position is given only to the privileged-level members of the Labor Party. He was shocked to hear information over the radio that was contrary to what he learned through his strict ideological education. He defected and now he is working at an intelligence agency in South Korea. There are probably not very many such young, privileged, and highly educated Labor Party members who listen to radio broadcasting, but reaching these elite is an important step toward triggering change within North Korea. Even though there are countless obstacles facing internal reform in the North, the impact of changing the minds of the country's elite should not be underestimated.

The Challenge of Advancing North Korean Human Rights under the Moon Administration

South Korean NGOs focus their efforts on a multi-faceted approach, especially in relation to information influx. However, there are many problems that NGOs cannot tackle due to their limited resources and circumstances. The role of the government is thus critical, especially in South Korean society, where donation culture is not deeply rooted.

The Moon administration has been even more silent on North Korean human rights issues than preceding progressive governments. While I am not suggesting that the current South Korean government has an outright policy of suppressing human rights activities, several pieces of evidence point to the current administration's reluctance to support the North Korean human rights movement. One of President Moon's first post-inauguration actions was to include North Korean human rights groups in an investigation of the "White List," groups that had benefited from the previous conservative administration. In the fall of 2017, the prosecution conducted investigations of some ten NGOs, tracking donation accounts as well as personal accounts of the employees. The names of the organizations were exposed to the media. Although no illegal activity was found, news of the investigation itself hurt the reputation and credibility of the organizations, leading some of them to close their doors.

In addition, on October 24, 2018 there was a side event on North Korean human rights at the UN headquarters to celebrate the seventieth anniversary of the UN Universal Declaration of Human Rights.[23] The event was initially planned as a large-scale international conference with speakers, including Thae Yong-ho. Yet the event was under "extraordinary pressure, never, ever seen before."[24] For instance, the Moon government prevented Thae from speaking at the conference and cut virtually all sources of funding for the event; as a result, it was canceled. The Moon administration also cut funding for the Association of North Korean Defectors in 2018, established in 1999 by Hwang Jang-Yop. Consequently, the organization had to shut down in early 2020 due to financial difficulties. It had been financially supported by the government for almost twenty years, including for ten years under the two previous progressive governments.

---

23 This detailed information was gathered directly by me as a member of SNK, which was one of the coordinating and participating organizations of the event.

24 Noted by Greg Scarlatoiu, one of the organizing committee members, at "Thinking Strategically about Human Rights Challenges in Negotiations with North Korea" Heritage Foundation, October 29, 2018, https://www.heritage.org/event/thinking-strategically-about-human-rights-challenges-negotiations-north-korea.

More importantly, in September 2018 there was a military agreement between Moon Jae-in and Kim Jong-un that included a ban on information balloon and leaflet activities. Many NGOs have attested that any medium for information influx, such as USBs, that are discovered by South Korean authorities have been confiscated, especially when the contents criticize the North Korean regime. Other signs of negligence include the shutdown of the North Korean Human Rights Foundation after twenty-one months of no activities since 2016, when the foundation was created. The Moon administration has also been delaying the nomination of the ambassador-at-large on North Korean human rights since August 2017. The North Korean Human Rights Report publication project, which is prescribed in the North Korean Human Rights Act, went back to square one. The Moon administration banned North Korean reporters from major newspapers from participating in various events hosted by the Ministry of Unification.

Moreover, the Moon government significantly decreased its budget on North Korean human rights issues in 2019. Specifically, the budget for the North Korean Human Rights Foundation was reduced by 92.6 percent. The North Korean information system budget has also been decreased by more than half.[25] The 2020 budget was cut further. For instance, the budget for establishing and implementing policy for North Korea human rights improvement was reduced by 59.5 percent, while the operation of the North Korean Human Rights Foundation was given 0.5 billion won, lowering its budget by 37.5 percent.[26]

These developments have alarmed many, including Christian Whiton, former State Department senior adviser and an established expert on North Korea, who said, "The tendency of [the Moon administration] to appease North Korea really seems to have gotten out of control."[27] In August 2020, the administration started a massive probe into twenty-five

---

25   Yeon-hee Yang, "U.S. Experts Say the Moon Administration's Budget Reduction on North Korea Human Right Activities Is a Betrayal" [in Korean], 펜앤드마이크 [Pen and Mic], https://www.pennmike.com/news/articleView.html?idxno=9542.
26   Ki-ho Han, "Ministry of Unification's Increase in Inter-Korea Cooperation Reserve Funds vs. Sharp Reduction in the Budget for North Korea Human Right Activities" [in Korean], 펜앤드마이크 [Pen and Mic], December 13, 2019, http://www.pennmike.com/news/articleView.html?idxno=25900.
27   Eunjung Cho, "Former U.S. Officials Chastise Seoul over Treatment of N. Korean Rights Groups," VOA News, August 13, 2020, https://www.voanews.com/east-asia-pacific/former-us-officials-chastise-seoul-over-treatment-n-korean-rights-groups.

North Korean human rights NGOs, in addition to the Unification Ministry canceling the corporate licenses of two NGOs for sending leaflets into the North. What this means is that the NGOs can no longer hold fundraisers and apply for tax exemptions, effectively cutting off their lifelines.[28] That is why thirteen former U.S. officials from both major U.S. political parties sent an open letter to President Moon saying that his administration "is undermining North Korea's human rights movement."[29]

In addition, in June 2020 Korean Congress member Kim Hong-gul, ruling party lawmaker and the youngest son of the late president Kim Dae-jung, proposed a bill that defined leaflets as a "national security risk element" and forced NGOs to obtain authorization from the Minister of Unification, shortly after Kim Yo-jong expressed harsh criticism and threats against NGO leaflet activities. These government measures—constraining the ability of NGOs to send leaflets into the North and the massive probe into NGOs—have been criticized both by the international community as well as the UN for turning back the clock on human rights for the purpose of appeasing the North Korean regime.[30]

This kind of environment has not been seen in any other administration. One reason the administration is dismissing human rights while being tolerant of the North Korean regime is their positive view of Pyongyang. For instance, during a public speech in Kenya, former South Korean prime minister Lee Nak-Yeon praised Kim Jong-un as "a leader who thinks of the livelihoods of people as being the most important thing among everything."[31] Representative Song Yong-gil from the ruling party explained North Korea's political system as a "family-oriented state with the goal of the happiest country in the world."[32]

---

28   A provisional injunction relief was sought against the cancellation of the corporate license of the two NGOs, which was granted by the court.

29   Cho, "Former U.S. Officials Chastise Seoul."

30   Robert King, former special envoy for North Korea human rights, said, "They're willing to abandon the principles of human rights," while opining on the recent actions by the Moon administration. See Cho, "Former U.S. Officials Chastise Seoul."

31   Joo-hyeong Hong, "Prime Minister Lee Nak-yeon, 'The Advent of People-Centered Leaders in North Korea'" [in Korean], *Sege Ilbo*, July 20, 2018, http://www.segye.com/newsView/20180720004735. See also Seo Yoo-geun, "Lee Nak-yeon Followed North Korea Propaganda Media Uriminsokkiri.com" [in Korean], *Chosun Ilbo*, December 16, 2019, https://news.chosun.com/site/data/html_dir/2019/12/16/2019121600110.html.

32   Jo Eui-jun, "Song Yong-gil: 'North Korea Is Recovering since Their Nuclear Development. . . . [It] Is a Family-Oriented State to Pursue the Happiness [of the

And in 2018, a special advisor for President Moon hung up on a VOA reporter, saying, "We have nothing to say to the propaganda machine of the United States."[33] Those remarks may reflect the general view of the Moon Jae-in administration.

Of particular note is the tendency of ruling party members to paint North Korean defectors as traitors. Assemblywoman Lim Su-kyung insulted a North Korean defector as a "bastard betrayer" and "son of a bitch."[34] During her college year as a student leader, Lim had crossed the 38th parallel to meet Kim Il-sung in 1989. Extremists like Lim may not represent the ruling party's official view, yet another representative, Choi Jae-sung, openly accused defectors of "spreading garbage-like information to make money"[35] after Lim's comments were widely covered in newspapers. It is also particularly worth mentioning that Im Jong-seok, who as a prominent student activist in the 1980s had helped arrange Lim's crossing to the North, would later serve as chief of staff and special advisor for foreign affairs to President Moon.

It may then be inevitable that North Korean human rights activities in South Korea will continue to face significant difficulties under the current South Korean government, which has consistently been silent about North Korea's hereditary dictatorship and provocations.

The Future

A multi-faceted approach is critical and imperative in devising solutions for the issues of North Korean human rights violations. As important as it is to get information into North Korea, advocacy activities that inform South Korea about North Korea's human rights abuses are also vital. Although the previous conservative administrations were somewhat more generous toward North Korean human

---

People]'" [in Korean], *Chosun Ilbo*, October 15, 2018, http://news.chosun.com/site/data/html_dir/2018/10/15/2018101500266.html.

33   Taken from the reporter's post on their Facebook timeline on September 15, 2018. Names omitted for anonymity.

34   Channel A, "'Defectors Are Betrayers,' a Blunt Remark from Congresswoman Lim Su-kyung," DongA.com, June 3, 2012, https://www.donga.com/news/article/all/20120603/46727959/2.

35   Kim Byung-chae and Dong-ha Kim, "Rep. Choi Jae-sung Accuses Defectors of 'Spreading Garbage-Like Information'" [in Korean], *Munhwa Ilbo*, June 7, 2012, http://www.munhwa.com/news/view.html?no=2012060701070323236004.

rights groups, none offered direct support for the North Korean human rights community. There is a general and significant South Korean disregard/insensitivity toward North Korean human rights issues that transcends the particular tendency of any given administration. This disregard leads to a vicious cycle of further neglecting North Korean human rights issues because the issues do not bring votes to politicians or clicks to the media. Despite South Korea's vibrant civil society, many South Koreans' sense of human rights seems to stop right before the DMZ.

Even though conservative administrations have been more generous toward North Korean NGOs, they have never offered sufficient support. Roughly thirty NGOs operated on an annual budget of four billion won in 2011. Three billion won was provided by the U.S. government and the remaining one billion won by Europe and Japan (~200 million won), private donations (~500 million won), and the South Korean government (~300 million won).[36] For perspective, in 2011 two hours of shortwave radio broadcasting daily for a year cost 100 million won.[37] At that time, most of the funding for broadcasting came from foreign sources (80 percent), while only 10 percent was covered by the Lee Myong-bak administration. This strongly suggests that South Korean government financial and institutional support must be increased.

Content is as important as access to information. The popularity of entertainment content has increased among North Koreans and such cultural infiltration has inspired many North Koreans to defect. However, as the survey results show, whether entertainment content helps North Koreans understand and accept democratic values is a separate matter. Television dramas and movies can provoke or nurture some North Koreans' curiosity about the outside world. But it is questionable whether such content can translate into social movement and collective action in a situation in which people do not have an opportunity to learn the value of political mobilization as a means of achieving

---

36   Huh Moon-myung, "An Interview with Ha Tae-Kyeong, Chairman of 'Open North Korea Broadcasting,' a North Korean Broadcast Media" [in Korean], *Donga Daily*, February 7, 2011, http://www.donga.com/news/article/all/20110207/34617 609/1.

37   Medium-wave broadcasting, which costs multiple times this amount, is operated only by SNK. As such, the analysis focuses on the more commonly used shortwave broadcasting.

social change. One key to the human rights problem and the liberation of North Koreans, therefore, lies in discrediting the regime's ideology in the minds of North Koreans. In this regard, it is necessary to inform them how ideology is being shaped, manipulated, and abused by Pyongyang. Producing and delivering quality information is imperative for the democratic change of North Korea.

As Gi-Wook Shin has noted, "While it is easy to condemn Pyongyang on moral grounds, it is much more challenging to come up with a practical solution."[38] Even if one hopes for an improvement in the North Korean human rights situation, hope is not a strategy. As long as tyranny continues in North Korea, the power to transform from inside will still be lacking. Governments and NGOs must propel the transformation. The most urgent need with respect to North Korea is to create a greater influx of truthful information into the country. Regardless of the form—whether it is delivered as leaflets, news, or movies—the more information enters, the more North Koreans will be able to gain the power to proactively work for change.

---

38   Gi-Wook Shin, "Finding a Way Forward on Human Rights in North Korea," *Nikkei Asian Review*, January 29, 2015, https://asia.nikkei.com/Politics/Gi-Wook -Shin-Finding-a-way-forward-on-human-rights-in-North-Korea.

Appendix A

The Challenge of Determining Which South Korean NGOs Work on North Korean Human Rights

Table 5.1 alone is insufficient to accurately understand the current state of North Korean human rights organizations. Many organizations are not registered with the Ministry of Unification (MOU); moreover, the criteria for classifying "North Korean human rights improvement organizations" ("human rights organizations," for short) are ambiguous since many groups combine human rights and humanitarian activities. Accordingly, the author selected representative organizations that have been most actively engaged in North Korean human rights activities up to the time of writing and summarized them in table A.1 below. Table A.1 includes organizations not registered with the MOU or those registered yet not officially classified as "North Korean human rights organizations."

TABLE A.1 Key South Korean NGOs working for North Korean human rights

Name	Founding year	Key activities
Organization "A"[a]	1985	Providing leadership training to people in North Korea; sending information into the North.
Citizens' Alliance for North Korean Human Rights (NKHR)	1996	Organizing conferences, concerts, and art exhibitions; running education and resettlement programs for North Korean youth in South Korea.
Helping Hands Korea (Catacombs)[b]	1996	Providing logistical support to escapees in China to guide them to safe haven in neighboring countries; providing necessities and aid to children.
Save North Korea (SNK, formerly Commission to Help North Korea Refugees)	1999	Collecting petition signatures and submitting to the UN and other international organizations and governments; broadcasting mid-wave AM radio; aiding the rescue of North Korean refugees; leading the airlift in 2004; operating diverse projects for helping North Korean defectors as well as increasing international awareness.
Dorihana	1999	Offering settlement and self-support assistance programs for North Korean refugees such as career counseling, livelihood support, legal aid; running an international school since 2009.
Network for North Korean Democracy and Human Rights (Nknet)	1999	Running Daily NK, an online newspaper having in-North Korea source networks; offering training programs, seminars, exhibitions, speaker series, and international conferences.
Refuge Pnan	1999	Assisting North Korean refugees in China; providing legal aid for asylum seekers in Korea; running "Jayoutuh School" for North Korea defectors.
Korean War Abductees' Family Union (KWAFU)	2000	Investigating abduction cases, restoring the honor of abductees, and securing the passage of a special law making the government exercise its duty to protect abducted citizens.

(continued)

Name	Founding year	Key activities
Database Center for North Korean Human Rights	2003	Collecting, analyzing, and sorting information about the North Korean government's human rights violations; protecting and supporting victims of such cases.
NK Watch[c]	2003	Holding exhibitions of various photos and drawings, hosting campaigns and speeches, rescuing North Korean refugees in China, providing talks on human rights in North Korea to the young.
Free NK Radio[c]	2004	Broadcasting shortwave radio programs.
People for Successful Corean Reunification (PSCORE)[d]	2006	Submitting written statements to the UN Human Rights Council; speaking at the sessions; attending council meetings and holding parallel events within its sessions.
North Korea Strategy Center (NKSC)[c]	2007	Working with over 150 North Korean defectors; sending over 40,000 DVDs, 400 radio sets, and 4,000 USBs into North Korea.
North Korea Intellectuals Solidarity[c]	2008	Conducting academic research on North Korea and unification and the development and progression of North Korea; cultivating the skills of North Korean defector intellectuals and fostering younger generations; smuggling USB drives and DVDs into North Korea.
1969 KAL Abductees' Families Association[e]	2009	Researching, campaigning, and advocating to determine the fate and whereabouts of the KAL abductees; bringing about their repatriation.
Now Action & Unity for Human Rights (NAUH)	2010	Organizing awareness campaigns; hosting cultural exchanges between South and North Korean young adults; participating in radio broadcasts that relay news of freedom for North Korea; helping rescue operations of North Korean refugees.
International Coalition to Stop Crimes against Humanity in North Korea (ICNK)[f]	2011	Lobbying governments, publishing op-eds, and working the corridors at the UN; comprises over 40 groups, including the major international human rights NGOs and groups from a variety of Asian and other countries.
No Chain[c]	2012	Sending outside information and content into North Korea via helium balloons, human smugglers, and helicopter drones.
Lawyers for Human Rights and Unification of Korea	2013	The first lawyer group focused on improving the human rights of North Korea; conducting public interest lawsuits, legal advice, petition for legislation, and educational research.
Transitional Justice Working Group (TJWG)	2014	Collecting, documenting, and visualizing evidence of crimes against humanity in North Korea in efforts to hold perpetrators accountable and to bring victims' needs and rights to mainstream awareness; working on capacity-building projects for Korean civil society.
Yonsei Center for Human Liberty	2014	Organizing conferences including the Seoul Dialogue, the largest conference in South Korea on North Korean human rights, and UN Seoul Office First-Year Anniversary Commemorative Symposium; launching the Sages Group on North Korean human rights.
Unification Media Group (UMG)	2015	An independent multimedia consortium comprising Daily NK, an internet periodical reporting on all aspects of North Korea; Radio Free Chosun, which broadcasts content targeting North Korean citizens; and Open North Korea Radio.

NOTE: [a]Non-Korean-led; [b]American-led; [c] defector-led; [d]in special consultative status with the UN Economic and Social Council since 2012; [e]composed mainly of the family members of the South Korean abductees of the KAL YS-11 flight that was hijacked by North Korea in 1969; [f]coalition of the various NGOs listed in this table.

SOURCE: The websites for each organization as well as the National Endowment for Democracy (https://www.ned.org/).

There is no official data publicly available on North Korean human rights organizations. Thus, it is necessary to examine the status of organizations registered with the MOU to grasp the process of change in North Korean human rights activities. As the registration record changes in real-time, historical data can only be identified based on prior research. As shown in Table 5.1, out of a total of 430 organizations registered with the MOU, 34 were registered as "human rights organizations" as of January 2020. (As of September 14, 2021, the total number of organizations had increased to 454. But subcategories including human rights improvement, humanitarian assistance, and education had been deleted and could no longer be confirmed.)

Until the early 2000s, few North Korean human rights organizations existed. According to one study, as of August 1, 2002, out of a total of 99 organizations registered with the MOU, only three were engaged in North Korean human rights improvement.[39] Even in 2006, when the number of organizations approved by the MOU increased to 181, "only a few" were North Korean human rights organizations. Until 2006, the MOU did not separately categorize North Korean human rights organizations. The 99 organizations registered with the MOU in 2002 included 41 organizations dealing with overall unification activities, 24 academic research organizations, 17 organizations focused on exchanges and cooperation, 16 humanitarian aid organizations, and one unification education organization.[40] In 2006, there were 51 organizations dedicated to unification activities, 32 academic research organizations, 8 exchange and cooperation organizations, 87 social and cultural organizations, 2 concerning the Kaesong Industrial Complex, and 1 unification education organization.[41]

Many North Korean human rights organizations are not registered with the Ministry of Unification; some are registered with other government agencies, some have not registered intentionally, while others have not registered due to various restrictions. MOU-registered organizations are established based on the Rules on the Establishment and Supervision of Non-Profit Corporations Governed

---

39   Je Seong-ho, "Improvement of North Korean Human Rights and the Role of NGOs" [in Korean], *Unification Strategy Studies* 12, no. 2 (2003): 271–300.
40   Je, "Improvement of North Korean Human Rights."
41   Lee Jong-seon, "The Roles of NGOs in Korea for Human Rights of North Korean Defectors in China" [in Korean], *Ethics and Philosophy Education* 7 (2007): 175–94.

by the Ministry of Unification. Separately from these rules, non-profit organizations may be established and/or registered under the Assistance for Non-Profit, Non-Governmental Organization Act or the North Korean Refugees Protection and Settlement Support Act. For instance, organizations registered with the Ministry of Interior and Safety are established and registered based on the Non-Profit, Non-Governmental Organization Act.[42]

---

42   Because of the absence of a proper inter-ministerial cooperation system, the South Korean government's activities involving human rights in North Korea have not been limited to one central ministry. Since 1997 the Ministry of Unification (then the Ministry of National Unification) has been primarily in charge of North Korean human rights–related affairs after responsibility for North Korean defectors was transferred from the Ministry of Health and Social Affairs. Organizations such as the Ministry of Public Administration and Security, Ministry of Foreign Affairs, Ministry of Justice, National Human Rights Commission, and the National Intelligence Service have also directly or indirectly supported North Korean human rights activities.

Government-level support for North Korean defectors began in 1962 upon the enactment of the Special Assistance Act for Persons of National Merit and Defectors to South Korea. Because North Korean defectors were given a status equivalent to those of national merit, they were managed by the Office of Veterans Administration. Afterward, relevant duties were transferred to the Ministry of Patriots and Veterans Affairs, which then re-transferred to the Ministry of Health and Welfare with the enactment of the Act on the Protection of North Korean Defectors in 1993. Accordingly, the social perception of North Korean defectors changed from those of national merit to the socially underprivileged. Fortunately, in January 1997, with the enactment of the North Korean Refugees Protection and Settlement Support Act, North Korean defectors became regarded as the main agents of unification rather than the marginalized. This change triggered the relevant responsibilities to be transferred to the then Ministry of National Unification.

Since that time, the role of local governments has gradually been emphasized, and the general trend has been that administration has shifted from the central to provincial governments. As such, the Ministry of Security and Public Administration, which has jurisdiction over local governments, has been working to support North Korean refugees and human rights activities since 2009.

6 The Changing Information Environment in North Korea

Nat Kretchun

Reporters without Borders' 2019 World Press Freedom Index once again ranked North Korea second to last, above only Turkmenistan.[1] While such global rankings do correctly reflect that North Korea remains among the most closed information environments in the world, they can obscure trends within the country, which are more dynamic and pronounced than most casual observers would imagine. The information environment within North Korea has changed drastically over the past quarter century, trending up from an extremely low base toward greater openness and access before, more recently, retrenching.

The most recent available data provides the strongest evidence to date that access to information is falling off from a period of relative openness during the Kim Jong-il era, when authorities were largely unable to police an influx of illicit media that occurred in the wake of the Arduous March.[2] While substantial numbers of North Koreans continue today to access outside news and information via multiple sources, there are numerous indications that citizens are increasingly concerned with being detected by authorities and media access behaviors that were previously normalized, if still illegal, may once again be considered highly sensitive and risky. Furthermore,

---

1 Reporters Without Borders, "Freedom of the Press Index," https://rsf.org/en/ranking.
2 For details on North Korea's famine in the mid-to-late 1990s, see Stephan Haggard and Marcus Noland, *Famine in North Korea: Markets, Aid, and Reform* (New York: Columbia University Press, 2007).

through technical analyses of North Korean media devices we are beginning to understand the full scope of authorities' ambition with regard to the construction of an automated system of technical information control. These recent findings in aggregate strongly support the notion that the regime is successfully moving toward a new information control system that fundamentally reorients several previously understood truths about information access and information flows within North Korea.

The information control system North Korean authorities are constructing is broadly characterized by an effort to move communications and media consumption onto state-controlled networks via state-sanctioned devices. While not yet fully implemented, this information control strategy is well conceptualized and strategically designed. It has taken into careful account the relative strengths and weaknesses of the regime and its grip on control vis-à-vis its domestic population, and has arrived at a forward-looking, technologically enabled roadmap for reestablishing control over the information environment. As such it is likely to be quite effective in curbing media flows into and within North Korea. Furthermore, it has done so in light of a realistic assessment of the country's likely future development trajectory—that is, toward a more complete and entrenched market economy.

If North Koreans are to maintain access to meaningful levels of access to outside information or fully realize the information-sharing potential of increasingly accessible modern devices, new channels for information access through or around the North Korean government's information control systems will be necessary. However, significant barriers to the development and deployment of such channels exist.

In an attempt to describe the quickly changing nature of information flows into and within North Korea, this chapter will present a summary of the current information environment in the country today and examine emerging evidence of the government's new information control strategy. It will then infer some of the authorities' goals and competing priorities in setting up an information control system and discuss the system's likely impact on important information dynamics, before concluding with a discussion of potential countermeasures in light of this new information control system. This chapter draws largely on quantitative and qualitative studies of North Korean refugees, defectors, and travelers as well as technical analyses of North Korean hardware and software, conducted primarily for the U.S. Agency for Global Media and the U.S. Department of State.

North Korea's Information Environment Today

Current efforts to supply outside information and media to North Korea are by and large reactions to the post-famine opening of the information environment that began in the late 1990s.[3] The famine effectively hobbled the North Korean economy and surveillance state. As North Koreans turned to informal market activities for survival, information and media flowed into and within the country at unprecedented levels, opening up its citizens to not only information from China but a plethora of new media content, including South Korean soap operas and films. By the time researchers outside the country were making initial attempts to estimate the depth and breadth of outside media penetration into the country, all indications were that most North Koreans had already been directly exposed to some form of outside information. Radio broadcasts from non-governmental organization (NGO) stations targeting North Korea added to the reach of established outside broadcasts such as Voice of America and Radio Free Asia. Popular throughout the region for high production value and compelling narratives, South Korean entertainment media circulated throughout North Korea over increasingly robust supply chains and was consumed on a complex and modern array of digital devices including DVD players, laptops, and even some of North Korea's first legal mobile phones. Throughout the Kim Jong-il era, a trend toward greater, more socially normalized consumption of outside information continued.

However, in the latter years of Kim Jong-il's life, even as North Korean citizens' access to foreign media continued to grow, North Korean authorities, having regained some measure of economic stability after the collapse of the socialist economy, began taking initial steps to reestablish control over information flows.

The current information environment represents a transition period in which proactive efforts to disseminate information into North Korea generally assume a relatively more open, post-famine, pre-networked information control apparatus. Yet, simultaneously, the government has begun implementing a far more technologically savvy information

---

3 One notable exception to this are Korean language radio broadcasts, such as those from the Voice of America whose history stretch back to the Second World War.

control strategy than it previously had the capacity to do. As a result, from a technology perspective, the information landscape is a mix of relatively less controlled legacy devices and far more locked-down modern devices, both of which impact the types of information citizens can access as well as their susceptibility to surveillance.

Findings from surveys of defectors, refugees, and travelers, for which fieldwork concluded in late 2018,[4] reinforce a number of general truths about the contemporary North Korean information environment. Many North Koreans receive outside information across a number of distinct delivery channels including word of mouth, terrestrial broadcast in the form of radio and television, and physically exchanged digital media via USB and SD cards. However, channels for access are limited and the survey findings offer few indications of significant innovations in content delivery for foreign media that have the potential to expand reach.

Radio

From a broader information environment perspective, regardless of the many changes stemming from the introduction of new technologies, foreign radio presents a unique offering within North Korea that continues to maintain an influential, if demographically delimited, audience. Survey findings suggest the presence of a meaningfully large foreign radio audience in North Korea.[5] While qualitative research highlights a number of distinct motivations for foreign radio listening, including curiosity about the outside world and information

---

4   The United States Agency for Global Media (USAGM) commissioned this survey through InterMedia, who interviewed 350 North Koreans who had left the North between 2016 and 2018. The report has not been made public. See Robert King, "North Koreans Want External Information, But Kim Jong-Un Seeks to Limit Access," CSIS, May 15, 2019, https://www.csis.org/analysis/north-koreans-want-external-information-kim-jong-un-seeks-limit-access.

5   For instance, the USAGM's 2015 Refugee, Defector and Traveler Survey found that 29 percent of the sample had listened to foreign radio. While these surveys are not statistically comparable, year-on-year figures ranging from slightly less than 20 percent to over a third of the sample are generally observed. See Nat Kretchun, Catherine Lee, and Seamus Tuohy, *Compromising Connectivity: Information Dynamics between the State and Society in a Digitizing North Korea*, InterMedia, February 1, 2017, https://www.aquietopening.org/compromising-connectivity.

on economic market conditions in China and elsewhere, foreign radio is often cited as a highly trusted source of information among the listening population.[6] For those in search of alternative sources of information about North Korea, foreign radio constitutes by far the most accessible, richest source, as multiple state and non-state broadcasts broadcast to audiences within North Korea with targeted programming.

One interesting recent development is the degree to which radio listening has become almost completely synonymous with foreign radio listening. Survey data suggests that as many as 90 percent of all radio listeners were tuning into foreign broadcasts.[7] This makes some sense, given the increasing richness of the media environment and the relatively limited and antiquated official radio broadcast offering.

However, this has a number of potentially worrying implications. Such a complete overlap between radio listeners and listeners of illegal foreign radio broadcasts, if recognized by authorities, has the potential to reduce the amount of plausible deniability that was previously associated with radio listenership. Those who were covertly tuning into illegal foreign broadcasts were harder to detect in a large population of legal domestic radio listeners. Close association of radio listening generally with illegal listening specifically could further sensitize an already quite risky behavior. While this could eventually lead to a wholesale ban on radios, North Korea continues to broadcast official content via radio, and there remain some important contexts in which official radio is more widely consumed.[8] Thus, it is likely that while sensitivity associated with radios and radio listening behaviors will persist, a ban is not likely until North Korean authorities move away from radio as a messaging tool.

An interesting recent divergence from previous findings is in the relationship between awareness and listenership to foreign radio broadcasts. In the U.S. Agency for Global Media's (USAGM) 2015 survey and before, there was almost perfect overlap between those who were aware of specific foreign broadcasts and those who listened. More recently, however, this relationship has broken down and there are

---

6   Kretchun, Lee, and Tuohy, *Compromising Connectivity*.
7   Kretchun, Lee, and Tuohy, *Compromising Connectivity*.
8   These range from car journeys to soldiers stationed in areas without access to television.

increasingly greater numbers of North Koreans who are aware of foreign broadcasts but choose not to listen.

There are a number of possible explanations for this. The names of foreign broadcasters do occasionally appear as the subject of ire in North Korean media, and it is possible that some survey respondents could have learned about the broadcasts from state media. It is also possible, as listening to such broadcasts has grown more sensitive, some proportion of those who learned about broadcasts from friends and family are now unwilling to take the risk to listen.

Thus, while radio listening rates do not appear to be dropping off precipitously there are a number of signs, including a relatively older listenership, that suggest listenership may decline in the future.

Television

With nearly universal access, television is mass media in North Korea and as such is currently the most important means through which the North Korean authorities message their citizens. Even though far fewer North Koreans appear to be listening to official radio broadcasts, survey findings consistently suggest that nearly all North Koreans watch state central television broadcasting.[9] Although North Korean TV still broadcasts an incredibly narrow range of programming by international standards, the production quality has been visibly improving in recent years and some updates have been made to the content of broadcasts as well.

For that same reason, TV also holds great potential to allow foreign broadcasts to reach large swaths of the North Korean populace with real-time, visually compelling content. While technology and terrain impose geographic limitations on the potential for broadcasts to seep into North Korea across both the Chinese or South Korean borders, all indications are that those within broadcast range are quite likely to tune in. Survey findings suggest that foreign broadcast viewership is common in areas where broadcasts are accessible and overall viewership appears to have increased during a period in which South Korea targeted North Korean viewers more intentionally with terrestrial broadcasts that formerly simply bled over.[10] While the potential exists for broadcast TV to more impactfully serve those within broadcast

---

9   2018 USAGM Survey of North Korea Refugees, Defectors, and Travelers.
10   Kretchun, Lee, and Tuohy, *Compromising Connectivity*.

range through content created specifically for North Korean audiences, no targeted content is currently broadcast.

Non-networked digital media

The large majority of North Koreans who have consumed foreign media content have done so via some form of non-networked digital media, be it DVD, USB, or Notel. DVD players and USB drives are the primary technologies facilitating the flow of recorded digital foreign media. Nearly every respondent who reported having viewed foreign digital content said they did so through a DVD player and four-fifths used USB drives as well.[11] Nevertheless, more than one in ten mention using a cell phone to access foreign content, though it is not clear that the phones were on a network.

Recent government crackdowns have re-sensitized consumption and sharing behaviors, as well as the distribution channels for these physical media. Since the signature system that prevents unsanctioned files and apps from loading on North Korean phones also deletes unsanctioned media, the state networked–based information control strategy may not bode well for the long-term viability of non-networked forms of digital foreign media consumption. That said, demand for foreign dramas, films and music persists, and we can expect non-networked digital media to continue to circulate in North Korea despite emerging threats.

Mobile phones and networked devices

Both in terms of breadth and intensity of use, North Korea has truly entered the mobile phone age, and use patterns are developing quickly. Previously, mobile phones often were shared between family or friends or rented as needed; today, they are quickly becoming personal proximate devices, mirroring how they are used in much of the rest of the world. Mobile phones are increasingly an integral part of North Korean society and the functioning of its economy, and they are connecting North Koreans to one another in ways previously inconceivable.

At the same time, mobile phones represent a new frontier in censorship technology and a boon to North Korea's security services. Indeed, mobile phones represent the most fully realized vision of the principles

---

11   2018 USAGM Survey of North Korea Refugees, Defectors and Travelers.

of North Korea's new digital information control strategy in real-world application.

In qualitative research, North Koreans have reported some awareness that their phones might be monitored by authorities.[12] Generally, North Koreans are very used to employing an array of operational security techniques so they can have sensitive discussions or engage in sensitive activities without detection. This includes such behaviors as limiting call duration, storing SD cards separately from devices, having sanctioned content on devices for plausible deniability, etc. Even though fewer than 4 percent of phone users said they were as comfortable speaking about sensitive topics on the phone as they would be in person,[13] as North Koreans become more reliant on mobile phones, their ability to communicate safely becomes increasingly difficult.

When asked about a range of relatively sensitive or risky behaviors such as listening to foreign music, watching foreign dramas or films, or reading foreign ebooks or texts, appreciable numbers of phone users reported having engaged in such activities despite their sensitivity.

However, when asked about the timing of these activities, most of them occurred in the past. This is in general accordance with the full rollout of the software-based content control system colloquially known as the "signature system." Whereas early mobile phone adopters used their phones as a media nexus, utilizing the advanced features of the mobile phones to share and consume illicit content, after the rollout of the signature system, qualitative research suggests that most of the activities described above became technically impossible on most North Korean phones.[14] While it is possible that some models of phones could not be updated to fully implement the signature system's software-based controls, it is clear that most of the illegal activity described happened at least two years prior to the survey.

North Korean authorities have demonstrated their strategic and technical sophistication in designing and implementing mobile phone-based censorship and surveillance solutions. However, authorities cannot inhibit the most fundamental functionality of mobile phones as interpersonal communications devices. Thus, many of the most substantial impacts that could arise as a result of the introduction of

---

12   Interviews with thirty-four recent defectors conducted by the author and colleagues in South Korea as part of research for *Compromising Connectivity*.

13   2018 USAGM Survey of North Korea Refugees, Defectors, and Travelers.

14   Interviews for *Compromising Connectivity*. See footnote 12.

mobile phones in North Korea are tied to the ability to facilitate new connections between North Korean citizens.

With that in mind, the 2018 USAGM Refugee, Defector and Traveler Study included two questions aimed at better understanding the size and character of the human networks with which survey respondents connect via their mobile phones. The size of the network among the subsample of domestic phone users roughly fell into three roughly equal groups—approximately one-third of phone owners had networks of 20 or fewer contracts, one-third had networks of between 20 and 50 contacts, and one-third boasted networks of 50 or more contacts.[15] While it is reasonable to assume that most respondents did not regularly contact all those in their networks, it does dispel the notion that many phone users only connect with a small handful of close family and friends.

Proactive Information Dissemination Efforts

Given the relative inaccessibility of North Korea, the huge security risks associated with operating inside the country or in the Chinese border area, the significant financial resources necessary to attempt such operations and the increasingly restrictive sanctions, it is extremely difficult for civil society organizations to play a role in promoting freedom of information as they do in many other countries. While there are South Korean and defector-led civil society organizations working independently on information freedom in North Korea, most of the larger and more active examples are U.S. government funded via the State Department's Bureau of Democracy Human Rights and Labor or the National Endowment for Democracy. These groups are generally attempting to curate content on removable media devices such as USB drives and micro-SD cards and then disseminate those physical devices into the country. Beyond these efforts, U.S. international broadcasters Voice of America and Radio Free Asia send shortwave and AM broadcasts to the North alongside a number of other nationally sponsored radio broadcasts, such as those from South Korea or Japan. While there are some nascent efforts to investigate and potentially pursue more technologically sophisticated forms of information dissemination, those efforts are largely still in their infancy compared to the state of development of North Korea's emerging information control apparatus.

---

15   2018 USAGM Survey of North Korea Refugees, Defectors, and Travelers.

North Korea's Emerging
Information Control System

As the information space in North Korea opened post-famine, despite increases in the technological sophistication of the devices used to consume foreign media—exemplified by a broad transition from DVDs to USB drives to share foreign content—the introduction of devices and the proliferation of content was uneven, idiosyncratic, and inefficient as a result of the phenomena's illegality. Somewhat counterintuitively, those very traits made it difficult for authorities to crack down on foreign information flows. In a context in which there was a great deal of plausible deniability (legal devices being used for illegal content consumption, for instance), remote monitoring was nearly impossible because devices were unnetworked, security agents were susceptible to bribes, and there was no single stream or source of illegal media to focus efforts on because distribution was so fragmented. Authorities would either have to muster huge resources to attempt to rebuild the mass human surveillance apparatus of the Kim Il-sung era or find a new solution to control a fundamentally altered information environment.

Authorities have clearly chosen the latter path, embracing new forms of digital technology that, when paired with their distinct technological sophistication advantage over their own citizens, they have calculated gives them greater, not less, control.

From the high-level state perspective, North Korean authorities appear to be attempting to reestablish control over the information and media its citizens receive in order to make domestic control a less potentially volatile and less resource-intensive endeavor. By legalizing and making available more, not fewer, digital technologies and, for the first time, opening up digital networked communications to ordinary citizens, the regime is reasserting control by taking steps to modernize rather than trying to recreate the information control structures of yore. This potentially solves many of the information control problems that characterized the laxity of the post-famine era.

Based on recent trends in surveillance and policing in North Korea,[16] it is not difficult to imagine an idealized conception of the information

---

16   Information interviews (see footnote 12) as well as technical analyses of North Korean devices undertaken as part of the research for *Compromising Connectivity*.

environment post-implementation of this new control strategy. North Koreans would consume media and communicate over networks totally under authorities' control. This would be facilitated by outlawing and inspecting for non-network devices, such as Notels and DVD players, which cannot be remotely censored and surveilled, and tightly policing the border with China to stem the physical inflow of unsanctioned media.

The censorship and surveillance power implied by shifting communications and media consumption behaviors to state-controlled devices are already on display in the functionality of North Korea's cell phones. Through network-level controls on the Koryolink and Kang Song NET networks and device-level software and hardware interventions, the North Korean government has made it extremely difficult to use mobile phones to access any unsanctioned or outside content.

Once a viable means to consume and share illegal foreign media content, authorities have completely removed mobile phones from the web of devices used to circulate and view foreign media content inside North Korea. This was achieved through multiple layers of control. Authorities are able to mandate the use of certain handsets, the software for which is built to North Korean government specifications and prevents access to all non-approved content and applications via a sophisticated system of digital signatures. These handsets are then connected to digital networks also under complete government control. This combination of digital device and network controls, coupled with specially tasked human security forces[17] who conduct inspections for illegal devices and content, is likely to continue to increase the level of difficulty and risk associated with accessing foreign media. In addition, North Korean authorities have shown the capacity to quickly iterate and evolve these control tactics. Examinations of North Korean software provide indications of quick learning. While it is often difficult to confirm if or how certain technological capabilities for surveillance and censorship are employed in routine practice, evidence of their growing capabilities is clear.

---

17   Security units such as Group 109 are tasked with enforcing laws relating to ideological crimes. While this currently consists of searching devices for illegal content, it is likely that as the North Korean government's control strategy matures, content is likely to be policed remotely through on-network devices, and human security units will be more focused on detecting illegal non-networked media devices.

The New Information Control
Calculus and Trade-Offs

Information control goals

As laid out above, while far from complete in its implementation, the recent survey findings and technical analyses of North Korean software do suggest that North Korean authorities continue to make progress toward reestablishment of greater information control. However, their focus is not singular, and it can be inferred that authorities have and must balance a number of competing priorities in constructing a complex, functional information control scheme. Those priorities feature the obvious goals of improved censorship and surveillance but also include other priorities such as economic facilitation and garnering popular support.

Censorship. Perhaps the central aim of many of the recent information control innovations in North Korea, authorities are attempting to create a "clean" information environment in which citizens use approved networked devices that technologically prevent the consumption and spread of unsanctioned content. For this purpose, the signature system North Korea has implemented, which allows only sanctioned, signed files and apps to run, has proven very successful at ensuring and maintaining "clean" digital networks. Examinations of North Korean software suggest that this is often prioritized over other areas such as surveillance or economic facilitation in implementation when those are mutually incompatible. Unable to load unsanctioned content, only 1 percent of respondents reported sending information they would personally classify as sensitive. The government's desire for an information environment free of ideologically unorthodox elements is apparent in North Korean law and official communications.

Surveillance. Increasingly widespread cell phone adoption has helped authorities to modernize a core function of the state by enabling much more sophisticated remote surveillance of cell phone owners, a far more resource-efficient approach than North Korea's traditional human surveillance apparatus. Although survey data speaks more directly to crackdowns enacted via human surveillance—such as 65 percent of the sample of the most recent USAGM Refugee Defector and

Traveler Study[18] having been inspected by Group 109—software and hardware analysis reveals a number of technological surveillance features that are present on North Korean cell phones and tablets, from the watermarking of files to establish digital chains of custody to Trace Viewer,[19] an application that provides digital assistance to human surveillance by taking unerasable snapshots of phone activity that security personnel can easily inspect.

While authorities' network- and device-level controls over phones and tablets on networks in North Korea mean that the proliferation of these devices has undoubtedly improved North Korea's centralized surveillance capabilities, when in direct conflict with censorship features, software implementations have generally prioritized censorship over surveillance. It is unclear how data collected via technologically aided remote surveillance maps with traditional human surveillance and bureaucratic reporting structures. Further research in this direction is needed.

Economic facilitation. Although the North Korean state may be trying to capture and control more of the market-based economic activity occurring within its borders, both official pronouncements and tangible reforms suggest that North Korean authorities have come to terms with a more marketized economic future. Mobile phones have the ability to facilitate market-based economic transactions, the primary driver of much of what (limited) internal economic growth the country is seeing.

In recent surveys, more than half of mobile phone users reported using their mobile phones to conduct business outside their official occupations.[20] Further, the human networks being leveraged by North Korean mobile phone users are surprisingly large and robust despite restrictions on physical travel. Nearly half of mobile phone users' phone contact lists included people outside their home province and included contacts in Pyongyang and along the Chinese border. The median mobile phone user in the sample had over thirty contacts in their phone's contact list.

---

18   2018 USAGM Survey of North Korea Refugees, Defectors, and Travelers.
19   Florian Grunow, Niklaus Schiess, and Manuel Lubetzki first publicly revealed the existence of the Trace Viewer function in a talk at the Chaos Computer Club (see "Woolim—Lifting the Fog on DPRK's Latest Tablet PC," https://media.ccc.de/v/33c3-8143-woolim_lifting_the_fog_on_dprk_s_latest_tablet_pc).
20   2018 USAGM Survey of North Korea Refugees, Defectors and Travelers.

Public support. Authorities have leveraged the increasing availability of modern information and communications technology devices such as mobile phones and tablets to project modernity to the domestic population. Qualitative interview findings among defectors suggest that many North Koreans believe that authorities introduced mobile phones to make citizens' lives better. This positive view of authorities' motives comes despite the widespread belief that mobile phones might be monitored by authorities. North Korean official media commonly and prominently features the use of mobile phones in state-produced content, not only demonstrating authorities' endorsement of their use but also employing the devices as a vehicle for projecting greater modernity and the government's success in economic management.

North Korea's information control trade-offs

Even as authorities have been able to largely curb the potential for unsanctioned media to circulate via mobile phones, they have chosen to allow millions of North Korean citizens to have mobile phones. The introduction and proliferation of these devices, which constitute the cornerstone of North Korea's new information controls strategy, bring with them a complex set of trade-offs, serving multiple government priorities but also introducing new social and economic dynamics that the government will have to contend with.

The essence of the calculated trade-off inherent in North Korea's new approach to information control is that in return for far greater and more resource-efficient censorship and surveillance capabilities, the widespread introduction of networked technologies signals a shift away from one of the core tenets of North Korea's previous social and information control strategy: isolation. Previously, North Korean authorities went to great lengths to prevent extensive horizontal connections between individual citizens, attempting to channel as many communications as possible vertically through state structures. However, with the widespread introduction of mobile phones, that is no longer possible. As is the case in many restricted information environments, word of mouth is the single most important source of trusted information. Mobile phones, and in the future potentially other networked devices, supercharge word-of-mouth networks, allowing North Korean citizens to communicate with one another far more quickly and over greater geographic expanses than ever before. Even if the government continues to tightly restrict physical movement, North Koreans are no longer as isolated as they once were, to both the benefit and potential peril of the government.

Shifting Dynamics in a New Information Control Landscape

Given both the realities of the information environment today and what appears to be true about North Korea's emerging information controls system, a number of prevailing dynamics that describe the way information flows within North Korea and interacts with the government's competing information control goals are in flux.

Dynamics worthy of special consideration include cleanliness, velocity, and dispersion. Under their new control strategy, authorities are seeking to sharply curb access to unsanctioned content through a combination of automated censorship, remote surveillance, and human crackdowns. This is already showing visible signs of success. However, velocity and dispersion are more complicated dynamics about which the regime is making less clear trade-offs.

"Cleanliness"

While some outstanding questions around the overall information control system design remain, for example with regard to the inclusion of tracking technologies (such as watermarking) in North Korean Android systems, most digital control innovations the authorities have pursued are focused on producing a digital information environment that is automatically scrubbed of all unsanctioned content. In early deployments on cell phones, the environment produced by the signature system is *so* clean that many important, state-sanctioned activities would be rendered impossible. It seems likely that authorities may have to take a step back from the pure cleanliness of the digital environment produced by the current implementation of the signature system if they hope to realize some of the economic benefits of these emerging digital networks. Already, partial attempts to address this difficult balance are apparent in the form of a software called "pigeon." Pigeon is an officially produced piece of software that allows officials to electronically sign their own files, allowing them to load on multiple devices. However, even as authorities explore the right balance, they have clearly established their ability and willingness to enforce extremely clean locked-down network environments.

Velocity

Information and media flows in North Korea remain extremely slow by modern international standards. However, mobile phones (and potentially other networked technologies that may soon be widely introduced as part of a new information control strategy) have already begun to increase the speed of information exchange and suggest the potential for much faster circulation still. The cleanliness of the networked digital environment discussed above, coupled with one-to-one information exchange dynamics,[21] have limited this increase in speed to certain forms of information within groups that have some form of offline (if often indirect or second- or third-degree) relationship. However, within those constraints, the velocity of information exchange has increased markedly. This is particularly noticeable in business and smuggling activities. Information exchanges that were once very slow and complicated to arrange are now done via mobile phones instantaneously. Authorities likely view most of the effects of this increase in information flow velocity as positive developments, ones that help drive greater economic efficiency in ways that directly or indirectly benefit the authorities. However, now that norms, behaviors, and expectations around rapid information sharing have been established, barriers to narrowly dictating what can be shared or how connections to new contacts are made could make control quite difficult, apart from completely shutting down mobile networks. Techniques ranging from undermining censorship software to simply using semi-coded language and making small behavioral tweaks could allow forms of unsanctioned content to ride the network rails in ways that could be difficult for authorities to monitor and could facilitate individuals who are testing the limits of permissible information sharing. Qualitative interviews with recent defectors reinforce this notion, with interviewees reporting the use of coded language in gray market business transactions.[22]

---

21   While North Koreans with mobile phones can text one another, there are no social media that would allow individuals to engage in one-to-many or micro-broadcast communications.

22   Interviews for *Compromising Connectivity*.

Dispersion

Isolation in multiple forms—physical, ideological, social—was a hallmark of North Korean social control policy under Kim Il-sung. Individuals had few opportunities to establish connections with those outside of their family, work, school, and neighborhood associations. This had the effect of limiting information sharing outside of small local nodes, with the prominent exception of the apparatuses of the state, which sent party guidance down and local information back to the center. While North Koreans still cannot not travel freely, the market economy has brought more opportunity for travel and interactions with those beyond their traditionally limited local connections. Thus, by creating more far-flung contacts and maintaining them via mobile phones, North Koreans have not only created vital inter-node connections, but they can now share information between these nodes instantaneously. As noted earlier, recent survey findings support the notion that North Koreans now have both a large number of and geographically diverse contacts with whom they communicate via mobile phone.

For networked technologies to continue to bring the government more gains in information control and economic facilitation than liabilities in the form of citizens' ability to communicate with one another more freely, it is critical that authorities are able to credibly enforce a "clean" digitally networked environment. If that condition is not met and citizens find ways to introduce significant amounts of unsanctioned content, the increases in the velocity and dispersion of information flows will pose far greater information control problems for authorities than they faced in a pre-networked era.

Evolving Dissemination Opportunities

While the outlines of North Korea's digital information control strategy are clear and it appears to be strategically designed and iteratively implemented, its rollout is not yet a fait accompli and its success not guaranteed. In the context of an emerging information control strategy designed to push citizens onto state-controlled digital networks that can be efficiently censored and surveilled, there are two general categories of potential technical solutions that civil society groups and others might pursue as countermeasures. These include utilizing or creating alternative information infrastructures and undermining government control over state networks such that they could be used for unsanctioned content.

Alternative infrastructures

Legacy technologies such as radio or terrestrial TV continue to be the most viable way to deliver outside news to North Korean citizens and have established, if somewhat limited, audiences. Exploring ways to create new delivery channels outside of government-controlled networks will be a key challenge for those seeking to promote access to information in North Korea. To attract audiences within the context of the new information controls regime, compelling, high-fidelity visual content will have to be delivered in a way that is difficult or impossible to detect remotely to devices that are easily concealable or that are modified versions of legal devices. As those requirements suggest, there are multiple challenges to be overcome in order to establish new channels of information. However, as authorities do more to push media and communications streams onto state-controlled networks and increased border security makes the distribution of physical materials through China more difficult, a modern information delivery infrastructure that is wholly separate from state networks is likely to be vital to supplying North Koreans with outside content.

Satellite and peer-to-peer communications or content caching technologies are among the potential infrastructural solutions currently being researched and tested for use in North Korea. These solutions, in effect, represent modern iterations on principles that work in practice in North Korea today. Satellite, much like broadcast media, can be beamed across the whole of the country, is difficult or expensive to jam, leaves little persistent evidence of what content was accessed, and viewers are not easily remotely identified by receipt of the signal alone. Furthermore, satellite has the ability to overcome some of the geographical limitations of broadcast media and could deliver targeted, high-quality modern visual media. While there are broadcast challenges, the principal hurdles at present appear to be how to design antennae and receivers that are sufficiently concealable and affordable to be feasibly used in North Korea, given the security risks.

Peer-to-peer communication solutions, by contrast, offer the potential to modernize and digitize the hand-to-hand content sharing behaviors associated with USB and SD cards today, without the need to traverse state-controlled digital networks. While there are many potential implementations of this principle, the fundamental goal would be to mirror the content consumption and sharing functions that mobile phones offer in much of the world, while avoiding state networks and operating systems that provide authorities with easy vectors for censorship and surveillance. They also create the potential for far greater internal content circulation thereby reducing the need to smuggle significant amounts of largely redundant content across North Korea's tightly controlled borders. While this approach holds promise, parallel challenges related to reducing risk for users, affordability, and popularization strategies are yet to be overcome.

Undermining technical information controls

Many of North Korea's new digital information controls are designed in recognition of the government's technological sophistication advantage over its own citizens. However, the North Korean government does not maintain such an advantage over external actors. Careful study of the principles, practices, and techniques guiding the development of digital information controls are likely to uncover options to directly or indirectly undermine these controls, thereby allowing North Koreans to gain greater information access and shield themselves from some forms of digital surveillance. Efforts to undermine North Korea's technical information controls are enticing, as they would allow for North Koreans to use widely available, legal devices to access unsanctioned content, which would significantly lower the bar to receiving illicit content for those with lower risk tolerances.

Further, over a slightly longer timeline, we should expect the capacity for North Korean citizens to understand and undermine elements of the government's digital information control system to increase. While they start at a significant disadvantage—and don't have the luxury of broad access to the kind of technical knowledge that would facilitate a sophisticated "hacking" culture—North Korean citizens have a long history of making hardware modifications in order to access outside information or increase their own safety and security when engaging in sensitive behaviors. The longer North Koreans are exposed to digital technologies and the greater number of people who are trained in computer science, the more likely it will be that North Korea's citizen hacking tradition moves into the digital age.[23] For those outside the country looking to catalyze such an effect, studying the implementation and evolution of North Korea's digital information control techniques will allow an understanding of these technologies to filter back into the country and may even result in the development of tools that aid in dismantling these technological controls.

---

23   While limited and difficult to verify, there are already anecdotal reports of those with technical training disabling elements of the censorship system on individual mobile phones.

7 North Korea's Response to Foreign Information

Martyn Williams

This chapter will examine North Korea's response to the increasing amount of foreign material that is flowing into the country from three perspectives: legal, ideological, and technological. It is based on interviews with 41 North Korean escapees (defectors); these were conducted in Seoul, South Korea, in February, March, and August 2019, originally for a report published in December 2019 by the Committee for Human Rights in North Korea. The escapees represent a cross-section of ages and jobs, and a total of 19 were female and 22 were male. About half escaped in the 2010s, with others escaping earlier. The majority came from North Hamgyong Province, but some were from Pyongyang, Ryanggang, and North Pyongan provinces. This chapter is adapted from that report, *Digital Trenches: North Korea's Information Counter-Offensive*, and also draws on state media news articles and my own library of daily North Korean television footage.[1]

The digitization of electronics and communications technology has been the biggest catalyst for the spread of foreign content inside North Korea over the past two decades. Digital media has made it easier and cheaper to smuggle, distribute, consume, and copy illicit content and these capabilities increase every year. North Korea has always battled against this inward flow of news and entertainment, but its opposition stepped up a notch after the ascent of Kim Jong-un in 2011. While it continues to rely on tools of the past, such as house raids and random street checks,

---

1 Martyn Williams, *Digital Trenches: North Korea's Information Counter-Offensive* (Washington, DC: Committee for Human Rights in North Korea), December 2019, https://www.hrnk.org/uploads/pdfs/Williams_Digital_Trenches_Web_FINAL.pdf.

the government is increasingly turning to digital tools to fight digital technology. This includes subverting open-source technology, such as the Android operating system, to serve its means. But as North Korea's digital response gets more sophisticated, the rise of the market economy and collapse of the state supply system have led to a sharp rise in bribery that is undercutting the battle. North Korea's domestically produced content continues to be uninspiring and heavily skewed toward obvious propaganda, but the state is showing early signs of adapting to the digital age.

The Problem

In any tightly controlled country, the free flow of information is a major concern for the state. Much of the state's hold over its people is based on a top-down system in which the people are fed a diet of information designed to keep them under control. Communications between citizens and from the outside can undermine state legitimacy by offering an alternate source of information that, whether fact or rumor, can destabilize the ruling elite.

In North Korea, where state control of the people is extreme, the government has built the tightest information control system in the world. People are fed a centrally controlled stream of propaganda that offers a single view and are punished if they seek out an alternate view. For the North Korean state, anything that deviates from state propaganda risks undermining it and casting doubt on the entire leadership and system.

The Legal Response to the Influx of Foreign Media

North Korea's evolving struggle with foreign information can be seen through updates to its criminal code from 2009, 2012, and 2015, which have shifted the focus of punishment away from the simple possession and consumption of content to its importation and distribution. In general, there are now shorter penalties for small offenders and longer penalties for more serious offenses. In most cases, smugglers are targeted with new penalties when it is not their first offense.

The North Korean criminal code

The portion of the criminal code covering the "Importing and Distribution of Decadent Culture" is a good example of these recent changes. It targets "a person who, without authorization, imports, creates, distributes, or illegally keeps drawings, photos, books, or electronic content like video recordings which contain decadent, carnal or foul contents." [2] As article 193 in 2009, it called for punishment by reform through labor of less than two years for most offenses, or up to five years if the offense was deemed "grave." It also called for a sentence of between five and ten years for pornographic content. In 2012, renumbered as article 183, the maximum penalty for the lowest level of offense was softened from two years to one year in a labor brigade, and the specific penalty for pornographic content was removed. In 2015 article 183 was further revised with the introduction of a new punishment of up to five years of reform by labor in cases where someone "imports, creates, or keeps such content frequently or in large quantity." Both "large" and "frequently" are not defined in the criminal code, leaving some latitude for judges. It also saw the return of the five- to ten-year sentence, this time for anything judged "severe." While the law doesn't spell out what "severe" means, North Koreans generally accept different levels of risk with different genres of content. The lowest-risk material includes movies from countries such as China, India, and Russia, a step higher are movies and soap operas from the United States and South Korea, and the riskiest content is anything that directly attacks the North Korean system or its leaders, anything political, anything religious, and all pornography. Similar changes can be seen in article 184, which covers decadent acts, article 185, which deals with reception of foreign broadcasts, article 221, which deals with illegal border crossing, and article 214, which controls the publication of material. In each case, the laws have been refocused to hit those in distribution roles more heavily.

Taken together, it appears the state has accepted that it is losing the battle against foreign content and instead is putting its efforts into the more serious aspects. Of course, the leniency or severity of sentencing can be affected by the political or domestic security climate at the time of prosecution, so in reality citizens can expect sentences that go beyond what the law allows.

Bribery

The increased willingness of lower-level security force workers to accept bribes is undermining the battle against foreign content. Escapees

---

2   The English translation of the North Korean Criminal Code is provided by the Committee for Human Rights in North Korea.

say that local Ministry of Public Security officials are most likely to accept bribes, especially when the alleged crimes involve lower-risk content. It is more difficult to bribe provincial- and national-level officers of the Ministry of State Security, especially if the content in question is "severe" or in large quantities. The rise of bribery has followed the collapse of the public distribution system, which has left security officials in a much less comfortable position than before, and the rise of the *donju* class, which has created a new group of wealthy citizens with money to spend.[3]

Escapees told me that the amount required depends on the alleged crime and the perceived social status of the offender; the amount required is usually large enough to put financial stress on an individual or family, so a bribe still represents a challenge for many North Koreans. Some escapees I spoke to talked of bribes of a few U.S. dollars for a minor offense, which itself is several times the state monthly wage, but some said bribes of over a thousand dollars would be requested in the case someone was caught attempting to escape.

Not all North Koreans make money in the markets or through their own business ventures, so the emergence of bribery has created a two-tier justice system where the rich are able to get away with infractions that the poor cannot.

Officials in cities far away from Pyongyang are more likely to accept bribes than those in the capital. This is explained by the poorer economic situation and weaker ideology in the provinces and also a desire to avoid scrutiny from Pyongyang. Crime in distant cities can bring unwelcome oversight from the national government and cost local officials their jobs, so local security officers have a personal interest in maintaining the veneer of a well-run city. One escapee told me local police would often warn him of impending crackdowns by the Ministry of State Security so that he could stash his content in advance of a raid.

Smuggling and border security

North Korea began strengthening security along its northern border after Kim Jong-un came to power. The first thing to appear was new

---

3 Daniel Collinge, *The Price Is Rights: The Violation of the Right to an Adequate Standard of Living in the Democratic People's Republic of Korea* (Seoul, Korea: United Nations Human Rights Office, May 19, 2019), https://www.ohchr.org/Documents/Countries/KP/ThePriceIsRights_EN.pdf.

fencing, which now covers most of the border, and more recently a video-surveillance camera network has expanded and is said to cover the entire border with China.[4]

Since about 2014, border patrol guards have been rotated more frequently to avoid becoming too friendly with local citizens and smugglers. The video camera network plays a role too, as it watches border guards just as effectively as it surveils potential smugglers.

Street inspections

Random street inspections continue to be one way in which the security forces search for foreign content. They include both body checks and inspections of the contents of smartphones. In the latter, officers will check chat logs and look at the content of messages, to see if South Korean colloquialisms have been used in text messages. However, the emergence of thumbnail-size microSD cards has made things less risky for citizens: they are much more difficult to find during a search and, if there is risk of discovery, can be easily destroyed by snapping them in half.

House raids

Unannounced residential raids still take place. They do not require warrants and can happen at any time, leaving occupants constantly on edge if they are watching foreign media or have any in the home.[5] Nevertheless, the shrinking size of media has made things a bit easier for citizens. A single USB stick can store the equivalent of several VHS cassette tapes and is much easier to hide. MicroSD cards, mentioned above, are even smaller.

---

4   Kang Ji-won, "Things Still Tense in Border River Area after Purge of Jang Song-taek," Asiapress, June 20, 2014; on video surveillance efforts, see Jo Hyon, "Video Surveillance Network Expanded on China-North Korea Border," *Daily NK*, December 28, 2018, https://www.dailynk.com/english/video-surveillance-network -expanded-on-china-north-korea-border/; and Mun Dong-hui, "Surveillance Cameras Installed to Cover Entire Sino-North Korean Border Region," *Daily NK*, March 18, 2019, https://www.dailynk.com/english/surveillance-cameras-installed -to-cover-entire-sinonorth-korean-border-region/.

5   Ken Gause, *Coercion, Control, Surveillance, and Punishment: An Examination of the North Korean Police State* (Washington, DC: Committee for Human Rights in North Korea, 2012), 43, https://www.hrnk.org/uploads/pdfs/HRNK_Ken-Gause _Web.pdf.

A key part of the state surveillance system continues to be the *inminban*[6] leader. Their duties include ascertaining if neighbors are watching foreign videos or listening to foreign radio broadcasts. A typical counter-strategy is to keep the volume low, but even that can attract attention. One escapee told me that they watched foreign content together with their *inminban* leader. This does not appear to be typical, but points to a general weakening of ideology and breakdown at the lower levels of the surveillance society.

Ideological Responses to the Influx of Foreign Media

The second arm of North Korea's defense against foreign content is ideological. North Koreans are exposed to ideological education from infancy, and it touches every element of their lives until they die.

The Propaganda and Agitation Department

Citizens are fed an unceasing, centrally controlled diet of propaganda. A vast control and censorship apparatus headed by the Propaganda and Agitation Department (PAD, 선전선동부) ensures that North Korean citizens are fed ideology through news reports, media, and artistic endeavors. As such, PAD works across the entirety of North Korea's media and arts sector to ensure that a common message is being delivered to the people, whether through a newspaper, television broadcast, movie, musical performance, or play. PAD also dictates the lectures that every North Korean (with the exception of Kim Jong-un) must attend each week.[7]

To carry out its job, it liaises closely with the Organizational Guidance Department (OGD), also under the Central Committee, to ensure that media messaging matches whatever programs the OGD is pushing across the country. Every month, PAD distributes guidelines to all media outlets that spell out propaganda themes that must be followed. The same themes are reflected in materials that work their way down to individuals.

PAD operates a pervasive control network that reaches into establishments including the Ministry of Culture and the Central Broadcasting

---

6   Neighborhood units.
7   Michael Madden, "KWP Propaganda and Agitation Department," NK Leadership Watch, November 2009.

Committee. By appointing, promoting, demoting, and dismissing thousands of workers in these sectors, it maintains effective control. PAD also places small teams of its own workers directly into publishing houses, movie studios, artistic troupes, and theater groups to oversee and approve the production of content at each phase of its creation. Work is continually referred to the PAD bureau in each organization and it is either approved or sent back with comments on how it should be changed. Once approved, it gets passed upward for further approval by the main PAD office.

The Kim family has always been closely associated with PAD. It was Kim Jong-il's first place of work after he graduated from Kim Il-sung University in 1964.[8] In 2015, one of the first visible moves into power of Kim Yo-jong, Kim Jong-un's sister, was her appointment as first vice director of PAD. She effectively controlled her brother's public image in that position, although it appears that role was taken over in April 2019 by Hyon Song Wol, former head of the Samjiyon Orchestra.[9]

Daily and weekly meetings

Regular meetings are an important part of the indoctrination system and serve to keep people in line. They occur at least weekly in every *inminban* across the country, but there are also daily workplace meetings. The latter often focus on whatever is being reported in the newspaper and attendees have an opportunity to discuss various issues. In practice, this means agreement with the view of the party and a pledge to support whatever is being asked of citizens.

The weekly meetings will often include a lecture, centrally dictated by PAD, on an important issue. Sometimes officials from the Ministry of State Security will participate and lecture on various subjects, including the evils of foreign content.

---

8 "Propaganda Agitation Department" [in Korean], North Korea Knowledge Dictionary, ROK Ministry of Unification, https://nkinfo.unikorea.go.kr/nkp/term/viewNkKnwldgDicary.do?pageIndex=1&dicaryId=128.

9 Michael Madden, "North Korea's New Propagandist?" *38 North*, August 14, 2015, https://www.38north.org/2015/08/mmadden081415/; "Kim Yo-jong in De Facto Power of PAD," *Daily NK*, July 20, 2015, https://www.dailynk.com/english/kim-yo-jong-in-de-facto-power-of-p/. Also see "State Media Hints at Growing Role for Hyon Song Wol in Party Propaganda Department," *NK News*, June 4, 2019, https://www.nknews.org/2019/06/state-media-hints-at-growing-role-for-hyon-song-wol-inparty-propaganda-department/.

Because the meetings are closed and cannot be monitored overseas, the state is free to deliver a much harsher message to its citizens than it can through broadcast media.

Technical Responses to the Influx of Foreign Media

Among all of the tools at the state's disposal in the battle against foreign media, none have advanced as much in the last few years as the technological ones. While the digitization of media was the catalyst that led to the mass spread of foreign content across the country, so too has the same technology been employed to help the government combat it.

In the early days of the digital revolution, the government often reacted to new technology by banning it. It was an immediate and simple solution to the problem, but not a long-term one. Despite such bans, products would inevitably get smuggled into the country anyway; bans also deprived the North Korean economy of the benefits that could come from technologies like cellular telephony and smartphones. In response, the government worked to modify how the technology could be used and deployed it in a controlled manner. Both cellular telephony and WiFi were initially introduced, then quickly banned when citizens found illicit uses for them. Eventually the state reintroduced them once it had managed to devise additional restrictions that locked down their use. Recently, some technologies such as IPTV (internet protocol television) streaming have been introduced, under strict government control from the beginning.

The pattern is clear. The North Korean government is getting increasingly sophisticated in the way it controls and engineers digital technology.

Cellular telephony

North Korea's first experience with mobile cellular technology was in 2002, when a network was launched in the Rajin-Sonbong (now Rason) Economic Zone. This 2G network was based on the European GSM standard and started by Bangkok-based Loxley Pacific. It attracted thousands of subscribers before being abruptly shut down by North Korean authorities in May 2004, just a year and a half after its launch. The reason for the sudden closure was never disclosed. However, it occurred less than a month after a huge explosion at a railway yard in Ryongchon near the Chinese border.

The explosion, which killed hundreds, occurred a few hours after a special train carrying Kim Jong-il had traveled through the area. Despite a general conclusion that it was the result of an accident, a rumor spread that it was an assassination attempt triggered by a cell phone. True or not, it seemed to be enough to spook the authorities as to the potential misuse of technology and they shut down the public cellular service shortly afterward.[10]

However, the government had clearly recognized the potential of cellular technology and a few years later in late 2008 reached a deal with Egypt's Orascom Telecom to launch a new network. That network, Koryolink, mirrors the fixed-line telephone network and is separated into two halves to control information flow. On one side are the phones used by North Korean citizens that can connect with other North Korean citizens and access the domestic intranet. The other side is used by foreigners, who have the ability to make and receive international calls and access the internet. The two portions of the network cannot communicate directly, shutting down the potential of those with international access from passing on information to those without. The result is that North Korea enjoys the benefits of cellular telephony without the risk of uncontrolled communications. It is a control system like no other in the world.[11]

Cell phone use in the border areas

To see what might happen without strict controls, one only needs to look to areas near the Chinese border. Signals from Chinese cellular towers effortlessly traverse the border and reach several kilometers inside North Korea, bringing with them a window into the outside world.[12] With a Chinese cellular signal and a smuggled phone with a Chinese SIM card, North Koreans have the ability to call any number in the world and can get unrestricted internet access.

---

10 "Thailand Urges N. Korea to Lift Mobile Phone Ban," *Kyodo News*, August 29, 2005.

11 "Koryolink Moves to Plug Censorship Loophole," North Korea Tech, September 2, 2014, https://www.northkoreatech.org/2014/09/02/koryolink-moves-to-plug-censorship-loophole/; see also Kang Mi-jin, "North Korea Targets Specific SIM Cards in Crackdown," *Daily NK*, July 31, 2017, https://www.dailynk.com/english/north-korea-targetsspecific-sim-c/.

12 Kim Joon-ho, "North Korea Expands Jamming, Surveillance of Chinese Cell Phones," Radio Free Asia, July 3, 2014, https://www.rfa.org/english/news/korea/jamming-07032014143126.html.

In response, the North Korean authorities are both jamming these cellular signals and attempting to locate the people making calls. The jamming operations are concentrated near population centers along the border, such as Sinuiju, Manpo, Hysean, and Hoeryong. To circumvent jamming, citizens must travel several kilometers away from town to receive a Chinese signal, according to reports; in some cases, they will climb hills in remote regions to catch weak signals from Chinese networks.

Sometimes, the authorities will switch the jamming off, which immediately makes it much easier for city-dwelling North Koreans to receive Chinese cellular signals, but there is a catch. If citizens make calls, the authorities will use direction-finding equipment to try and locate them. This equipment is expensive, sensitive gear from Germany's Rohde & Schwarz that was imported into North Korea in 2008 under the guise of an anti-surveillance system to protect its new Koryolink 3G network.[13]

As a result, citizens must go to considerable lengths to protect themselves. Phones must be kept switched off when not being used and when calls are made, they must be kept as short as possible. Some users will travel into the countryside or climb a hill, where they might get a better signal, while also having a better lookout post for anyone approaching.

The detection system isn't perfect: it has trouble differentiating between a legitimate North Korean phone and one connected to a Chinese network. To improve their chances of detection, the authorities have reportedly resorted to periodically shutting down the country's legitimate wireless network, which forces all North Korean phones offline and leaves only those connected to Chinese networks on air.[14]

The advent of high-speed 5G cellular in China will present another problem for North Korean authorities. It was reported in 2019 that

13   "North Korea's Koryolink: Built for Surveillance and Control," *38 North*, July 22, 2019, https://www.38north.org/2019/07/mwilliams072219/.

14   Moon Sung-hui, "North Korea Temporarily Closes Telecom Towers to Nab Chinese Mobile Users," Radio Free Asia, December 16, 2014, https://www.rfa .org/english/news/korea/crackdown-12152014134428.html; "N. Korea Clamping Down on People Making Phone Calls with South Koreans: Sources," *Yonhap News*, March 29, 2016, https://en.yna.co.kr/view/AEN20160329004300315. See also "North Korea Temporarily Closes Telecom Towers to Nab Chinese Mobile Users," Radio Free Asia, December 16, 2014.

some North Koreans had begun using WeChat to communicate and send video content into North Korea. The WeChat platform limits video to 100MB, which is a few minutes' worth of high-definition footage, but faster 5G networks and a different messaging platform could soon make it possible to send TV shows and movies across the cellular network in a short period of time.[15] When such technology arrives, it would remove the need to cross the physical border between the two countries and make the import of illicit content a safer, albeit still risky, operation.

The main limiting factor now is the time needed to download a longer video file such as a movie. These are typically around 1–2 gigabytes in size, which can take tens of minutes on current networks; 5G will reduce this to several minutes, although as the phones use newer frequency bands, their signals might be more easily detectable.

If data networks are used for cross-border information distribution, it can be expected that North Korean authorities will clamp down further on the use of phones near the border.

Technological blocks on smartphones and PCs

In networked repressive states, a common way of controlling what the population does online is to implement controls at the network level. In countries such as China and Iran, this usually involves blocking certain websites, censoring keywords, and keeping track of what users do online. In North Korea, the government has much greater control of the network. The entire infrastructure is state-run, and the security services are heavily integrated in the running of the telecommunications network. This gives the government a complete view of all network traffic. Even if the encryption built into North Korea's Naenara web browser is used, the government can still surveil traffic because it issued the encryption keys.

Over the last decade, the government has gotten increasingly sophisticated at clamping down on PCs and smartphones. It has cleverly reacted to the potential freedoms such digital devices can bring and subverted open-source software to prevent citizens from exploiting those

---

15   Mun Dong-hui, "North Koreans Turn to WeChat for Videos and Crossborder Communication," *Daily NK*, July 30, 2019, https://www.dailynk.com/english/north-koreans-turn-to-wechat-for-videos-and-crossborder-communication/.

freedoms. The system is comprehensive and appears to be successful. Computer security engineers have called North Korea's PC software "a surveillance mess and a privacy nightmare."[16]

User surveillance with Red Flag and Trace Viewer

Running in the background of every Android tablet and smartphone in North Korea is a process called "Red Flag." The software logs every page a user visits with the web browser and takes screenshots randomly during use of the tablet or phone. North Korean authorities have also included an app called "Trace Viewer" that allows users to see this database of collected screenshots but does not allow them to be deleted.[17] The system is sinister in its simplicity. It reminds users that everything they do on the device can be recorded and later viewed by officials, even if it does not take place online. As such, it insidiously forces North Koreans to self-censor in fear of a device check that might never happen.

File watermarking

North Korean engineers have added a file watermarking system to both the Red Star operating system for PCs and to their own version of Android smartphones. Each time a media file is opened on a device, a string of data based on either the hard drive's serial number or the phone's identification number is appended to the file. The watermarking is added to images, videos, and document files—anything that could carry illicit information.[18]

The watermark can be used to determine if a file has been opened on a particular machine or phone and, in the case of files that are passed from user to user, the string of devices used to access them. This means

16   Florian Grunow, "Lifting the Fog on Red Star OS," Chaos Computer Club Congress, December 27, 2015, https://media.ccc.de/v/32c3-7174-lifting_the_fog _on_red_star_os/related.

17   Florian Grunow, "Lifting the Fog on DPRK's Latest Tablet PC," Chaos Computer Club Congress, December 28, 2016; Florian Grunow and Niklaus Schiess, "Exploring North Korea's Cellphone Surveillance Technology," https://www.ernw .de/download/nospy6_exploring_north_koreas_survelliance_technology.pdf; Also see, "All That Glitters Is Not Gold: A Closer Look at North Korea's Ullim Tablet," 38 North, March 3, 2017, https://www.38north.org/2017/03/mwilliams030317/.

18   Grunow, "Lifting the Fog on Red Star OS."

that, given a single file, the watermarking could theoretically be used to determine the complete distribution path for the file, right back to the first person to open it on a North Korean device. Given enough files, a complex distribution map could be drawn up that reveals key points in the distribution network.

This capability is troubling, though there is currently no evidence that the government has a comprehensive national database of hard drive serial numbers. However, the Koryolink cellular operator records the international mobile equipment identity (IMEI) number of all phones it issues, so mobile users are potentially at a higher risk.

Digital signatures

North Korea's digital certificate system is effective and simple. It locks down a smartphone or tablet to the point that it becomes little more than a consumption device for state propaganda and personal memories. Its introduction began in 2012, when the government mandated that new software be downloaded on all smartphones in the country. The change added new controls that took away the ability to watch anything but state-sanctioned video files.

The level of thought that went into the introduction was evident in one simple feature: phones with the new software installed had signal bars that were red, instead of the original blue. This meant street inspectors could see at a glance if a phone had been updated as required, without having to delve into settings screens in phone menus.

When a file is opened on a device with the updated operating system, the app opening it checks to see if it has been digitally signed by one of two digital certificates: NATISIGN, a national signature derived from the North Korean government's digital certificate, or SELFSIGN, which comes from the device's own unique digital certificate.[19] Without one of these two signatures, files cannot be opened. Apps that use the digital signature system include the file browser, image gallery, music player, Android installer, PDF viewer, audio recorder, and text editor. In practice, this means that if a file was not created by the device or it did not come from the government, it cannot be played on the phone. It instantly rendered North Korean smartphones useless as devices for consuming illicit media. The system is also used on Android application

---

19   Grunow, "Lifting the Fog on Red Star OS."

files, meaning apps cannot be freely installed on smartphones and tablets unless they have the blessing of the government.

File integrity checks

The security software pre-loaded onto North Korean phones and computers would not be such a hurdle if it could be easily replaced, but it cannot. Beginning with Red Star OS in 2013, engineers added routines that check core files of the operating system against a preinstalled database. They look to see if any of the files have been changed or replaced and, depending on the file, will either warn the user or immediately reboot the device. If the latter happens, the machine can end up stuck in a loop of constant reboots and be useless to the user. This "bug" would have been obvious to programmers, so it was a conscious decision to render a PC useless rather than allow it to run with modified files.[20]

WiFi

North Korean authorities learned a lot from the introduction of WiFi on cell phones and computers in the late 2000s. At first it was viewed as a harmless technology, but that soon changed. At least one embassy in Pyongyang set up an open WiFi access point in 2013 so that anyone nearby would be able to connect and access the internet. According to one report, this access resulted in an increased demand to live in the neighborhood.[21] Soon after the report was published, North Korea's State Radio Regulatory Department sent a letter to diplomatic missions and international organizations in Pyongyang informing them that WiFi was prohibited without government permission.[22] The letter all but confirmed the story when it said that WiFi signals "installed and being used without license, produce some effect upon our surroundings." It went on to instruct users to consult with the government if they wanted to use a WiFi network, or else risk a fine.

Having removed the immediate problem of open WiFi networks, the authorities' next step was a little more ambitious. They began removing

---

20   Grunow, "Lifting the Fog on DPRK's Latest Tablet PC."
21   North Korea Intellectual Solidarity, "평양시내 대사관주변의 집값천정부지로 뛰어 올라" [Prices of houses close to embassies rise in Pyongyang], August 6, 2014.
22   Leo Byrne, "North Korea Bans WiFi Networks for Foreigners," *NK News*, September 8, 2014, https://www.nknews.org/2014/09/northkorea-bans-wifi-networks-for-foreigners/.

WiFi from the phones themselves. Several subsequent generations of North Korean smartphones had the WiFi feature disabled in firmware, so it was impossible to switch on. This lasted for several years until, the government apparently believed that it could reintroduce WiFi on its own terms.

In September 2017, North Korea's first public WiFi network went into operation in Pyongyang. Called the Mirae network, it is available on the Mirae Scientists Street and in Kim Chaek University areas and requires an app that is preinstalled on some phones and tablets.[23] Details of the service are scarce but a KCTV report said that it requires a SIM card for use and showed a video of a card with the "Mirae" logo being inserted into a phone.[24]

Social Engineering as a Response

The introduction of new technology can have a profound effect on people, causing them to alter the habits of a lifetime over a short period of time, for better or for worse. Among a handful of technologies introduced to North Korea over the last few years, two are worth watching with respect to their effects on the consumption of foreign information.

Smartphone games

At first, it might seem unlikely that North Koreans would have access to a wide range of smartphone games. After all, North Korea's state media is not known for being lighthearted, but over the past few years, the number of games officially available has grown tremendously.

A modern North Korean smartphone, such as the Daeyang 8321, includes a catalog of 125 gaming apps, with titles such as "Special Operations Group," "Future Cities," and "Volleyball 2016." A handful are free, but most require payment.

In many countries, mobile gaming has become a major activity on smartphones, and it appears that the North Korean government has seized on this idea. The time spent playing a game will take away from

23   "Wi-Fi로 전민학습환경을 개선 / 무선망판형콤퓨터가 호평" [Demand grows for improving the learning environment with WiFi-capable computers], *Choson Sinbo*, August 8, 2018, http://chosonsinbo.com/2018/08/il-1814/.
24   Korean Central Television, "8 p.m. News Report," KCTV, October 21, 2018.

the overall free time that somebody has, and that includes time that might otherwise be spent watching a foreign drama or movie.

There is a precedent for this. Before smartphones, computer games already played this role in homes where several users shared a single laptop. While a family member played games, the laptop couldn't be used to watch foreign content. The use of smartphone games to steer people away from foreign content is perhaps more subtle than expanding state television content. While numerous escapees in their twenties told of the boredom of watching state television, many were interested in computer games.

IPTV services

IPTV services stream live video channels and on-demand programming across the national intranet and have been a research focus of North Korean IT groups since at least 2012. In recent years, state media has reported several times on a system called "Manbang," developed by the Manbang Information and Technology Supply Center.[25] The set-top box for the service is sourced from Aisat, a Chinese electronics maker, and the Manbang TV service is accessed through a set-top box connected to the national intranet through a DSL (digital subscriber line) data connection over the telephone network.

The IPTV system appears to be a subtle way the state is expanding access to its ecosystem to lock more people into the programming. Using Manbang, viewers can access a number of live television channels including Korean Central Television and several Pyongyang-only channels such as Ryongnamsan TV, Mansudae TV, and Sports TV. The additional channels give viewers outside of Pyongyang a choice in programming for the first time, making it a little more likely they might stay within the state media system. Of the additional channels, Ryongnamsan TV includes foreign movies and Sports TV offers global sporting events. Man TV also features a library of on-demand video, including children's TV shows and movies. Through Man TV, state media can now offer something to watch before KCTV signs on at three o'clock each afternoon. Before Man TV, most of the country received only KCTV. The additional content means viewers are less likely to be pushed toward illicit content out of boredom.

---

25   Korean Central Television, news program viewed by author, August 16, 2016.

Conclusion

From conversations with escapees, it is easy to conclude that official attitudes are changing toward foreign content in North Korea. After all, many talk about its pervasiveness and speak of watching it with family, friends, and even officials who are meant to be controlling its spread. Laws have also been reduced, and the death penalty is rarely handed out for what has become a more common offense. However, to assume things are getting better would be a mistake. The state is far from giving up control over what North Koreans watch and listen to.

The North Korean system remains firmly in control of people's lives and has not shown any signs of major instability, although the government does appear to understand that it risks losing the propaganda battle. In March 2019, Kim Jong-un called on Workers' Party propaganda officials to work harder on their indoctrination efforts:

> Under the present drastically changing situation, the grand goal of struggle that we want to achieve demands us, as we always have, put more sincere and greater effort into inspiring the ideological and spiritual strength of the popular masses, who are the masters of the revolution and construction.[26]

The State still has the benefit of years of brainwashing on its side and a powerful security apparatus to keep people in line. Citizens might not be executed as commonly as before for watching foreign content, but they are still at risk of losing everything should they be caught. This is especially true for the lowest levels of society. The rise in bribery risks the creation of a two-class society, where illicit consumption shifts toward the rich and well connected, while the poor avoid it because they cannot pay the bribes.

The criminal code revisions represent a slight softening of attitude toward the consumption of foreign media, but also a refocusing of efforts to crack down on distributors. If successful, this could throw established supply chains into chaos and lead to fewer distribution routes for foreign content and a higher cost.

While digital technology has created new pathways for foreign content, the increased networking of products could work against information freedom and eventually lead to the creation of an even more

---

26 *Rodong Sinmun*, March 9, 2019.

Orwellian society. Although media reporting in many countries has highlighted the uncomfortable amount of data collected by companies like Facebook, Google, and Uber, North Koreans have not seen this and so are a soft target. The government's total control over smartphone software means it would be relatively simple to include tracking and surveillance software should it wish to do so. There are no signs that it has taken this step yet, but it could be a serious threat to the population. Aside from the most obvious risks, such as user tracking through GPS and surveillance of text messages, there are frightening possibilities, such as the use of the microphone to surveil nearby conversations or detect what content is being watched.

The North Korean state has proven over time to be adept at countering the flow of information into the country, and for this reason, the future remains bleak. While each new technology or innovation represents a new chance to provide North Koreans with greater access to information, continuing development and innovation will be essential to stay a step ahead of the state.

III. Human Rights and Denuclearization

8 Human Rights Advocacy in the Time of Nuclear Stalemate

The Interrelationship between Pressuring North Korea on Human Rights and Denuclearization

Tae-Ung Baik

At its 120th session in Geneva during the week of February 10–14, 2020, the UN Human Rights Council Working Group on Enforced or Involuntary Disappearances (WGEID) dealt with 597 cases of enforced disappearance from various states, including 43 in the Democratic People's Republic of Korea (DPRK).[1] As of 2020, the WGEID had around 275 outstanding cases of disappearances that allegedly involved the DPRK. Acting as a communication channel between family members of victims of enforced disappearance and the relevant authorities, the WGEID transmits cases to the governments concerned asking for information on the fate or whereabouts of the

This article was supported by the Strategic Research Institute Program for Korean Studies through the Ministry of Education of the Republic of Korea and Korean Studies Promotion Service of the Academy of Korean Studies (AKS-2020-SRI-2200001).

---

1   The WGEID, one of the special procedures of the UN Human Rights Council, receives petitions for enforced disappearances and requests its member states to investigate the fates and whereabouts of the disappeared. It communicates with governments through general allegations or other letters, and submits the results of thematic studies to the UN Human Rights Council and the UN General Assembly. At present, the UN Human Rights Council has about 57 special procedures, including 14 country-specific mandates and 43 thematic mandates with 80 independent experts. The WGEID was established in 1980, the oldest procedure in the UN Special Procedures, and is comprised of five members appointed from each of the five regions of the world being supported by Geneva-based secretariat staffs. The regular sessional meeting of the WGEID covers cases of enforced disappearances, including new petitions and existing cases, and discusses ways to resolve the issues with various government representatives, civil society representatives, and the victims.

disappeared people. Each year it sends a reminder to these governments, reiterating requests for information on all outstanding cases. During the session, the WGEID again raised its concerns about the lack of cooperation from the DPRK, which continues to send identical replies to the transmitted cases.[2]

While campaigns for denuclearization and peace negotiations were taking place through the North-South Korean summits and the North Korea–U.S. summits, there has been increasing concern that human rights issues in North Korea were not being properly considered. In fact, UN Special Rapporteur on DPRK Human Rights Tomas Ojea Quintana wrote in his 2019 report, "Despite the fact that there is no sign of improvement in the situation of people's human rights in the DPRK, human rights considerations have not been part of the agenda in the peace talks to date." He emphasized that "peace, if achieved, will be significant for the citizens of the DPRK only if it guarantees them an improvement in the exercise of their most fundamental rights."[3]

During the Human Rights Council's Universal Periodic Review (UPR) of North Korea in May 2019, the country sent a ten-member delegation to represent the government. During the review, the DPRK accepted 186 recommendations made by Human Rights Council members, even if it rejected another 63. It is obvious that the DPRK can no longer deny the concept of human rights. However, North Korea still generally responds to the international community's calls for human rights changes with categorical rejections, under the rationale that these criticisms are based on inaccurate information from hostile forces. It is indeed not an easy task to push North Korea to improve human rights conditions and toward judicial system reform.

A tougher and more complicated issue is how the international community can pursue human rights improvement in DPRK while the world is primarily focused on the country's denuclearization. The short answer to the problem is that human rights issues should not be sacrificed in the pursuit of denuclearization. In fact, we should be able to find an optimal way to raise both denuclearization and human rights issues in DPRK at the same time.

---

2   See, for example, UN General Assembly, Communications Transmitted, Cases Examined, Observations Made and Other Activities Conducted by the Working Group on Enforced or Involuntary Disappearances, A/HRC/WGEID/118/1, ¶46 (July 30, 2019).

3   UN General Assembly, Situation of Human Rights in the Democratic People's Republic of Korea, A/74/275/Rev.1, ¶1, ¶66 (September 20, 2019).

Human Rights in the DPRK

The human rights issue is one of the key problems in DPRK.[4] However, it has been often put second to other issues. North Korea is most commonly depicted as a regional and global security threat, and its development of nuclear weapons and long-range missiles is considered a serious regional danger. Another aspect of North Korea drawing international attention are its various humanitarian crises, such as the continual food shortages inflicting suffering on its people and the great number of refugees living illegally in China. The North's human rights problem, therefore, has often been viewed by the international community as less serious a concern than security or humanitarian problems, even if there is abundant evidence showing that human rights violations in the country are alarmingly grave and compelling. Torture, extrajudicial killing and disappearance, suppression of freedom of expression and association, and other breaches of fundamental human rights are widespread and systematic in North Korea.[5]

The United Nations has appointed a special rapporteur on DPRK human rights since 2004,[6] and, in March 2013, the UN Human Rights Council established the Commission of Inquiry (COI) on Human Rights in the Democratic People's Republic of Korea to investigate the systematic, widespread, and grave violations of human rights.[7] The COI report was submitted on February 17, 2014, and it recommended that the UN Security Council should refer crimes against humanity in North Korea to the International Criminal Court.[8] North Korea tends to respond to these international criticisms with a flat denial.

---

4   For more information, see Tae-Ung Baik, "Non-judicial Punishments of Political Offenses in North Korea—With a Focus on Kwanriso," *American Journal of Comparative Law* 64, no. 4 (December 1, 2016): 891–930.

5   See Human Rights Watch, *The Invisible Exodus: North Koreans in the People's Republic of China* 14, no. 8 (November 2002) (written by Tae-Ung Baik, Dinah Pokempner, and Mike Jendrzejczyk).

6   UN Commission on Human Rights, Resolution 2004/13, Situation of Human Rights in the Democratic People's Republic of Korea, E/CN.4/RES/2004/13 (April 15, 2004).

7   UN General Assembly, Human Rights Council, Situation of Human Rights in the Democratic People's Republic of Korea, A/HRC/RES/22/13 (April 9, 2013).

8   Human Rights Council, Report of the Detailed Findings of the Commission of Inquiry on Human Rights in the Democratic People's Republic of Korea, A/HRC/25/CRP.1, ¶1211 (February 7, 2014).

Strategies for Human Rights Advocacy

The UN COI on human rights in North Korea in its report asserted, "Systematic, widespread, and gross human rights violations have been, and are being, committed by the Democratic People's Republic of Korea, its institutions, and officials."[9] It proposed that "the United Nations must ensure that those most responsible for the crimes against humanity committed in North Korea are held accountable," and that the measures should be combined "with a reinforced human rights dialogue, the promotion of incremental change through more people-to-people contact and an inter-Korean agenda for reconciliation."[10] The greater emphasis of the COI report seems to be put on the accountability of the regime rather than the promotion and protection of human rights, which has prompted North Korea to strongly denounce the report. Although the COI report has successfully captured global attention, it was not successful in converting its human rights criticisms into efforts to make actual and incremental changes in the country.[11]

Some may question whether, under the current regime, there is any hope at all for a legal system that protects human rights. We remember similar skepticism with regard to Russia and China. In fact, North Korea is following China's example of legal change, even if the speed is slow. For a long time, the only reference to human rights in North Korean legislation was article 5 of the Criminal Procedure Act, adopted in 1992, stipulating that "The State should thoroughly protect human rights in dealing with criminal cases."[12] However, in 2009 North Korea amended its constitution and added an expression of human rights to it, following China's lead. Article 8 of the amended constitution provides that "the State shall defend the interests of the working people including the workers, peasants, soldiers, and working intellectuals," and "respect and protect human rights." In another sign of progress, as stated above, North Korea responded to the recommendations for changes made during the UPR. North

---

9   A/HRC/25/CRP.1, ¶1211.

10   A/HRC/25/CRP.1, ¶1218.

11   This section, "Strategies for Human Rights Advocacy," heavily relies on Baik, "Non-judicial Punishments."

12   As of 2012, it remains included in the Act as article 6.

Korea has accepted 197 recommendations in 2019, and 114 in May 2014, in contrast to its complete rejection of all UPR recommendations in 2009.[13]

In terms of normative development, North Korea is not an exception, and it also demonstrates the gradual infusion of human rights norms into domestic legal systems. Risse-Kappen and Sikkink, using their "spiral model" argument, explain the process of human rights development as a gradual one. The development of human rights and democracy happens, they say, as successive phases of repression, denial, tactical concession, prescriptive status, and rule-consistent behavior.[14] Considered in this light, North Korea apparently cannot continue its total repression and denial stages, and it needs to move toward a human rights protection system.

These gradual changes should be carefully considered in the process of advocacy for promotion and protection of human rights in North Korea. It would be very hard to single out any one approach as the best way to promote human rights in North Korea. Some seem to prioritize humanitarian issues, while others put more emphasis on the DPRK's violations of civil and political rights than on engagement.[15]

The Kim Dae-Jung (1998–2003) and Roh Moo-Hyun (2003–08) administrations in South Korea pursued an engagement policy with North Korea. Kim Dae-Jung's so-called Sunshine Policy, which endeavored to use appeasement as a lever for change in North Korea, was internationally known.[16] However, under these lenient policies, the Kim and Roh governments were less active in advocating for human rights issues in North Korea. They refused to participate in the introduction of UN resolutions on North Korean human rights. When the first UN resolution on North Korean human rights was put forward for adoption in the Commission on Human Rights in April 2003, South Korea chose to

---

13   See Louis Charbonneau, "U.N. Sees Signs of North Korea Softening in Human Rights Dialogue," Reuters, October 28, 2014, http://reut.rs/1wzRdEK.

14   See Thomas Risse, Stephen C. Ropp, and Kathryn Sikkink, eds., *The Power of Human Rights: International Norms and Domestic Change* (New York: Cambridge University Press, 1999), 20–35.

15   See UN General Assembly, Situation of Human Rights in the Democratic People's Republic of Korea, A/60/306 (August 29, 2005).

16   See Chung-in Moon, "The Sunshine Policy and the Korean Summit: Assessments and Prospects," in *The Future of North Korea*, edited by Tsuneo Akaha (London: Routledge, 2001).

abstain from voting.[17] The Roh Moo-Hyun administration voted for a resolution on North Korean human rights at the UN General Assembly for the first time in December 2006.[18] The administrations hesitated from raising human rights issues because they worried that direct criticism against the regime might restrict opportunities for the South to continue its engagement and cooperation with the North.[19] This approach was widely criticized by conservative groups in South Korea and by the international community. In fact, this idea—that human rights criticisms of North Korea can jeopardize South Korea's cooperative relationship with the North—has never been proven true. South Korean progressives need to learn that advocacy for human rights in North Korea does not have to jeopardize the promotion of a peace and reunification agenda on the Korean Peninsula.

European states took a different approach when they normalized diplomatic relations with North Korea in 2000. The EU and some of the European states had demanded that human rights should be one of the agenda items in the dialogue,[20] and the North Korean government agreed to include human rights as a main agenda item in the negotiation for the normalization of relations with the EU and other European states.[21] As noted above, the North Korean government also adopted an expression of human rights in the 2009 amendment to its constitution. When the international community presents sound, fact-based

---

17   See UN Commission on Human Rights, Resolution 2003/10, Situation of Human Rights in the Democratic People's Republic of Korea, E/CN.4/RES/2003/10 (April 16, 2003), https://www.refworld.org/docid/43f313210.html.
18   Mincheol Kim and Hawon Lee, "Ministry of Foreign Affairs 'Voted for UN Resolution for Human Rights in North Korea'" [in Korean], *Chosun Ilbo*, November 17, 2006.
19   For example, Kim Dae-Jung tried to defend the Sunshine Policy as a form of human rights policy. When he and his North Korean policy aides were criticized by conservative blocs, he rebutted by saying that offering food aid to North Korea was one of the most important human rights protection activities. Jo Jung-an, "Kim Dae-jung: 'The Sunshine Policy Has Become a Way to Realize Human Rights and Democratization in North Korea,'" *Korea Times*, November 24, 2006, http://www.pluskorea.net/sub_read.html?uid=1434&section=section1.
20   See "The EC—Democratic People's Republic of Korea (DPRK): Country Strategy Paper 2001–2004," 5, 18–19, http://eeas.europa.eu/korea_north/docs/01_04_en.pdf.
21   North Korea knowingly made the concession to proceed with the normalization of diplomatic relations with the EU. When the EUparticipated in the adoption of the Human Rights Resolution on North Korea in the United Nations in 2003, North Korea's dialoguewith the EU stopped.

illustrations of the North's human rights violations, the regime cannot ignore such criticisms, and in fact it has demonstrated a tendency to take measures to mitigate the situation.[22]

In dealing with North Korean human rights issues, we often encounter conflicting approaches: Whether to emphasize engagement or whether to pursue complete isolation; whether to maintain an objective stance or to engage in an aggressive political campaign; whether to promote dialogue and cooperation or to initiate harsh criticism and pressure; and whether to propose cooperation or to intensify confrontation. The optimal strategies for the promotion and protection of North Korean human rights will not be found in taking only one set of approaches from the above list. Rather it is more important to understand and carefully consider the country's complicated internal dynamics so that we do not sacrifice the human rights of the people of North Korea for some other unrelated causes.

Origins of DPRK's Human Rights Violations

Among other DPRK human rights violations, the practice of sending political offenders and their family members to a *kwanriso*[23] without appropriate judicial process is clearly in violation of international human rights law. The International Covenant on Civil and Political Rights (ICCPR) article 9 states, " No one shall be subjected to arbitrary arrest or detention," and "No one shall be deprived of his liberty except on such grounds and in accordance with such procedure as are established by law."[24] Article 8 also provides that "No one shall be required to perform forced or compulsory labor."[25] The non-judicial punishment of political offenders by sending them to a *kwanriso* is definitely in violation of the ICCPR. It is also in violation of the same covenant's right to liberty of movement and freedom to choose residence,[26] and could

---

22 A good example showing this tendency are the continuous amendments of the Criminal Act and Criminal Procedure Act.

23 A *kwanriso* can be literally translated as an "administrative camp," but the facility is used for punishing political offenses and a site of frequent human rights violations. For more information, see Baik, "Non-judicial Punishments."

24 Office of the UN High Commissioner for Human Rights, "International Covenant on Civil and Political Rights (ICCPR)," December 16, 1966, art. 9.1, https://www.ohchr.org/EN/ProfessionalInterest/Pages/CCPR.aspx.

25 ICCPR, art. 8.3(a).

26 ICCPR, art. 12.

also be considered a case of enforced disappearance. The treatment of *kwanriso* residents also constitutes serious human rights violations, which could amount to the crime of humanity as persecution.[27] Are these human rights violations happening because of flaws in North Korea's criminal laws and procedures? Are they a result of DPRK law enforcement agencies not complying with existing laws? Or are these violations not a legal problem, but something attributable to the general system? In fact, North Korea's human rights violations cannot be attributed to any one of these reasons, but are a consequence of inter-related problems in the entire penal system.

First, human rights violations in North Korea's process of criminal justice can be ascribed to flaws in the law. North Korea's Criminal Act and Criminal Procedure Act have provisions that are incompatible with international human rights standards. Clearly, the excessively broad definitions of "anti-national crimes" and the insufficient procedural safeguards of defendants' rights are legal flaws that are significant origins of North Korea's human rights violations. The North's fundamental penal principle of prioritizing social education over legal punishment seems to be another significant reason for human rights violations through extra-judicial punishment and administrative measures. In particular, the non-judicial punishment of political offenses by sending the principals and their family members to a *kwanriso* can never be justified under the North Korean legal system.

Second, even if they are far from sufficient, the pre-existing procedural rights in the current legal system are often neglected. For example, the provisions in the Criminal Procedure Act like the maximum periods of investigation, trial, and detention, the rights not to be subject to torture or coerced interrogation, and the right to be tried in front of a judge are not fully respected. Indeed, there are many occasions where human rights infringements happen in violation of the existing law. Similarly, DPRK law enforcement agents are aware that torture, cruel treatment, and the abuse of power are not permitted, but they violate their own laws. This chain of impunity is another significant contributing factor to human rights violations.

---

27   Under article 7.1(h) of the Rome Statute of the International Criminal Court, "persecution" is a crime against humanity, and is defined as "intentional and severe deprivations of the fundamental rights contrary to international law by reason of the identity of group or collectivity."

Third, the government lacks a strong will to eliminate human rights violation in the penal process, especially in the treatment of political offenders. The government and the Korean Workers' Party should be blamed for not taking decisive measures to abolish the wrongful practice, the abuse of power, and governmental sponsorship of illegal acts. Given that there are so many complicated factors to consider, efforts to improve human rights conditions in North Korea should be very cautious and deliberate. The most important caveat is to ensure that any criticism is based upon concrete facts and can lead the country to make real changes.

The Origins of the DPRK Nuclear Crisis and the Need for Change

North Korea started its nuclear development program as a desperate effort to survive after the end of the Cold War. It pursued nuclear weapons to overcome economic difficulties and to achieve military self-defense and security guarantees. In fact, fundamental changes have taken place in Northeast Asia's security map as a result of North Korea's development of missiles, including intercontinental ballistic missiles, and nuclear weapons.

Kim Jong Un, Supreme Leader since 2011 and chairman of the Workers' Party since 2012, decided to move from a military-first policy to the so-called *Byeongjin* ("parallel development") policy in May 2013. Under *Byeongjin*, formally adopted by the Central Committee of the Workers' Party to promote simultaneous nuclear and economic development, North Korea declared its completion of nuclear development in November 2017. According to a 2001 Rand report, the long-term U.S. objective for Asia was prevention of the rise of a regional hegemon, maintenance of regional stability, and management of Asia's transformation.[28] The report also stated that the basic U.S. strategy against North Korea was to prevent the proliferation of weapons of mass destruction and prevent attacks against the United States and her allies. The North's declaration of developing nuclear weapons capable of reaching U.S. territory clearly challenged this strategy.

---

28 Zalmay Khalilzad et al., *The United States and Asia: Toward a New U.S. Strategy and Force Posture* (Santa Monica, CA: RAND, 2001).

During this time, there were also changes in the political environ-ment surrounding the Korean Peninsula, including growing tensions among the states in the region. China strove to claim its position as new rising great power; Japan, through a revision of article 9 of its constitution, sought to be a normal state that can wage war. Russia, with its annexation of Crimea, began to emphasize its presence in Asia. At the same time, the United States began pursuing its pivot to Asia. In South Korea, Park Geun Hye's regime ended with impeachment, backed by the candlelight demonstration movement in 2017. The Moon Jae-In government started to pursue changes in the inter-Korean relationship and former president Donald Trump responded positively to the request for a dialogue with North Korea. In 2018 and 2019, in-ter-Korean, North Korea–China, and North Korea–U.S. summits took place and seemed to fundamentally change the atmosphere around the Korean Peninsula. However, after the failure to reach any agreement in Hanoi in March 2019, the dialogue seemed to reach a stalemate, and the prospects for achieving complete denuclearization and a permanent peace regime in the region are still unclear.

In order to promote long-term peace and stability on the Korean Peninsula, denuclearization is indispensable. However, if demands for nuclear weapon dismantlement are set as preconditions for any dia-logue and cooperation, no progress seems to be possible. A more pru-dent approach needs to be developed. The Biden administration seems to be developing an understanding that the nuclear issue must be pur-sued through a step-by-step approach, under a well-articulated gradual and mutual course of action.

The first step for actual denuclearization is the freezing of nuclear weapon and missile development, which can be gradually followed by nuclear weapons reductions and, ultimately, the fundamental dismantle-ment of nuclear weapons. It is fortunate that the two U.S.–DPRK sum-mits in 2018–19 contributed to the freezing of North Korea's heated escalation of nuclear weapons development. However, progress is no longer being made, and will not be made unless additional actions are taken. The South Korean government is seeking a partial lifting of U.N. sanctions while enhancing its efforts to engage with North Korea, in pursuit of a gradual resolution of the nuclear and missile issues. A com-plete resolution may take some time, but Seoul seeks to lift some sanc-tions in exchange for steps taken toward denuclearization, as part of a broader diplomatic engagement. It also wants to consider a declaration of an end to the Korean War and eventually a peace treaty as possible negotiation chips.[29]

Beijing has proposed to resolve the nuclear issue through dialogue between the two Koreas as well as between North Korea and the United States. It has suggested a principle of mutual suspension (suspending North Korea's nuclear and missile programs and simultaneous suspending large-scale South Korea–U.S. joint military drills) and parallel efforts (both denuclearization of the Korean Peninsula and establishment of a peace regime on the Korean Peninsula).

In the North Korean economy, decisive changes are taking place. North Korea has been trying to promote foreign exchange, slightly opening up its markets. Since the enactment of the Foreign Investment Act in 1984, North Korea had enacted various laws to solicit international investment and to promote cooperation with foreign companies, including the Foreign Investment Act (1992), Equity Joint Venture Act (1994), Contractual Joint Ventures Act (1995), Law on Taxes on Foreign-Invested Enterprise & Foreigners, Foreign Exchange Control Act, External Civil Relations Act, and External Economic Arbitration Act. Pyongyang created twenty-five special economic zones (SEZs), including the Rason SEZ, the Mount Kumgang Tourist Region, and the Hwanggumpyong and Wihwa Islands SEZs.[30] The special economic zones were created to attract foreign companies and technologies and to cultivate international markets, and North Korea says that SEZs were created to transform its socialist market-based foreign exchanges into capitalist markets. Even though joint ventures between South and North Korea had some positive results, the cooperation has been on hold: Mt. Kumgang Tourist Region was suspended in July 2008,[31] and the Kaesong Industrial Region was suspended in the wake of the North Korea's nuclear test in 2016. Worse still, North Korea blew up its liaison office in Kaesong in 2020. International sanctions and the COVID-19 pandemic also serve as barriers to cooperative relationships.

---

29   The end-of-war declaration and peace treaty were supposed to follow the armistice agreement at the end of the Korean War in 1953, but are still pending after almost seventy years.

30   Kim Chul Joon, "The Establishment and Development Status of Special Economic Zones in North Korea" [in Korean], *International Korean Studies* no. 16 (2016).

31   Nearly two million South Korean tourists visited Mt. Kumgang in North Korea up until July 2008.

Neverless, the time has come to reconsider the containment approach, in light of the lack of progress in denuclearization. Inter-Korean exchanges and cooperation should not be put off pending the full resolution of the nuclear issue. Instead, mutual exchange and cooperation should be expanded as work is done to secure the first stage of the freezing of weapons development and move into the second phase of nuclear/conventional arms reduction, with complete denuclearization the final goal. With increased economic cooperation through the North's SEZs, including Kaesong back in operation, Pyongyang will be more incentivized to consider taking further action toward the dismantlement of its nuclear weapons.

Talks between the two Koreas should continue to push North Korea toward these three phases of freeze/reduction/dismantlement and a return to the nonproliferation treaty system; dialogues should be held for the establishment of a lasting peace regime on the Korean Peninsula and a peace treaty with a regional security guarantee.

Conclusion

There are no quick fixes for the security issues on the Korean Peninsula. However, North Korea's possession of nuclear weapons and intercontinental missiles means the world can no longer disregard the challenges. Hoping for drastic regime change has proved to be an illusion. While pursuing denuclearization, we cannot abandon human rights concerns. Real change—in security and in human rights—will be possible only through broad engagement.

In the process of pursuing human rights improvements in North Korea, the following four principles should be kept in mind. First, consistent efforts for engagement should be made without sacrificing high human rights standards. The security and humanitarian dimensions of North Korean issues may make it hard to focus on the problems of human rights issues, but we should never give up our efforts to promote human rights in the country. Human rights engagement does not exclude criticizing or pressuring Pyongyang, and human rights standards should be openly maintained. Second, more efforts for technical cooperation in the areas of human rights protection should be exerted. For example, the North Korean authorities would benefit from efforts at cooperation and consultation to promote reform of their judicial system, especially in the criminal justice system. North Korean law enforcement needs to immediately learn how to collect evidence without relying on interrogations under torture, as well as the advantages of doing so. If North Korea initiates reform in its criminal investigatory, legal, and law enforcement processes, it will create substantial momentum toward the promotion of human rights in North Korea. Third, although human rights discourse inevitably entails some political implications, we should try to maintain political neutrality by preserving a human-centered approach. Where there is human suffering, the government is under an obligation to take measures to alleviate the problem, without resorting to excuses to justify such violations. Finally, we should rely on the power of the moral values that human rights embody. We can and should convince the regime that human rights violations are, in fact, against their own belief system as well. No matter how slow the development of a human rights protection system may be, we can be optimistic because the accumulation of small changes will better protect of the rights of North Koreans.

Creativity is necessary in pursuing a human rights agenda against North Korea. Wielding human rights as an abstract political slogan may be counterproductive. Instead, sometimes it makes sense to focus on specific human rights violations, ones that occur in a specific time and place, so that we can demand immediate remedies for these cases. The information gathered by the UN Working Group on Enforced or Involuntary Disappearances, the UN Accountability Project, the South Korean Office for Recording North Korean Human Rights Violations, or many NGOs will play an important role in promoting human rights in North Korea. The cases of human rights violations documented by the stakeholders concerning violations at various levels in North Korea may be used to request the punishment of, for example, specific perpetrators of sexual violence committed in a given detention center (*jibgyulso*), reeducation center (*kyohwaso*), or administrative camp (*kwanriso*), or instead for broader policy changes. If the information is concrete enough, the requests for action and remedy can be very specific. When the identities of specific perpetrators and the detailed contexts of the charges are known, it may be possible to challenge the systemic concealment of the incidents in question.

Demands for changes for human rights condition in North Korea should not be given up in the name of denuclearization, when in fact advocacy for human rights can actually help in the process. By adhering to the basic principles of human rights advocacy I have out-lined above—engagement without sacrificing standards, willingness to offer technical cooperation, maintaining political neutrality, and rely-ing on the moral value of human rights—it is possible to work toward denuclearization and the safeguarding of human rights in North Korea at the same time.

9 The Error of Zero-Sum Thinking about Human Rights and U.S. Denuclearization Policy

Victor Cha

In July 2020, the South Korean unification ministry released a document announcing its punitive actions against two North Korean defector-run organizations for sending balloons filled with rice, money, and anti-North Korean regime pamphlets across the northern border.[1] These organizations would be charged with violating domestic law and would have their licenses revoked, rendering them ineligible for government funding. The unification ministry's suspension of the non-governmental organizations (NGOs) followed shortly after North Korean leadership complaints about the balloon launches.[2] The messages in these balloons, according to the NGOs, "[carried] the truth about the Kim family: They are not gods, they are human, and they

Thanks to Andy Lim for research assistance and for comments from participants in the annual Koret conference at the Shorenstein Asia-Pacific Research Center on March 13, 2020. An earlier and different version of this paper appeared in Victor Cha, *Regaining Lost Ground in the North Korean Human Rights Movement* (George W. Bush Institute, March 19, 2020), https://www.bushcenter.org/publications/resources-reports/reports/north-korea-human-rights-movement.html.

---

1 Ministry of Unification, "ROK Government's Stance on Leaflet Campaigns and North Korean Human Rights," (Seoul: Unification Ministry, 2020); Wonju Yi, "UN Rapporteur: Inspection of Activist Groups Should Not Undermine Efforts to Improve N.K. Rights Situation," *Yonhap News*, July 30, 2020, accessed July 31, 2020, https://en.yna.co.kr/view/AEN20200730010500325.

2 Byung-joon Koh, "S. Korea to Legislate Ban on Anti-Pyongyang Leaflet Campaign after N.K. Threats," *Yonhap News*, June 4, 2020, https://en.yna.co.kr/view/AEN20200604000655325?section=nk/nk.

must be resisted. The truth is what the Kim dynasty is most afraid of."[3] One of the leaders of the suspended human rights organizations wrote in the *Washington Post*, "We send food and information into North Korea. Why is Seoul trying to stop us?"[4] While the Moon Jae-in government has political and policy reasons for undertaking these restrictive measures, this clampdown might not have been possible just a few years ago amid heightened international momentum surrounding the fight to improve the human condition in North Korea.

North Korea remains today one of the worst human rights disasters in the modern era. The government suppresses all freedoms of its citizens, including the right to organize, to travel, and to worship. The only political expressions that are permitted are ones that demonstrate complete fidelity to the state and to its leader. Over 120,000 citizens sit in political gulags that remain outside of international monitoring.[5] North Korea is one of the few industrialized societies in the modern era to have suffered a famine in the mid-1990s due to economic mismanagement, not lack of resources.[6] Though the famine killed as many as one million North Koreans, the ruling elite remains well fed and well heeled. An entire generation of North Korean youth today grows up malnourished and physically and mentally stunted (preschoolers are up to 13 cm shorter and 7 kg lighter than those in the South) even as the regime pours national resources into nuclear weapons and ballistic missiles.[7]

---

3   Sang Hak Park, "We Send Food and Information into North Korea. Why Is Seoul Trying to Stop Us?" *Washington Post,* July 13, 2020, https://www.washingtonpost.com/opinions/2020/07/13/we-send-food-information-into-north-korea-why-is-seoul-trying-stop-us/.
4   Park, "We Send Food and Information into North Korea."
5   David Hawk, *North Korea's Hidden Gulag: Interpreting Reports of Changes in the Prison Camps* (Washington, DC: Committee for Human Rights in North Korea, August 27, 2013), https://www.hrnk.org/uploads/pdfs/NKHiddenGulag_DavidHawk(2).pdf; Cholhwan Kang and Pierre Rigoulot, *The Aquariums of Pyongyang: Ten Years in the North Korean Gulag* (New York: Basic, 2001); David Hawk, *The Hidden Gulag: The Lives and Voices of "Those Who Are Sent to the Mountains: Exposing Crimes Against Humanity in North Korea's Vast Prison System,* 2nd ed. (Washington, DC: U.S. Committee for Human Rights in North Korea, 2012); and Carl Gerschman, "Review Essay: A Voice from the North Korean Gulag," *Journal of Democracy* 24, no. 2 (April 2013): 165–73.
6   Stephen Haggard and Marcus Noland, *Witness to Transformation* (Washington, DC: Peterson Institute for International Economics, 2011); Andrew Natsios, *The Great North Korean Famine* (Washington, DC: U.S. Institute of Peace, 2001).
7   Daniel Schwekendiek, "Height and Weight Differences Between North and South Korea," *Journal of Biosocial Science* 41, no. 1 (January 2009): 51–55; Soo-

While it is not uncommon to lament the many abuses of citizens inside of North Korea, there is a crisis brewing outside of the country with regard to human rights policy. It gets fairly little attention in the media because the headlines habitually focus on the prospects for more summit diplomacy between North Korean leader Kim Jong-un and his American and South Korean counterparts. The world seems to have forgotten about the efforts begun only six years ago to address the human rights challenges in North Korea.

This chapter will consist of four parts. I will describe the silent crisis that has arisen regarding human rights policy on North Korea. Second, I will argue that the lost ground on human rights stems from two zero-sum dynamics: the United States sees a zero-sum relationship between pressing for human rights and denuclearization negotiations, while South Korea sees a zero-sum relationship between pressing for human rights and inter-Korean engagement. Third, I will enumerate practical ways to integrate human rights issues with mainstream U.S. denuclearization policies, including the consideration of some first steps or potential low-hanging fruit in the health and humanitarian sectors to better integrate policy. Finally, the chapter will entertain some "out-of-the-box" ideas to improve the human condition in North Korea that challenges U.S. policy conventions.

The purpose of this chapter is not to define a human rights agenda to pursue with North Korea. Other authors in this volume address the topic. Instead, this chapter's purpose is more narrow. It is to identify a "policy logic" for mainstream decision-makers in the national security and denuclearization space that explains how and why human rights is not just important to address, but also integral to formulating a successful policy. In this regard, I argue against the dominant zero-sum policy pathology that human rights and denuclearization are two discrete and opposing issues—they are not, and they should lend themselves to natural policy integration. I also argue against the widely accepted belief that integrating the two issue-areas is value-neutral or value-negative for U.S.-DPRK denuclearization negotiations. On the contrary, this is a value-added proposition both for the United States and the DPRK. The challenge is to create the right policy framework

---

Kyung Lee, "North Korean Children: Nutrition and Growth," *Annals of Pediatric Endocrinology & Metabolism* 22, no.4 (December 2017): 231–39; Hazel Smith, "Nutrition and Health in North Korea: What's New, What's Changed and Why It Matters," *North Korean Review* 12, no. 1 (Spring 2016): 7–34.

such that there are incentives for both parties to be responsive to human rights issues.

Lost Ground

In 2014, the world witnessed a groundswell of activity and support after the release of the historic United Nations Commission of Inquiry (COI) report on North Korean human rights. The report was widely praised as the most comprehensive account of human rights abuses in North Korea. One of the primary recommendations of this 400-page authoritative document was to bring the North Korean leader, as well as officials in the State Security Department (SSD), Ministry of People's Security, the Korean People's Army, the Office of the Public Prosecutor, the judiciary and the Workers' Party of Korea before the International Criminal Court for crimes against humanity.[8]

Subsequent to the COI, the UN Security Council added North Korea's human rights abuses to its formal agenda in 2014, 2015, 2016, and 2017, and discussed it in a non-public session in 2020.[9] Following a recommendation in the report, the Office of the High Commissioner for Human Rights (OHCHR) opened a Seoul field office in June 2015 to better monitor and document the human rights situation in North Korea.[10] A panel of independent experts—including a lawyer in the Supreme Court of Bangladesh and a former member of the UN COI— was created by the UN Human Rights Council in March 2016 to recommend practical mechanisms for accountability.[11] One of their recommendations led to the creation of the DPRK Accountability Project

---

8   UN General Assembly, Report of the Commission of Inquiry on Human Rights in the Democratic People's Republic of Korea, A/HRC/25/63 (February 7, 2014), annex I, "Correspondence with the Supreme Leader of the Democratic People's Republic of Korea and First Secretary of the Workers' Party of Korea, Kim Jong-un," 23–25.

9   Human Rights Watch, "North Korea: Events of 2018," https://www.hrw.org/world-report/2019/country-chapters/north-korea.

10   UN News, "New UN Office Opens in Seoul to Monitor Human Rights Issues in DPR Korea," June 23, 2015, https://news.un.org/en/story/2015/06/502362-new-un-office-opens-seoul-monitor-human-rights-issues-dpr-korea.

11   UN Human Rights Office of the High Commissioner, "Group of Independent Experts on Accountability Pursuant to Human Rights Council Resolution 31/18 on the Situation of Human Rights in the Democratic People's Republic of Korea," https://www.ohchr.org/EN/HRBodies/SP/CountriesMandates/KP/Pages/GroupofIndependentExpertsonAccountability.aspx.

in March 2017, which strengthened the Seoul OHCHR office's capacity by adding international criminal justice experts to develop plans for eventual prosecution of North Korean officials.[12]

These developments led many experts and activists inside and outside of governments to believe that the abuse of human rights in North Korea—an issue that had floundered in the darkness for decades—was finally gaining the attention of the international community. The fervor behind a movement that once was seen as quixotic now looked very real, so much so that a senior U.S. official in 2016 stated publicly and boldly in a speech in Washington, D.C., that the world knows who the abusers are, what they are doing to the people, and promised that they would all be held accountable.[13] The world could point to concrete actions and a degree of international mobilization to help the people of North Korea.

In the past three years, however, this momentum to bring human dignity to the citizens of North Korea has ground to a halt. In 2018, the UN Security Council failed to renew a debate in its chambers on North Korean human rights abuses for the first time since the release of the COI report in 2014. An effort to put the issue back on the agenda failed in 2019 (although, as mentioned, a non-public discussion took place in December 2020). The Trump administration's focus on summit denuclearization diplomacy obscured any interest in taking up the human rights issue. Three meetings of the two leaders failed to produce a single statement or commitment to improving the lives of the North Korean people.

One of the developments that predated the COI was the creation of a refugee program for North Korean defectors to the United States in 2004, when President George W. Bush signed the North Korean Human Rights Act.[14] This made the United States the only country outside of South Korea to have legislated such a program. Though the numbers were small relative to South Korea, the program was symbolically important, effectively internationalizing the issue of North Koreans escaping political repression at home. However, as table 9.1 below shows,

---

12   Human Rights Watch, "UN: New Move on North Korea Crimes," March 24, 2017, https://www.hrw.org/news/2017/03/24/un-new-move-north-korea-crimes#.

13   Tom Malinowski, "Special Address at the Center for Strategic and International Studies," February 19, 2016, https://csis-website-prod.s3.amazonaws.com/s3fs-public/legacy_files/files/publication/20160226_TomMalinowski_Special_Address.pdf.

14   North Korean Human Rights Act of 2004, Pub. L. No. 108-333 (October 18, 2004).

the number of North Korean refugees coming to the United States under the 2004 North Korean Human Rights Act dwindled to zero by 2019. While there were several contributing factors to this decline, it only accentuated the "de-mobilization" of the human rights movement and reflected a general decline in escapees from North Korea to any country.[15]

Finally, South Korea has stopped co-sponsoring a UN General Assembly resolution on the human rights situation in North Korea, something it has done annually since 2008. The Moon Jae-in government also has slashed budgets supporting numerous human rights organizations operating in South Korea.[16] As noted above, the unification ministry explained the underlying rationale for these actions when it revoked licenses for the human rights NGOs Fighter for a Free North Korea and the Kunsaem Education Center. It argued that these activities complicated the government's official policy of inter-Korean economic cooperation and family reunions, effectively decreeing that there is only one way to pursue the human rights agenda.[17]

Zero-sum logic in the United States

The lost ground in the human rights movement stems from the predominant view in Washington and Seoul that there is a zero-sum relationship between advocating for human rights and pursuing denuclearization (for the United States) or inter-Korean engagement (for the ROK). Human rights activism is deemed a "policy expense" because it

---

15   See Roberta Cohen, "Admitting North Korean Refugees to the United States: Obstacles and Opportunities," Brookings Institution, September 20, 2011, https://www.brookings.edu/opinions/admitting-north-korean-refugees-to-the-united-states-obstacles-and-opportunities/; and Robert King, "Number of North Korea Defectors Drops to Lowest Level in Two Decades," CSIS, January 27, 2021, https://beyondparallel.csis.org/number-of-north-korean-defectors-drops-to-lowest-level-in-two-decades/.

16   Jeongmin Kim, "As North and South Korea Cosy up, Human Rights Groups Struggle for Cash," Reuters, June 27, 2018, https://www.reuters.com/article/us-northkorea-southkorea-rights/as-north-and-south-korea-cosy-up-human-rights-groups-struggle-for-cash-idUSKBN1JNoON; "South Korea Slashes North Korea Human Rights Budget, Raises Regime Aid," *Deutsche Welle*, September 3, 2018, https://www.dw.com/en/south-korea-slashes-north-korea-human-rights-budget-raises-regime-aid/a-45331031.

17   Ministry of Unification, "ROK Government's Stance on Leaflet Campaigns and North Korean Human Rights," July 2020, 3.

is unrealistic to expect Pyongyang to open their gulags (for example), and it is impractical because it offends North Korean interlocutors, which undermines pursuit of more practical goals.

Donald Trump's behavior wholly reflected this zero-sum mindset. The Trump administration started its term with an interest in highlighting North Korea's human rights abuses. As Robert King has written, almost ten percent of the president's first State of the Union speech in January 2018 was devoted to North Korea, with a significant portion focused on human rights.[18] The president said, "No regime has oppressed its own citizens more totally or brutally then the cruel dictatorship in North Korea."[19] Trump invited North Korean defector Ji Seong-ho to the speech and met with North Korean escapees in the White House. He notably relisted North Korea on the State Sponsor of Terrorism List and befriended the parents of Otto Warmbier, a University of Virginia student who was detained, was sentenced to prison, and eventually lapsed into a fatal coma while in North Korean custody. The United States also quietly provided small grants to sustain the activities of some of the NGOs that suffered funding cuts on the South Korean side.

However, as Trump prioritized a series of summit meetings with the North Korean leader, all designed to achieve a denuclearization agreement, the focus on human rights quickly dissipated. Instead, Trump started to refer to Kim as his good friend, "very sharp," and a "real leader"—hardly consonant with the language of the COI report.[20] Human rights was deemed distracting at best and disruptive at worst to the core goal of befriending Kim.

The absence of U.S. support has been evident in subtle but significant ways. In 2019, in an effort to put the human rights issue back on to its agenda, the UN Security Council could not achieve the nine-vote minimum to put the issue back on the agenda. The United States, which

---

18 Robert King, "North Korean Human Rights in the 2018 and 2019 State of the Union Addresses: What a Difference a Year Makes," CSIS, February 7, 2019, https://www.csis.org/analysis/north-korean-human-rights-2018-and-2019-state-union-addresses-what-difference-year-makes.

19 Cited in *North Korea Policy One Year after Hanoi: Hearing before the Subcommittee on East Asia, the Pacific, and International Cybersecurity Policy of the Comm. on Foreign Relations*, 116th Cong. (February 25, 2020) (Statement of Robert R. King, Senior Adviser, Center for Strategic and International Studies).

20 Tom Porter, "Why Shouldn't I Like Him? Trump Piled Praise on Kim Jong-un in His First Interview since Their Summit Collapse," *Business Insider*, March 1, 2019, https://www.businessinsider.com/trump-praises-kim-jong-un-vietnam-summit-2019-3.

TABLE 9.1 North Korean refugee resettlement in the United States

Year	Refugees resettled	Year	Refugees resettled
2006	9	2013	14
2007	28	2014	15
2008	38	2015	14
2009	18	2016	19
2010	17	2017	1
2011	16	2018	6
2012	23	2019	0

SOURCE: Interactive Reporting System, Refugee Processing Center, https://www.wrapsnet.org/.

was the potential ninth vote, pulled back its support at the eleventh hour, presumably in an effort not to complicate the president's self-professed affinity for the North Korea leader.[21]

In another important indicator, the number of North Korean refugees coming to the United States under the 2004 North Korean Human Rights Act dwindled to zero in 2019 (see table 9.1). Offering citizens a pathway out of a country that oppresses their civil and economic rights, the United States has always tied refugee resettlement—whether in Cuba, Vietnam, or the Soviet Union—with a proactive stance on human rights.

While the downturn in North Korean refugees stems from a number of factors beyond U.S. policy, including Sino–North Korean collusion to tighten border control, the numbers reflected a downward trend with six refugees in 2018 and only one in 2017.[22] By contrast, the highest number admitted in a year was in 2008, when 38 were resettled. A total of 220 North Korean refugees have come to the United States since the program first began in 2006, when nine resettled here.[23] As the only country outside of South Korea that passed legislation mandating a refugee resettlement program, the United States had led by example. The absence of U.S. leadership during the Trump administration—manifest in the four-year vacancy of the Congressionally mandated point position for North Korean human rights abuses—resulted

---

21   Edward Wong and Choe Sang-hun, "Trump Officials Block U.N. Meeting on Human Rights Abuses in North Korea," *New York Times*, December 9, 2019, https://www.nytimes.com/2019/12/09/world/asia/north-korea-trump.html.

22   "No N. Korean Defectors Admitted to U.S. Last Year: State Department Data," *Yonhap News*, January 7, 2020, https://en.yna.co.kr/view/AEN20200107007600325.

23   Interactive Reporting System, Refugee Processing Center, https://www.wrapsnet.org/.

in a silent but significant crisis. U.S. officials by their action clearly implied that there was a trade-off between human rights and security, and the threat posed by North Korea's nuclear weapons was the priority.

Rollback in South Korea

The Moon Jae-in administration has been conspicuously silent on the human rights situation in North Korea. Despite President Moon's numerous summit meetings with Kim Jong-un during 2018–19, the topic of human rights did not come up once. In that sense, Moon has behaved not unlike previous progressive governments because the human rights issue is normally owned by conservative, anti-Sunshine Policy advocates. However, Moon has differentiated himself from his predecessors in one important respect. The ROK government has actually broken new ground by moving beyond ambivalence to a proactive posture of rolling back human rights activities in South Korea.

Progressive governments in South Korea traditionally have not embraced the "name and shame" activist approach to human rights with North Korea, which includes awareness raising, publicity campaigns, sanctions, and documentation of crimes for eventual prosecution. It is not that these governments do not care about the abuses; instead, they prioritize inter-Korean cooperation over human rights activism. "Naming and shaming," in this view, only disincentivizes Pyongyang from responding positively to Seoul's Sunshine Policy engagement efforts. While this zero-sum view of human rights activism was informally internalized by the political left in Korea, it was codified under the Moon government. Nowhere was this more apparent than in the July 2020 Unification Ministry document suspending balloon launches and revoking the licenses of the associated organizations. While the ministry said that these launches were ineffective (in terms of the content of the balloons reaching North Korean people), the primary reason for punitive actions was that these activities drew the ire of Pyongyang, which then obstructed the government's self-declared "human rights" policy of inter-Korean engagement.[24] Thus, the July 2020 document is important because it effectively classifies all traditional "name and shame" human rights activities—which may obstruct inter-Korean engagement at the government level—as being invalid. Moreover, it rationalizes as

---

24 Ministry of Unification, "ROK Government's Stance on Leaflet Campaigns and North Korean Human Rights," July 2020.

justified any actions taken against human rights organizations or individuals if they potentially undermine official efforts at inter-Korean cooperation. In short, the only human rights agenda that is acceptable is the South Korean government's engagement policy. This is unprecedented and it is in this context that the world has witnessed a rollback of human rights activities in South Korea.

In November 2019, for example, the ROK government set a new precedent by forcibly repatriating two North Korean fishermen who had been captured in South Korean waters. The fishermen, who allegedly killed sixteen crew members to escape, had already professed their desire to defect; human rights activists feared their forced return would likely mean their death in North Korea. The South Korean repatriation was done secretly (until a press leak), and in violation of South Korea's own constitution, which grants citizenship to defectors.[25] The two escapees were not given access to attorneys or due process. During the same month, the ROK also did not co-sponsor a UN General Assembly resolution on the human rights situation in North Korea, something they have done annually since 2008. The Moon administration's actions were roundly criticized by human rights groups in a December 2019 joint letter, and also by the UN special rapporteur on human rights violations of North Korea, Tomás Quintana.[26]

Following from this zero-sum view of human rights activism and North Korean engagement, the Moon administration has not just stopped being an advocate for human rights, but has sought rollback measures. It has slashed government budgets for supporting human rights work, including ending nearly twenty years of funding for the Association of North Korean Defectors in December 2017, and a 92 percent budget cut for the North Korean Human Rights Foundation in 2018.[27] The

---

25   Sang Hun Choe, "2 North Koreans Tried to Defect. Did Seoul Send Them to Their Deaths?" *New York Times*, December 18, 2019, https://www.nytimes.com/2019/12/18/world/asia/north-korea-fishermen-defectors.html.

26   For the joint letter written and signed by 67 organizations, see "Letter to President Moon Jae-in RE: ROK's Stance on Human Rights in North Korea," Human Rights Watch, December 16, 2019, https://www.hrw.org/news/2019/12/16/letter-president-moon-jae-re-roks-stance-human-rights-north-korea; For Special Rapporteur Quintana's remarks, see Christy Lee, "UN Human Rights Expert: Seoul Sent Wrong Message to Pyongyang," VOA, December 19, 2019, https://www.voanews.com/east-asia-pacific/un-human-rights-expert-seoul-sent-wrong-message-pyongyang.

27   Jeongmin Kim, "As North and South Korea Cosy Up, Human Rights Groups Struggle for Cash," Reuters, June 27, 2018, https://www.reuters.com/article/us

government has yet to create one of the four bodies—the North Korean Human Rights Foundation—mandated by the North Korean Human Rights Act (NKHRA) that passed in September 2016. Seoul's support for the three other bodies created by this act has also been spotty.[28] The post for the ROK ambassador-at-large on North Korean human rights has remained vacant since September 2017, when the mandate for the previous ambassador, Lee Jung-hoon, expired.

The ROK government has made it more difficult for North Korean defectors and human rights activists in South Korea to carry out their work. Opportunities to shape the public policy discussion, such as media appearances and public lectures for defectors, have dried up—the result of an implicit government ban on critical voices.[29] Human rights groups have repeatedly decried the government's increasing interference with activists' press interviews, public speaking engagements, and advocacy work. Notable incidents include an April 2018 human rights conference involving North Korean defector Thae Yong-ho and interference from National Intelligence Service agents and an April 2018 episode involving South Korean policemen preventing North Korean defector and activist Lee Min-bok from launching balloons into North Korea—which he had done since 2003 without government interference. One U.S.-based expert characterized the government's actions as a "purging" of activist organizations that is "unprecedented" and far beyond anything that previous progressive governments have undertaken.[30] In an indication of the severity of the situation, human rights groups have sent open letters to both President Moon (April 2018) and to UN Special Rapporteur Quintana (February 2019) asking for help.[31]

-northkorea-southkorea-rights/as-north-and-south-korea-cosy-up-human-rights-groups-struggle-for-cash-idUSKBN1JN0ON; Julian Ryall, "South Korea Slashes North Korea Human Rights Budget, Raises Regime Aid," *Deutsche Welle*, September 3, 2018, https://www.dw.com/en/south-korea-slashes-north-korea-human-rights-budget-raises-regime-aid/a-45331031.

28   For an in-depth look at the implementation of NKHRA, see Teodora Gyupchanova, "Three Years since Its Passage, South Korea's North Korea Human Rights Law Stalls," *NK News*, August 7, 2019, https://www.nknews.org/2019/08/three-years-since-its-passage-south-koreas-north-korea-human-rights-law-stalls/.

29   Edward White and Kang Buseong, "N. Korean Defectors Worry about Seoul's Wooing of Kim Jong Un," *Financial Times*, September 19, 2019, https://www.ft.com/content/3acf1336-d9bf-11e9-8f9b-77216ebe1f17.

30   Email correspondence with U.S.-based human rights expert, August 4, 2020.

31   For the HRF letter to President Moon Jae-in, see "South Korea Silences North Korean Defectors to Appease Kim Jong-un," Human Rights Foundation, April 23,

Regaining Lost Ground

Policymakers view human rights as contrary to diplomacy for peace-building for South Korea, and contrary to denuclearization for the United States. This mindset has contributed to the demobilization on the human rights front over the past several years. The irony of the current predicament, however, is that human rights are an integral and unavoidable component of a comprehensive North Korea strategy. A deal with North Korea—whether on nuclear weapons or on a peace regime—is not possible without an improvement in the human condition. In the past, the United States privileged nuclear negotiations and South Korean administrations gave priority to North-South relations. It became a policy truism to accept that delicate negotiations would be made too indelicate by raising human rights with Pyongyang. Many negotiators (including the author when he was involved in the Six-Party Talks) feared that human rights would distract from the main issue of denuclearization, or even offend the regime and scuttle the talks.

The United States has followed this playbook for the past thirty years, and most recently in the past three summits with Kim Jong-un—but there is no evidence that avoiding human rights has helped the negotiations in any way. Despite these summits, the United States is no closer to a denuclearization agreement. Indeed, we are in the worst of all worlds: no denuclearization, no human rights improvement, and yet a mistaken belief that stifling one helps to achieve the other.

The United States has invariably lost ground in the past three years, but that ground is recoverable. The Biden administration provides an opportunity for America to refocus its attention on human rights in North Korea. A denuclearization deal with North Korea is still some distance away. The Trump administration's unique summit diplomacy had many flaws, but one thing it did do was to set a new precedent in U.S.-DPRK negotiations, having produced multiple historic face-to-face meetings with the North Korean leader. This unprecedented access

2018, https://hrf.org/press_posts/south-korea-silences-north-korean-defectors-to-appease-kim-jong-un/; for joint letter to Special Rapporteur Quintana, see "Joint Letter to UN Special Rapporteur: Defend the Free Speech of North Korean Defectors and Human Rights Activists in South Korea," North Korea Freedom Coalition, February 27, 2019, http://www.nkfreedom.org/2019/02/27/joint-letter-to-un-special-rapporteur-defend-the-free-speech-of-north-korean-defectors-and-human-rights-activists-in-south-korea/.

provides future U.S. administrations with the opportunity to bring this issue to the person single-handedly responsible for and capable of changing this situation. Maintaining this channel is one way to ensure that human rights are on the agenda moving forward, but it cannot be solely relied upon. What is required is a whole-of-government approach that internalizes the understanding that human rights and denuclearization work together and not in opposition to one another.

Principles for policy integration

Two steps are critical to cultivating a positive-sum view of the relationship between human rights policy and denuclearization diplomacy. First is the internalization of a set of policy principles that rejects the past zero-sum policy pathologies as unworkable, evidenced by the stunning absence of results despite decades of negotiations that muffled any discussion of human rights. The second step is to create a set of touchstones with which any future negotiations must engage if they are to successfully integrate human rights and denuclearization diplomacy into a single, comprehensive strategy.

The first principle we must accept is that integrating human rights into our strategy is not a choice, but a necessity. As the self-professed beacon of human freedom in the world, the United States has a moral obligation to place human rights at the top of its agenda with all partners. The failure to consistently uphold this principle has already encouraged regimes to take liberties with gross infringements on human dignity (e.g., Uighur prison camps, Hong Kong security law).

The second principle is that the denuclearization and human rights agendas are inextricably intertwined. This point cannot be overemphasized. It is key to the understanding of policy integration between human rights and denuclearization, but it is often missed. Whether through its forced labor exports, mining operations, or commerce related to sanctioned entities, North Korean revenues gained from human rights abuses help to finance the regime's proliferation activities.[32] Further-

---

32 Matthew Zweig, "North Korea's Use of Slave Labor Will Limit Any Prospective Sanctions Relief," Foundation for Defense of Democracies, February 27, 2019, https://www.fdd.org/analysis/2019/02/27/north-koreas-use-of-slave-labor-will-limit-any-prospective-sanctions-relief/; John Park and Jim Walsh, *Stopping North Korea, Inc.: Sanctions Effectiveness and Unintended Consequences* (Cambridge, MA: MIT Security Studies Program), August 2016, https://www.belfercenter.org/sites/default/files/legacy/files/Stopping%20North%20Korea%20Inc%20Park%20

more, respect for international norms, such as the non-proliferation efforts of the International Atomic Energy Agency (IAEA), of which the DPRK was a member and which includes 171 countries, and the International Declaration of Human Rights, of which the DPRK is still a member, legitimize and internationalize the commitments the DPRK needs to make. Failure to keep human rights commitments undermines denuclearization commitments.

The third principle for integrating human rights and denuclearization is that calling for human rights improvements in North Korea strengthens U.S. leverage in negotiations. North Korea's reaction to the groundswell of international sentiment in 2014 makes this eminently clear. In the aftermath of the COI report, the normally reclusive Pyongyang started to dispatch its diplomats all over Eurasia and Scandinavia to lobby their representatives against raising North Korean human rights in the UN Security Council and in General Assembly resolutions. The regime senses vulnerability on this issue like no other. The COI and its calling out of the regime's maltreatment of its citizens shattered the myth of North Korea's paradise and spotlighted the illegitimacy of the regime in the eyes of its own people.

The fourth principle is that mainstreaming human rights in the U.S.–North Korea agenda is politically smart. Bipartisanship in Congress on North Korean human rights remains strong, and this helps to make Pyongyang understand that a U.S. administration cannot simply ignore the issue as in the past. Congressional influence on the process is evident both in legislation and in sanctions. Congress unanimously passed and reauthorized the North Korea Human Rights Act (NKHRA) in 2018, reaffirming its commitment that human rights remain a key part of U.S. policy toward North Korea.[33] In late 2019, the Otto Warmbier North Korea Nuclear Sanctions and Enforcement Act was passed as a provision to the FY2020 National Defense Authorization Act (NDAA).[34] The legislation strengthens and expands U.S. sanctions against North Korea and its enablers, including Chinese banks.

and%20Walsh%20.pdf; Stephan Haggard and Marcus Noland, "Sanctioning North Korea: The Political Economy of Denuclearization and Proliferation," *Asian Survey* 50, no. 3 (May/June 2010): 539–68.

33   Robert King, "Congress Affirms Concern for North Korea Human Rights: Extends Human Rights Act," CSIS, July 12, 2018, https://www.csis.org/analysis/congress-affirms-concern-north-korea-human-rights-extends-human-rights-act.

34   "Van Hollen, Toomey, Brown, Portman Applaud North Korea Sanctions in Final NDAA Package," Chris Van Hollen website, December 18, 2019, https://www

This builds upon the foundation of sanctions and enforcement mechanisms mandated by significant laws such as the North Korea Sanctions and Policy Enhancement Act of 2016 (NKSPEA) and the 2017 Countering America's Adversaries Through Sanctions Act (CAATSA) championed by Congress.[35] Going forward, there is little likelihood that Congress will support any U.S.-DPRK agreements coming out of presidential summitry that do not address human rights. Moreover, sanctions lifting will not be possible under U.S. law without certifications on human rights improvements (this point is expanded on below).

Negotiating denuclearization with human rights

The fifth principle for countering the zero-sum logic on human rights is to recognize that the objective of denuclearization can be facilitated, rather than hampered, by a human rights agenda. As counterintuitive as this may sound, the two issues are tied more closely together today than ever before because of the evolution of the sanctions regime over the past two decades. For example, to the extent that any future U.S. administration will want to pick up the pieces from the Trump-Kim summit diplomacy, it will find that human rights helps to support U.S. objectives as specified in the June 2018 Singapore Summit:

1. The United States and the DPRK commit to establish new U.S.–DPRK relations in accordance with the desire of the peoples of the two countries for peace and prosperity.
2. The United States and the DPRK will join their efforts to build a lasting and stable peace regime on the Korean Peninsula.[36]

It is inconceivable that either of the stated objectives in clause 1 or clause 2—"new U.S.-DPRK relations" or "stable peace regime on

---

.vanhollen.senate.gov/news/press-releases/van-hollen-toomey-brown-portman
-applaud-north-korea-sanctions-in-final-ndaa-package.

35   For more on NKSPE, see North Korea Sanctions and Policy Enhancement Act of 2016, H.R. 757, 114th Cong., https://www.congress.gov/bill/114th-congress/ house-bill/757/text. For more on CAATSA, see U.S. Department of the Treasury, "Countering America's Adversaries through Sanctions Act," https://www.treasury .gov/resource-center/sanctions/Programs/Pages/caatsa.aspx.

36   See "Trump and Kim Joint Statement from the Singapore Summit," *Washington Post*, June 12, 2018, https://www.washingtonpost.com/news/politics/wp/ 2018/06/12/trump-and-kim-joint-statement-from-the-singapore-summit/.

the Korean Peninsula"—could be achieved without a fundamental transformation of political relations between the United States and the DPRK, and that transformation is impossible without an improvement in the human condition. Congress would not support such an outcome given its record of advocacy on human rights.

Moreover, for any future U.S. administration, a political transformation of relations and concomitant human rights improvements constitute the true challenge of returning to nuclear diplomacy with North Korea, not another "freeze" of the weapons program. That is, in the past three nuclear agreements, the United States has reached "step-by-step," "action-for-action" incremental and interim agreements suspending further nuclear bomb production and testing for sanctions-lifting and energy assistance. In the 1994 Agreed Framework, this was an IAEA-monitored freeze of Yongbyon in return for interim shipments of heavy fuel oil.[37] In the 2005 Six-Party Joint Statement, this was a freeze and partial dismantling of facilities at Yongbyon in return for energy assistance.[38] The United States has had a lot of experience with this type of negotiation, and thus, it would not be hard to achieve the same for a future U.S. administration.

The real challenge is how to move forward beyond this well-trodden plateau. Past diplomatic efforts in 1994 and 2005 failed because the next step was the verification phase—i.e., after the freeze on operations, the next step was a North Korean declaration of the nuclear inventory that would then be verified by inspectors. In the Six-Party agreement in late 2008, for example, the negotiations broke down because Pyongyang refused to provide a declaration that was credible and refused to allow any sort of verification of their nuclear holdings. One of the primary obstacles to the verification phase is the lack of trust between the two interlocutors. The DPRK does not trust the United States enough to reveal its inventory, and the United States doubts the veracity of any inventory declaration produced by the North. This level of distrust can only be overcome by a fundamental transformation of the political relationship between the two sides. Such a political transformation of relations is not possible without an improvement in the human rights condition.

---

37 Joel Wit, Daniel Poneman, and Robert Gallucci, *Going Critical: The First North Korean Nuclear Crisis* (Washington, DC: Brookings Institution, 2005).

38 Victor Cha, *The Impossible State: North Korea Past and Future* (New York: Ecco, 2013).

This is because a human rights commitment by North Korea as part of a nuclear deal would send a costly but credible signal. It would mark an unprecedented and novel step by Pyongyang that could signal the leadership's nod to real reform and to joining the community of nations. Without a human rights commitment, yet another freeze-for-freeze deal would not garner much credibility in Washington policy circles.

Finally, to demand human rights improvements is the only realistic way to facilitate the world's economic development and assistance to North Korea. President Trump touted the potential for North Korea to become an "economic rocket" if it commits to denuclearization, speculating on the possibility of condominiums, casinos, and beachfront properties on Wonsan, making North Korea potentially "an incredible place."[39] As flamboyant as the language was, Trump's words echo what has been the longstanding core quid pro quo for denuclearization—entrance into the community of nations and access to economic assistance. However, the reality is that the robust sanctions regime that has been established by Congress and the UN for both nuclear proliferation and human rights abuses over the past five years hamstrings any private sector engagement with the North. In the past, if nonproliferation concerns were addressed, then sanctions relaxation could potentially open the spigot of international assistance. Today, addressing nonproliferation concerns is a necessary but not sufficient condition for sanctions relaxation, because a bevy of sanctions remain in place for human rights violations.[40] This was the ultimate folly of the Trump approach. He promised Kim the prospect of Trump casinos on the beaches of Wonsan if he denuclearized, but the reality of the sanctions picture was that unless Trump also elicited human rights concessions from Kim, he could never deliver those casinos. U.S. companies, aid organizations, and international financial institutions like the World Bank and IMF would not, under U.S. law, be able to aid, invest, or trade with the North given human rights abuses in the supply chain.

---

39   Donald Trump's Twitter account (@realDonaldTrump), as cited in Daniel Politi, "Trump Foresees North Korea Becoming an 'Economic Rocket' Thanks to Brutal Dictator," Slate, February 9, 2019, https://slate.com/news-and-politics/2019/02/trump-north-korea-economic-rocket-kim-jong-un.html; and "Press Conference by President Trump," Capella Hotel, Singapore, June 12, 2018, https://trumpwhitehouse.archives.gov/briefings-statements/press-conference-president-trump/.

40   Eleanor Albert, "What to Know about Sanctions on North Korea," Council on Foreign Relations, July 16, 2019, https://www.cfr.org/backgrounder/what-know-about-sanctions-north-korea.

In sum, rather than a zero-sum game, human rights and denuclearization operate in a positive-sum game where each side is incentivized
to contend with human rights improvements. If Pyongyang wants sanctions relief, denuclearization is not a sufficient condition unless it is
accompanied by human rights improvements. And if the United States
wants the carrot of economic assistance to credibly alter North Korean
decision-making, then it must insist on human rights improvements
to unlock legal private sector interest in North Korean beaches and
mineral resources.

Thus, it is incumbent on any future U.S. administration to give
serious thought to policy integration; moreover, this is a responsibility unique to the United States. This is not to say that Seoul cannot
incorporate human rights issues into its own bilateral dialogue with
Pyongyang, but it cannot lead on nuclear policy integration because
that portfolio is held by Washington. The United States is reluctant to
subcontract this negotiation to Seoul, and North Korea remains resis-
tant to discussing nuclear weapons issues with South Korea.

Low-hanging fruit: Health and humanitarian assistance

How could North Korea engage on human rights? The chapters in this
volume lay out any number of ways. One possible opportunity presents
itself with the COVID-19 virus. As late as July 2021 there have been
no reported cases of COVID-19 in North Korea, but health experts
believe it is very likely that cases exist there.[41] There is a unique transmission vector given that China is the only country that has somewhat
regular travel with the isolated North. The absence of reported cases
in the DPRK could stem from the government's traditional opacity,
but it could also reflect the inability of health authorities to diagnose
cases. The DPRK lacks any testing equipment for COVID-19, and it
does not have trained personnel or adequate labs. The vulnerability of
the regime to the pandemic is evident in the draconian actions taken
by the government to protect itself. Not only has Pyongyang closed its

---

41   Sue Mi Terry, "Can North Korea Cope with the Coronavirus?" *Foreign Affairs*,
March 3, 2020, https://www.foreignaffairs.com/articles/north-korea/2020-03-03/
can-north-korea-cope-coronavirus; and Victor Cha, "Splendid Isolation: North
Korea and COVID-19," CSIS, April 30, 2020, https://www.csis.org/analysis/
splendid-isolation-north-korea-and-covid-19.

borders, but the government has instituted quarantine protocols more than twice the length of those usually recommended for the virus. The regime also recently banned citizens from public gatherings, including at restaurants. All of these actions are similar to ones taken in response to the Ebola virus, MERS, and SARs in previous years.[42] Because these quarantine measures are directed at traffic from China, the closed border has dramatically reduced commerce and resulted in as high as a 6 percent contraction in the North Korean economy in 2020, which is as bad as was experienced during the famine in the mid-1990s.[43] These extreme measures reflect the government's insecurity about the weakness of its state-based health infrastructure.

There is an opportunity to address human rights issues through health and humanitarian assistance. North Korea has maintained contact with UN agencies and NGOs and has requested more information about the virus, diagnostic kits, and health experts. While there would be similar concerns about North Korea's living up to international standards for verification and monitoring as NGOs have faced in the past, COVID-19 could provide a proximate issue, thus providing a means of engaging North Korea on human rights issues as a part of U.S. policy. The United States would do well to remove limits on NGO humanitarian assistance.

Whatever means are used to engage with North Korea on the human rights front, diplomacy must preserve four core standards with any assistance: (1) transparency in food aid; (2) fiscal transparency; (3) access to North Korean prison camps; and (4) improved access to information in the country.

Touchstones for policy

The Biden administration must consider concrete, actionable items to mainstream the human rights issue in bilateral relations with Pyongyang. North Korea policy should engage with the following touchstones on human rights:

42   Cha, "Splendid Isolation: North Korea and COVID-19."
43   Sam Kim, "Worst North Korea Economy in Two Decades Causing Kim to Lash Out," Bloomberg, June 22, 2020, https://www.bloomberg.com/news/articles/2020-06-22/worst-north-korea-economy-in-two-decades-pushing-kim-to-lash-out.

Demand rights first. The United States must establish a rights-first approach in future dealings with North Korea, acknowledging that achievement of the normalization, denuclearization, and peace regime objectives of the 2018 Singapore declaration requires an improvement in human rights.

Make a tangible first step. The United States must seek an initial tangible step from its next round of diplomacy (e.g., cooperation on issues of persons with disabilities or health-related issues, which are likely less threatening to the regime) in order to set a new precedent in negotiations and to establish non-nuclear issues for cooperation with the DPRK.

Establish a longer-term dialogue. The United States must establish a human rights dialogue as part of any path to normalization of political relations. This dialogue should seek achievement of specific goals as stated in the UN Commission of Inquiry Report. This dialogue could also be used to help North Korea remedy violations in the supply chain that would prevent private investment.

Appoint a U.S. human rights envoy. The White House must appoint a special envoy for human rights as mandated by Congress, but which remained unfilled through the Trump administration.

Resume humanitarian assistance. The United States should remove obstacles it has created to limit private NGO humanitarian assistance, should support UN humanitarian efforts, and should consider providing U.S. government aid when appropriate. Such assistance must meet international standards for verification and monitoring.

Set the bar for allies and partners. The United States must signal to China and the ROK that its engagement with North Korea and achievement of the U.S.-DPRK summit objectives of denuclearization and peace on the peninsula are not possible without tangible human rights improvements. China must stop refoulement—the practice of sending escapees back to North Korea. South Korea must stop suppressing NGO human rights activities.

Set a broader playing field. The human rights initiative is most effective as a global effort. The United States must re-energize the issue in the United Nations by seeking positive votes in the UN Security Council to debate North Korean human rights issues. Having rejoined the UN Human Rights Council in early 2021, the United States should find positive ways to engage with North Korea on human rights in the context of the council's Universal Periodic Review process. The ultimate purpose of these and other actions might be to create a Helsinki-like process addressing North Korea in East Asia.

Conclusion: The Role of Economic Rights

The points above would constitute a sturdy foundation for human rights to be included in a North Korea policy review by any U.S. administration. I admit that this would not be an easy task. North Korean provocations in the aftermath of U.S. elections often compel an incoming administration to focus on the immediate problem rather than experiment with new policy constructs. These are the constraints of policy.

However, if one were to throw aside all conventional policy realities and seek an "out-of-the-box" way to improve the human condition in North Korea, then the most practical and immediate measure would be to promote private economic rights in the country. While there is much that remains the same about the repressive North Korean state through three generations of leadership, the most significant socioeconomic agent for change has been the growth of markets. Largely a result of the Great Famine of the 1990s, markets have sprung up throughout the country, both official (well over 400) and unofficial ones, to help people to survive.[44] Micro-surveys of North Korean citizens in 2017–18 found that 100 percent of respondents believe that the government public distribution system does not provide enough for a good life and that 83 percent of respondents found outside goods gained from the market to have a larger impact on their daily lives than the distribution system.[45] In this sense, markets have created a separation of society from the state and an independence of thought as people cultivate their own livelihoods through markets rather than rely on the state.

44 Natsio, *Great Famine;* and Kay Seok, "North Korea's Transformation: Famine, Aid and Markets," Human Rights Watch, April 15, 2008, https://www.hrw.org/news/2008/04/15/north-koreas-transformation-famine-aid-and-markets.

45 Surveys were performed by the Beyond Parallel project at CSIS. Victor Cha and Lisa Collins, "The Markets: Private Economy and Capitalism in North Korea?" CSIS, August 26, 2018, https://beyondparallel.csis.org/markets-private-economy-capitalism-north-korea/.

And as ordinary citizens thrive in market life they have become more critical of the state. In the fall of 2017, just as the state was celebrating the "completion" of its nuclear deterrent, for example, 70 percent of survey respondents said that the nuclear program was not a source of national pride.[46] And the vast majority of respondents admitted that they knew of someone in private who would make jokes about or be critical of the government.[47] The North Korean government, moreover, is beholden to the growth of markets, both official and black, because of the inordinate hard currency tax revenues it collects, amounting to well over USD 50 million per year.[48]

Promoting the economic and consumer rights of North Korean citizens would improve their quality of life and help to foster a nascent civil society. I refer to this as an "out-of-the-box" recommendation because to implement it would require a paradigm shift in policy thinking in Washington, including the lifting of sanctions, education on market principles, access to international financial institutions, and direct foreign investment—exactly those things that the West withholds from the regime as rewards for denuclearization. Perhaps there will be a U.S. administration courageous (or desperate) enough to consider this.

In the course of denuclearization diplomacy with North Korea over the past three decades, every U.S. administration has said it would not succumb to buying the same horse again. President Trump broke past policy conventions by engaging in "top-down" summit diplomacy with a country where only one person makes decisions of consequence. But this approach yielded even less than past negotiations of which Trump was been so critical. A future U.S. administration could truly live up to advertising a "very different" policy to North Korea by integrating human rights into the diplomacy in ways that support the goal of final and fully verifiable denuclearization.

---

46   Victor Cha and Marie DuMond, "The Devil's Weapons: What Ordinary North Koreans Think of Their Nuclear Program," *Beyond Parallel*, March 2, 2018, https://beyondparallel.csis.org/devils-weapons-ordinary-north-koreans-think-nuclear-program/.

47   Victor Cha and Marie DuMond, "No Laughing Matter: North Koreans' Discontent and Daring Jokes," *Beyond Parallel*, November 2, 2016, https://beyondparallel.csis.org/no-laughing-matter-north-koreans-discontent-and-daring-jokes/. Methodology regarding the microsurveys is found in the article. While many of the findings comport with defector testimony, the *Beyond Parallel* microsurveys were done with North Korean citizens who have not defected.

48   Cha and Collins, "The Markets: Private Economy and Capitalism in North Korea?"

IV. Human Rights in Comparative Perspective

10 Germany's Lessons for Korea

Sean King

Germany,[1] like Korea, was divided in two after World War II. But while Germany was peacefully reunified in 1990 with the end of the Cold War, Korea remains split. The two Koreas even fought a bitter, vicious war from 1950 to 1953, which the two Germanies never did.

South Koreans, including many of the country's recent presidents, have since looked to Germany as a model for Korean reunification. But the German and Korean situations are very different. Not only was East Germany internationalist in nature while go-it-alone North Korea is ultranationalist, but West Germany also approached East Germany very differently from how South Korea approaches North Korea—perhaps most notably as it regards human rights.

Not enough Korea watchers fully understand what really happened in Germany and are thus prone to drawing false conclusions from its example. It is therefore worth comparing the two situations, with an emphasis on what actually happened in Germany,[2] so that we can learn from the former West Germany's aggressive humanitarian engagement

---

1 In addition to its occupation and subsequent division, Germany lost other territory after World War II, including some 40,000 square miles that was redrawn into Poland. Hence today's reunified Germany is smaller than wartime Germany. See Jabeen Bhatti, "Ousted by Poland in 1945, Germans Want Homes Back," *Wall Street Journal*, August 11, 2004, https://www.wsj.com/articles/SB109218743179488325.
2 I have never been to North Korea, but since 1997 have been to South Korea more times than I can remember. I was a 1986–87 high school exchange student in Ystad, Sweden, during which time I made the first two of four eventual visits to what was then East Germany. In fall 1991, one year after German reunification,

of the East (and, from the latter's eventual collapse). But given North Korea's uniquely closed and nationalist character, there is in truth only so much the South can do.

South Korean Fascination

German reunification is a source of fascination for South Koreans. It has been said South Koreans are more interested in German unification than Germans are.[3] South Korea's Unification Ministry spent six years studying the German example.[4] Annual mentions of German reunification in South Korean national newspapers[5] rarely drop below 500 and topped 1,100 as recently as 2018.[6] South Korean ambassador to Germany, Jong Bum Goo, said in 2018, "Germany and the city of Berlin are for most Koreans symbols of reunification."[7] A three-panel section of the Berlin Wall in Seoul's aptly named Berlin Plaza is labeled a "symbol of hope" for Korea.[8]

However, much of the resultant South Korean discussion has been about German reunification's logistics (e.g., transfer of legal systems and technical standards, infrastructure requirements, etc.) and its aftermath[9] (e.g., cost, rise of the political far-right in the former East Germany, etc.), as opposed to about how and why the two Germanies came to reunify in the first place.

And among those South Koreans who *have* taken time to think about what actually brought about German reunification, I can see,

---

I did an undergraduate semester abroad in Berlin. I speak some German but no Korean.

3 Victoria Kim, "The Fall of the Berlin Wall Once Gave South Korea Hope. Not Anymore," *Los Angeles Times,* December 4, 2019, https://www.latimes.com/world-nation/story/2019-12-04/berlin-wall-germany-south-korea-reunification.

4 Kim, "Fall of the Berlin Wall."

5 This figure does not include mentions in *Chosun Ilbo*. See Min Joo Kim and Rick Noack, "30 Years On, South Korea Remains Obsessed with the Fall of the Berlin Wall. Perhaps Too Much," *Washington Post*, November 9, 2019, https://www.washingtonpost.com/world/2019/11/09/years-south-korea-remains-obsessed-with-fall-berlin-wall-perhaps-too-much/.

6 Kim and Noack, "30 Years On, South Korea Remains Obsessed."

7 Madeline Chambers, "Reunified Germany Is in No Rush to Help Reconcile Korea," Reuters, February 5, 2019, https://www.reuters.com/article/us-germany-korea/reunified-germany-is-in-no-rush-to-help-reconcile-korea-idUSKCN1PU1C7.

8 Kim, "Fall of the Berlin Wall."

9 Kim, "Fall of the Berlin Wall."

from my own anecdotal conversations and observations over the years, too many have concluded that Germany reunified chiefly because West Germany reached out to the East—somehow implying that East Germany made a conscious decision to reunify with the West. This view not only misreads historical events but also misinterprets the foundational differences between multilateralist (and thus permeable) East Germany and "independent," largely sealed, xenophobic North Korea, as well as the very different approaches to their communist opposites taken by the former West Germany and today's South Korea.

Germany principally reunified not because West Germany extended the East a hand but because East Germany fell after the Soviet Union chose to no longer back it. Bonn's eastern outreach did contribute to East Germany's collapse by helping expose East Germans to the world outside (but may have also helped sustain the regime through payments and loans) and helped smooth the eventual but sudden reunification process. However, reunification itself was possible only because the East disappeared. This is a hard truth that many South Koreans, especially those on the nationalist left, seem to want to avoid acknowledging.

South Korean leaders often reference Germany's experience when discussing their own country's division. President Kim Dae-jung delivered a speech in March 2000 at Berlin's Free University (in the former West) entitled "Lessons of German Unification and the Korean Peninsula."[10] Kim made clear South Koreans' seeming preoccupation with late twentieth century German history when he said, "Today, I came here to learn about your experiences, which are extremely important for a president of Korea, which is still divided." Kim saw German reunification as an example, stating, "It is regrettable that the historic worldwide change has failed to produce an impact on the [Korean] peninsula." The first lesson he claimed to see was that "unification was possible because of West Germany's enormous potential, which was derived from democracy and a market economy." A second supposed lesson Kim identified was that Germany pursued its *Ostpolitik* toward East Germany as well as toward the countries of Central Europe, seeing his Sunshine Policy in the same vein. But as we will later see, West Germany's *Ostpolitik* was part of a much wider Soviet and Eastern European play. Hence it is not directly comparable to Kim's Korean-only Sunshine Policy.

---

10   Kim Dae-jung, "Address by President Kim Dae-jung of the Republic of Korea, Lessons of German Reunification and the Korean Peninsula," *Le Monde diplomatique*, March 9, 2000, https://www.monde-diplomatique.fr/dossiers/coree/A/1904.

President Park Geun-hye emphasized German reunification as an example for Korea during her 2014 "Dresden Declaration" speech at that city's University of Technology, in what had been East Germany.[11] She called for North-South people-to-people exchanges and family re-unions, co-prosperity through infrastructure development, and eventu-ally "integration between the peoples of North and South Korea." But how can North and South Koreans "integrate" unless either Pyongyang or Seoul gives way to the other? There has to be a winner. And, there has to be a loser. Hopefully, Seoul is the winner. North Korea's invec-tive in response to Park's Dresden speech,[12] comparing her to a bab-bling peasant, saying she "put thick makeup on her old, wrinkled face and rambled on," suggests Pyongyang grasped the logical conclusion of Park's reunification dream even if she herself did not enunciate it. That is, Park's reunification vision necessitates the North's eventual demise.

Earlier that year, Park rightly spoke of an "economic bonanza" in the event of Korean reunification.[13] German reunification was an eco-nomic loser, by the way, as Germany reunited during the *Eurosclerosis* period of economic stagnation from which, because of structural issues, much of Western Europe will likely never escape. A reunified Korea, however, would find itself in the world's most economically dynamic region, bordering what is today the world's second-largest economy (mainland China). Assuming a former North Korea could be subsumed into South Korea's various preferential trade agreements as the for-mer East Germany was subsumed into the European Community[14] and NATO upon German reunification, Korean companies would have an incentive to bring operations back *home*—in particular, from neighbor-ing mainland China—into what was North Korea. Costs would be less than in the former South, with a presumably eager workforce, yet with preferential access to major world markets (in some cases, tariff-free)

11   "Full Text of Park's Speech on N. Korea," *Korea Herald*, March 14, 2014, http://www.koreaherald.com/view.php?ud=20140328001400.

12   "North Korea Launches Misogynistic Tirade against South Korean President," *The Guardian*, April 4, 2014, https://www.theguardian.com/world/2014/apr/04/north-korea-misogynist-tirade-south-korean-president.

13   Matthew Winkler and Sam Kim, "Park Extols Korea Bonanza with a North-South Unification," Bloomberg, January 12, 2014, https://www.bloomberg.com/news/articles/2014-01-12/park-extols-korea-bonanza-with-a-north-south-unification.

14   Today's European Union (EU) was known as the European Community (EC) until 1994.

without having to worry about host country political interference, as when Beijing punished South Korean interests over Seoul's 2016 decision to allow deployment of America's Terminal High Altitude Aerial Defense (THAAD) anti-missile system in Seongju. What is more, resourceful North Koreans, especially since the breakdown of the North's public distribution system in the 1990s, have had to scratch and claw for much of what they have. The emergence of the *jangmadang* private markets demonstrates northern enterprise, suggesting that a reunified Korea, under Seoul's rule, could be a formidable economic force. East Germany, by contrast, had hardly any private business of any kind. North Koreans are way ahead of Cold War East Germans on this score.

Where I am less certain is the social and political prospects for Korean unification, as the two sides have been so thoroughly cut off for so long. What's more, as mentioned, they even fought a war against each other. Combining the Nazi and communist eras, East Germans had lived under dictatorship for "only" a combined fifty-six years when they finally got their freedom. As North Koreans went straight from a brutal Japanese colonization to the Kim family's ongoing multigenerational reign of terror, they have already been without their own freedom for a combined 110 years and counting. That's a lot to overcome when facing an entirely new world.

Shortly after his May 2017 election, current South Korean president Moon Jae-in too made a North–South Korean relations address in Berlin.[15] He did not offer unconditional cooperation with the North but did signal his desire for better relations with Pyongyang. He reaffirmed Seoul's alliance with Washington and called for denuclearization but emphasized, true to nationalist left form, that inter-Korean relations and eventual reunification must be achieved "by our nation itself." No German could have ever said such a thing, as the two Germanies were under postwar occupation.

Origins

We cannot understand the differences between the German and Korean situations without knowing each country's history. Germany was only first united in 1871 while Korea had already been one for a millennium.

---

15   Moon Jae-in, "Address at the Körber Foundation, Germany," July 6, 2017, https://english1.president.go.kr/briefingspeeches/speeches/65.

Germany started the Second World War that resulted in its division, while Korea was a victim during said period at the hands of German ally Japan. Some Germans even accepted their country's division as deserved punishment for their wartime atrocities and sins. Koreans, on the other hand, suffered twice through no fault of their own.

Cold War

Both divisions were supposed to be temporary but again, unlike the two Koreas, the two Germanies never fought each other (this fact cannot be emphasized often enough). East Germany (formally known as the German Democratic Republic [GDR] aided, abetted and harbored terrorists (e.g., Carlos the Jackal,[16] Baader Meinhof,[17] etc.) who carried out attacks in Western Europe, including in West Germany. The Palestine Liberation Organization (PLO) even had an East Berlin office.[18] East Germany's *Ministerium für Staatssicherheit* (Ministry for State Security, or Stasi) secret police spied on its own citizens and penetrated the highest levels of West German government and society. But as a rule, East German forces and agents themselves did not kill West Germans. North Korea, on the other hand, specifically targets South Koreans: for example, the 1983 Rangoon bombing aimed at then South Korean president Chun Doo-hwan[19] and the North's downing of Korean Air Flight 858 in 1987,[20] en route from Baghdad to Seoul, so as to scare people away from attending the 1988 Seoul Summer Olympics.

---

16   Tony Paterson, "Rescued from the Shredder, Carlos the Jackal's Missing Years," *The Independent,* October 30, 2010, https://www.independent.co.uk/news/world/europe/rescued-from-the-shredder-carlos-the-jackals-missing-years-2120492.html.
17   Neal Ascherson, "A Terror Campaign of Love and Hate," *The Guardian,* September 27, 2008, https://www.theguardian.com/world/2008/sep/28/germany.terrorism.
18   Jeffrey Herf, "East Germany's Eurocentric Definition of Terrorism," The Wilson Center, June 12, 2017, https://www.wilsoncenter.org/blog-post/east-germanys-eurocentric-definition-counterterrorism.
19   William Chapman, "North Korean Leader's Son Blamed for Rangoon Bombing," *Washington Post,* December 3, 1983, https://www.washingtonpost.com/archive/politics/1983/12/03/north-korean-leaders-son-blamed-for-rangoon-bombing/ddec34cc-9c12-4fc6-bf75-36057091aa4e/.
20   Paula Hancocks and Jake Kwon, "Ex-North Korean Spy Recounts Olympic Plot to Blow Up Plane," CNN, January 26, 2018, https://www.cnn.com/2018/01/22/asia/north-korea-secret-agent-blew-up-plane-intl/index.html.

Globalist vs. Nationalist

East German leader Walter Ulbricht badgered Soviet leader Nikita Khrushchev into finally letting him build the Berlin Wall in 1961,[21] as the GDR was hemorrhaging refugees to West Berlin. This is not unlike North Korea's Kim Il-sung's having harangued Khrushchev's predecessor, Josef Stalin, until Moscow signed off on Kim's 1950 invasion of South Korea. (Kim was also lobbying China's Mao Zedong at the time.)

But for the most part, the two Germanies were dutiful client states, distancing themselves from Nazi Germany's shameful history, as part of a worldwide struggle between patrons Washington and Moscow. They made war reparations,[22] hoping to be accepted as new states by the countries Germany had attacked.

Meanwhile, as the two Germanies were trying to be less German, the two Koreas were shooting it out to claim Korea's place in the world. And by rewriting Kim family history to assert that Kim Il-sung launched anti-Japanese guerilla attacks from the foot of allegedly sacred Mount Paektu (from where Korea's mythical founder, Tangun, is said to have descended in 2333 BCE to spawn the Korean race), and that second leader Kim Jong-il was born there, the Kim regime falsely claims some kind of divine right to rule while trying to reunify the peninsula on its terms.[23]

East Germany vs. North Korea

East Germany was a much smaller part of all Germany than North Korea is of all Korea. East Germany's population of 16 million[24] was

---

21 Hope M. Harrison, *Driving the Soviets Up the Wall: Soviet-East German Relations, 1953–1961* (Princeton, NJ: Princeton University Press, 2003), 170.

22 Georgios Karkampasis, "What Happened to the German War Reparations after the End of WWII" (master's thesis, Centre for European Studies, May 2016), https://www.researchgate.net/publication/305719680_What_Happened_to_the _German_War_Reparations_after_the_end_of_WWII.

23 Jean H. Lee, "Parsing the Propaganda: What to Make of Kim Jong Un on a White Horse," Wilson Center Asia Dispatches, October 29, 2019, https://www.wilsoncenter .org/blog-post/parsing-the-propaganda-what-to-make-kim-jong-un-white-horse.

24 United States Department of State, Bureau of Public Affairs, "German Democratic Republic, Background Notes," November 1–8, 1984, https://pubmed.ncbi .nlm.nih.gov/12178098/.

a quarter of West Germany's population of 63 million,[25] only a fifth of reunited Germany. North Korea's population of 26 million[26] is just over half of South Korea's population of 51 million[27] and would thus constitute one third of a reunited Korea. North Korea's land mass is larger than South Korea's, while East Germany's territory was much smaller than West Germany's. Hence a former North Korea should have more say in a reunited Korea than the highly marginalized former East has had in reunified Germany. Another major difference was the existence of West Berlin, which was, in practical terms, a piece of West Germany deep inside the East.[28] East Berliners saw West Berlin every day, just over the Berlin Wall, on their way to work, or school. They could hear David Bowie's June 1987 outdoor concert at the Reichstag,[29] in what was Berlin's British sector, and see Coca-Cola billboards. Imagine, if you will, a *South* Pyongyang where North Koreans, on their way to Kim Il-sung Square for an anti-U.S. rally, could crane their necks and see, in real life, K-pop billboards, or their upwardly mobile rivals driving the latest Hyundai sedans. Unthinkable.

Ideology

Most importantly, as unfree as it was, East Germany was vehemently anti-nationalist. East Germans were global communists. They were communists who happened to be German. German nationalism was for them as an evil to be eradicated once and for all. They saw the very notion of Germany itself as a problem. East German leaders came to embrace Germany's division.

---

25   Aaron O'Neill, "Population of East and West Germany 1950–2016," Statista, October 11, 2019, https://www.statista.com/statistics/1054199/population-of-east-and-west-germany/.

26   Worldometer, https://www.worldometers.info/world-population/north-korea-population/.

27   Worldometer, https://www.worldometers.info/world-population/south-korea-population/.

28   West Berlin technically was not part of West Germany, as it was formally under postwar Allied control until German unification in 1990. Hence West Berliners didn't have to serve in the West German military.

29   Max Fisher, "David Bowie at the Berlin Wall: The Incredible Story of a Concert and Its Role in History," Vox, January 11, 2016, https://www.vox.com/2016/1/11/10749546/david-bowie-berlin-wall-heroes.

East Germany espoused, officially at least, multiculturalism,[30] branding itself the only anti-racist, anti-fascist German state.[31] It castigated West Germany as the inheritor of Nazism. East Germany trumpeted working class solidarity beyond culture, nationality, and race. This runs counter to nineteenth-century German and Korean nationalism rooted in the ideas of ancestry, culture, and race.[32] East German authorities approved of its citizens mingling with politically acceptable foreigners and opposed any race-based conditions to marriage.[33] South Korea's military, meanwhile, only first allowed mixed-race Koreans to serve in 2006, while North Korea openly criticizes the South for tolerating intermarriage.[34]

North Korea's Kim monarchy is an ultra-Korean nationalist cult that has pursued its uniquely perverse brand of communism (which the American Enterprise Institute's Nicholas Eberstadt has called *racial socialism*[35]) in hopes of achieving its version of reunification. East Germans got wise to North Korea's retrograde ideology[36] and closely monitored its diplomats in the GDR, even infiltrating and reporting on events at its embassy in East Berlin. East German diplomats in Pyongyang cabled home, complaining Kim Il-sung was writing the Soviet

---

30   The former East Germany is the political base for today's far-right, anti-immigrant Alternativ für Deutschland (AfD) opposition. However, there was also underreported racist sentiment, violence, and even murder in the GDR days. Students and contract workers from places like Mozambique, Cuba, and Vietnam were among the targets.

31   Sven Felix Kellerhoff, "In der DDR gab es Neonazis. Sie lynchten Gastarbeiter," *Welt,* August 19, 2016, https://www.welt.de/geschichte/article157749931/In-der-DDR-gab-es-Neonazis-Sie-lynchten-Gastarbeiter.html.

32   Gi-Wook Shin, "The Perils of Populist Nationalism," Shorenstein Asia-Pacific Research Center, September 2019, 2, https://fsi-live.s3.us-west-1.amazonaws.com/s3fs-public/shin_perils_of_populist_nationalism.pdf.

33   Sara Pugach, "African Students and the Politics of Race and Gender in the German Democratic Republic," in *Comrades of Color: East Germany in the Cold War World,* edited by Quinn Slobodian (New York: Berghahn Books, 2015), 131.

34   Peter Maass, "Radioactive Nationalism," *New York Times,* October 22, 2006, https://www.nytimes.com/2006/10/22/magazine/radioactive-nationalism.html.

35   "We Need a Long Game for North Korea: A Conversation with Nicholas Eberstadt," Heritage Foundation, Summer 2018 Insider, August 13, 2018, https://www.heritage.org/insider/summer-2018-insider/we-need-long-game-north-korea.

36   Mark Hallam, "North Korea Cables Reveal East Germany's Deep-Rooted Suspicion of Kim Regime," *Deutsche Welle,* February 8, 2018, https://www.dw.com/en/north-korea-cables-reveal-east-germanys-deep-rooted-suspicion-of-kim-regime/a-42160823.

Union out of Korea's liberation history (of course, taking all the credit for himself).

East Germany was always poorer than the West, telling its citizens that West Germans were on balance richer because the West did not take care of its poor and exploited its working class (standard communist fare). But North Korea, which was once richer than the South, tells its people South Koreans are materially better off because Seoul has outsourced its sovereignty to foreign forces (i.e., U.S. troops), thus forsaking South Koreans' Korean-ness.[37]

Going It Alone

North Korea boasts of its supposed independence, publicly rejecting any foreign direction or interference. For example, it proudly crosses ally Beijing on weapons tests. But East Germany talked up its Soviet allegiance at every turn. Chinese troops had left North Korea by 1958 while 380,000 Soviet troops were in East Germany when the Berlin Wall fell.[38] East Germany housed Soviet nukes[39] while Pyongyang blasts Seoul for having had U.S. nukes on its soil until 1991. As Kim Jong-un's uncle, Jang Song-thaek (who was executed in 2014 after allegedly advocating for PRC-style economic reforms and building up a power base too big for his own good) found out the hard way, getting close to Beijing can be dangerous for North Koreans. But final East German head of state Erich Honecker schemed with Soviet leader Leonid Brezhnev, in 1971, to overthrow Ulbricht.[40] Being tight with Moscow advanced East Germans' careers while it resulted in charges of flunkeyism against North Koreans, especially after Stalin's death as Kim Il-sung began to build out his personality cult at home.

North Korea's *Rodong Sinmun* newspaper and Soviet daily *Pravda* editorialized against each other in the early 1960s while East German

---

37   B.R. Myers, *The Cleanest Race* (Brooklyn, NY: Melville House, 2010), 154.

38   Ciarán Fahey, "The Forbidden City: Inside the Abandoned Soviet Camp of Wünsdorf," *The Guardian*, January 11, 2017, https://www.theguardian.com/cities/2017/jan/11/forbidden-city-inside-abandoned-soviet-camp-wunsdorf-east -germany.

39   Louise Branson, "Soviets Say Missiles Are Deployed in East Germany," UPI, January 17, 1984, https://www.upi.com/Archives/1984/01/17/Soviets-say-missiles -are-deployed-in-East-Germany/6356443163600/.

40   Edward Norman Peterson, *The Secret Police and the Revolution: The Fall of the German Democratic Republic* (Westport, CT: Praeger, 2002), 9.

newsstands, even at transit highway rest stops to and from West Berlin, sold publications from around the East Bloc.[41] No foreign media is on offer in North Korea. East Germany celebrated Soviet achievements with as much enthusiasm as it did its own. Cosmonaut Yuri Gagarin was given a 1961 hero's parade in East Berlin, and children played on Sputnik jungle gyms.[42]

Statues of Lenin, not of any East German leader, stood tall across the GDR. North Korea, by contrast, attributes everything it has ever achieved to the Kim family.

Western Connection

Because it was more interested in being communist than being *German*, East Germany was ideologically freer to engage West Germany as just another state, in ways that North Korea *cannot* engage the South because it purports to be the only one true Korea. This made East Germany more vulnerable to outside information and influence in ways that North Korea cannot be.

After the Germanies effectively recognized each other through their 1972 Basic Treaty (which also enabled them to both formally enter the United Nations and cleared the way for the United States to establish diplomatic relations with the GDR), East Germany amended its constitution, in 1974, to declare that it was now "forever and irrevocably" linked with the Soviet Union.[43] It also—worlds apart from North Korea's unification fixation—deleted its article 8 commitment to German reunification, further deleting the words "Germany" and "German nation."[44] It changed the identification stickers on its cars from D for Deustchland (Germany) to DDR for Deustche Demokratische Republik (German Democratic Republic).[45] Honecker himself said

---

41 Newsstands are visible in 1985 in "Trafikmagasinet besöker DDR 1985—Das Verkehrsmagazin im SVT besucht die DDR," Youtube, https://www.youtube.com/watch?v=SpQxb4NHH4c.

42 Darijana Hahn, "Zeitgeschichte auf dem Kinderspielplatz" [Contemporary history in the children's playground], *Stadt+Grün*, April 5, 2021, https://stadtundgruen.de/artikel/zeitgeschichte-auf-dem-kinderspielplatz-15879.html.

43 See the entry for October 7, 1974, at "Chronicle 1974," Chronik der Mauer [Chronicle of the Wall].

44 "East Germany: Relations with West Germany," Country Data, http://www.country-data.com/cgi-bin/query/r-5139.html.

45 See the entry for January 1, 1974, at "Chronicle 1974," Chronik der Mauer [Chronicle of the wall], http://www.country-data.com/cgi-bin/query/r-5139.html.

East and West Germany would never reunify, even though he was from what was West Germany. His *Abgrenzung* (demarcation) policy sought to foster a distinct East German national identity.[46]

Human Rights Comparisons and Contrasts

Human rights can be a politically loaded term that means different things to different people. Of the thirty articles in the United Nations Declaration of Human Rights,[47] however, East Germany and North Korea have been serial violators of most, if not all. The rights to liberty and protection against arbitrary arrest immediately come to mind. But as it regards other rights like the freedom of movement within a state, freedom to travel abroad, freedom of religion, freedom of assembly, access to outside media, and having enough to eat, East Germany was far less oppressive than North Korea is.

East Germany did not welcome scrutiny of its human rights record but (because it was part of a multinational communist coalition and more and less followed the Soviet Union's lead) it at least signed the 1975 Helsinki Accords, whose Basket III provision guaranteed certain human rights, including the fundamental right to travel.[48] North Korea usually protests, or storms out of, meetings that even mention human rights. The UN Commission of Inquiry (COI) on Human Rights in the Democratic Republic of Korea's (DPRK) horrifying 2014 report, led by Honorable Justice Michael Kirby of Australia, laid bare for all to see the true depravity of the North Korean regime. The report recommended referring the North Korean leadership, including Kim Jong-un, to the International Criminal Court (ICC), in The Hague.[49] Such a referral has never actually been made, but whenever the subject is brought up, North Korean officials go into a panicked, global full-court press to

---

46   "East Germany: Relations with West Germany."

47   "Universal Declaration of Human Rights," United Nations, https://www.un
.org/en/about-us/universal-declaration-of-human-rights.

48   "The Helsinki Process and the OSCE," Commission on Security and Cooperation in Europe, https://www.csce.gov/about-csce/helsinki-process-and-osce.

49   Troy Stangarone, "Could North Korea Be Sent to the International Criminal
Court over Kim Jong-nam?" Korean Economic Institute of America, https://keia
.org/the-peninsula/could-north-korea-be-sent-to-the-international-criminal-court
-over-kim-jong-nam/.

ward it off. Then North Korean foreign minister Ri Su Yong even visited the General Assembly to challenge the COI's findings.[50]

But while nowhere near as bad as North Korea, East Germany was still a bad place where people's rights were violated daily. Citizens were under constant surveillance. They voted, but had no real voice in choosing their political leaders. Families and friends informed on each other for the Stasi. Innocent people were denied promotions and university spots for not having the correct views. East Germany incarcerated 250,000 political prisoners during its forty-one years of existence.[51] But there were not East German prison camps, or gulags, as there are in North Korea. Also, unlike North Korea, East Germans did not go to jail for the "crimes" of their family members, ones they themselves did not commit. An East German defector's family members may have received some punishment upon a relative's successful escape, but nothing compared to the standard North Korean multigenerational, family incarceration for "transgressions" as seemingly minor as consuming South Korean media. East Germans were also never born in jails and forced to live out their days there in brutal physical service to the state as they are in North Korea.

More than one thousand East Germans died trying to escape, not only at the Berlin Wall but also along the much longer inner-German rural border and on the Baltic coast in attempts to reach West Germany or Scandinavia.[52] But they were allowed, with some restrictions, to travel to most other communist countries. Billboards for state airline Interflug advertised flights to Moscow, Prague, and Hanoi. Some lucky newlyweds even went to Cuba on their honeymoons. Families took summer vacations to Hungary, where they could rendezvous with West German relatives, much easier than the meticulously scrutinized North-South family reunions for which President Park called in her Dresden speech. The North-South reunions—painfully few, carefully staged, and closely supervised—pale in comparison to the opportunities per-

---

50   David Hawk, "North Korea Responds to the UN Commission of Inquiry," 38 North, October 16, 2014, https://www.38north.org/2014/10/dhawk101614/.

51   Elisabeth Jahn, "East Germany's Inescapable Hohenschönhausen Prison," *Deutsche Welle,* October 9, 2014, https://www.dw.com/en/east-germanys-inescapable-hohensch%C3%B6nhausen-prison/a-17982535.

52   Kate Connolly, "'More than 1,000 Died' Trying to Flee East Germany," *The Independent,* August 13, 2003, https://www.telegraph.co.uk/news/worldnews/europe/germany/1438720/More-than-1000-died-trying-to-flee-East-Germany.html.

haps millions of East and West Germans enjoyed to informally meet during the Cold War.

Visiting other relatively less oppressive communist countries (in particular, Hungary, which was a usual rite of passage for East German high school students where they could, for example, buy Western sports gear and records) led East Germans to want, and to expect, more from their own government after they returned home. In fact, it was Hungary's 1989 opening of its border with Austria that helped kick-start the fall of the Berlin Wall, as East Germans already in Hungary could freely cross the border into Austria, where they were welcomed by Vienna-based West German consular officials (these events started a chain reaction back home). North Koreans, except for a very select few, cannot even visit mainland China or Russia. And those increasingly fewer (because of expulsions and sanctions) sent abroad to earn hard currency for the regime hardly ever get to see anything of their host countries outside their strictly controlled work sites.

Unlike North Koreans who have traditionally needed permission to travel within the DPRK and who must earn the right to live in capital Pyongyang, East Germans could move freely within the GDR. Resettling in another East German city was admittedly perhaps not always so easy and only fully vetted citizens could live near the border with West Berlin or West Germany. But someone in Dresden would not think twice about a spontaneous day trip to East Berlin for the opera or to Leipzig for a soccer game. The same cannot be said for North Koreans.

Aside from the occasional military defection, the Demilitarized Zone (DMZ) separating the two Koreas is sealed shut with virtually no one crossing in either direction. But East Germany's western borders were much more porous than most appreciate. East German pensioners came and went as they pleased, as they were no longer considered useful to the state, although many could not afford the trips. Upon mutual recognition between the two Germanies in 1972, roughly 40,000 East Germans of all ages were allowed to visit the West each year,[53] conditional on them leaving behind family members to ensure their return.

But in 1986, East German leaders thought the West might appear less alluring if people could go there more easily.[54] But just the opposite happened, as word of fellow East Germans' experiences *da drüben*

---

53 David Childs, *Fall of the GDR* (London: Routledge, 2001), 29.

54 Robert J. McCartney, "E. Germany Relaxes Curbs on Working Citizens' Visits to West," *Washington Post*, April 16, 1988, https://www.washingtonpost.com/

("over there") spread, resulting in only more East Germans wanting to see it for themselves; 573,000 East Germans took advantage of these relaxed rules to visit West Germany in 1986, 1.2 million in 1987, and 2.2 million in 1988.[55] Hence a significant proportion of East Germany's 16 million people had already visited the West *before* the Berlin Wall opened that fateful November 1989 night.

East Germans also had another human right of theirs regularly violated, although perhaps to their advantage. Thousands of East German activists, artists, and intellectuals, like musician Wolf Bierman in 1976, were exiled to the West.[56] Bierman's stepdaughter, punk rocker Nina Hagen, followed him. Some exiles would later appear on anti-GDR programming beamed back into the East. East Germans would sometimes get arrested on purpose (for political crimes) just so they could be charged and then kicked out of the country.[57] But in North Korea, dissidents are never deported. Rather, they are sent to camps or executed.

From the day the inner-German border was truly sealed,[58] when the Berlin Wall was constructed in 1961 until it opened in 1989, 3.5 million East Germans had resettled in West Germany. This compares to only 29,000 North Koreans who have reached South Korea since the Korean War, as of 2016.[59] Given the population difference, this means in relative terms there are 400 times fewer North Koreans living in South Korea today than there were East Germans in West Germany.[60]

German travel went both ways. West Germans (and, most other foreign nationals, for that matter) were free to visit East Germany. Between

---

archive/politics/1988/04/17/e-germany-relaxes-curbs-on-working-citizens-visits
-to-west/bf53ec1a-a4a5-4168-a171-759393155c9b/.

55   David Childs, "The SED Faces the Challengers of Ostpolitik and Glasnost," in *East Germany in Comparative Perspective*, eds. David Childs, Thomas A Baylis, and Marilyn Rueschemeyer (London: Routledge, 1988), 5.

56   "The Exile of Wolf Biermann," BBC Sounds, November 24, 2017, https://www.bbc.co.uk/sounds/play/w3csvtsf.

57   June Carolyn Erlick, "Many Exiles Quietly Going into the East," *South Florida Sun-Sentinel*, November 14, 1989, https://www.sun-sentinel.com/news/fl-xpm -1989-11-14-8902090802-story.html.

58   East Germany sealed its rural border with West Germany in 1952 but East Germans could get out by crossing from East Berlin into West Berlin, until the Berlin Wall was built in 1961.

59   Ruediger Frank, "The Unification Cases of Germany and Korea: A Dangerous Comparison (Part 1 of 2)," 38 North, November 3, 2016, https://www.38north .org/2016/11/rfrank110316/.

60   Frank, "The Unification Cases of Germany and Korea."

January and April 1984 alone, for example, there were 897,000 West German visits to East Germany and East Berlin.[61] My Western Berlin host parents kept photo albums of their 1980s GDR travels. Visas were required and movements monitored, but for transit to and from West Berlin through the East, one could just show up unannounced at the border, pay the necessary fees, get a visa, and travel through (so long as you did not deviate from your route). The same held true for day visits within East Berlin. East Germany needed the hard currency and West Germany wanted the human contact. This is how I always got into the East, paying DM 5 (US $3) for each transit and DM 30 ($17) for each East Berlin day visit. I limited my interaction with locals and did not do anything to draw attention to myself, but was otherwise free to roam East Berlin with no required stops. Anyone who has visited North Korea tells me they have had a much more *managed* travel experience there. And, there is no transiting North Korea en route to mainland China and/or Russia—any talk of a Moscow-Seoul rail line is today pure fantasy.

For those East Germans with a phone, they could sometimes talk to family and friends in the West. They could also exchange letters, even though East German authorities read everything. No contact of any kind exists between North and South Koreans today.

West Germany vs. South Korea

But not only was East Germany very different from North Korea, Bonn's approach to East Berlin could be very different from Seoul's approach to Pyongyang. West Germany was, from its 1949 inception, a democracy and human rights model citizen. South Korea, however, was guilty of its own human rights abuses and only began to democratize in the late 1980s.

And while South Korea's nationalist left presidents have sent aid north seemingly without condition, West Germany's chancellors, both on the left and right, almost always ensured there was a humanitarian "pay for" in exchange for any assistance that it sent east. When Bonn extended East Berlin a DM 1 billion ($553 million) banking credit in 1983, the latter agreed to remove much of the automatic weaponry (directed at East Germans attempting to escape) along the inner-German

---

61   "East Germany: Relations with West Germany."

border.[62] East Berlin also thereafter eliminated the minimum currency requirement for children visiting the GDR and reduced that for West German pensioners from DM 25 ($14) to DM 15 ($8).[63]

West Germany even paid for the freedom of 33,755 political prisoners, transferring them out of East German jails to the West.[64] The unfortunate result was DM 3.5 billion ($1.9 billion) going into East German government coffers,[65] but Bonn's motivation was noble. It was always looking to get East Germans out of East Germany. Seoul is nowhere nearly as aggressive trying to get North Koreans out. In fact, South Korean defectors and human rights activists rightly claim the Moon Jae-in administration has deemphasized North Korean human rights while leaning on state media outlets to keep North Korean defectors off the air, so as not to upset Pyongyang.[66]

Seoul regrettably chose not to co-sponsor an annual 2019 North Korean UN human rights resolution so as to assuage Kim Jong-un, thinking such a move might help resurrect inter-Korean governmental dialogue.[67] President Trump did not help matters when at his direction the United States blocked a meeting of the UN Security Council to discuss North Korean human rights the following month, in hopes that it would bring Kim Jong-un back to the nuclear negotiating table.[68]

---

62   Office of European Analysis, Directorate of Intelligence, "Background and Implications for the DM One Billion Credit to East Germany," Central Intelligence Agency Reading Room, October 27, 1983, https://www.cia.gov/readingroom/docs/CIA-RDP02-06156R000100550001-2.pdf.

63   Office of European Analysis, Directorate of Intelligence, "Background and Implications."

64   "Race to Remember Berlin Wall Victims, 30 Years On," AFP, August 17, 2019, https://www.france24.com/en/20190817-race-to-remember-berlin-wall-victims-30-years-on.

65   "Race to Remember Berlin Wall Victims, 30 Years On."

66   Edward White and Kang Buseong, "N. Korean Defectors Worry about Seoul's Wooing of Kim Jong Un," *Financial Times*, September 18, 2019, https://www.ft.com/content/3acf1336-d9bf-11e9-8f9b-77216ebe1f17.

67   Colum Lynch, "South Korea Declines to Co-Sponsor North Korea Human Rights Resolution for First Time Since 2008," *Foreign Policy*, November 15, 2019, https://foreignpolicy.com/2019/11/15/south-korea-declines-cosponsor-north-korea-human-rights-un-resolution-first-time-since-2008/.

68   Colum Lynch and Robbie Gramer, "Desperate to Save Diplomacy, White House Blocks U.N. Meeting on North Korean Atrocities," *Foreign Policy*, December 9, 2019, https://foreignpolicy.com/2019/12/09/white-house-blocks-un-meeting-north-korea-atrocities-trump-kim/.

Sometimes it seems as if South Korean nongovernmental organizations (NGOs) are on their own, trying the best they can to help their fellow Koreans in the North. In comparison, West German environmental NGOs, in particular, were very active regarding East Germany and often enjoyed official West German encouragement.

But West Germany's dealings with the East were not always honorable. The GDR, from 1972 to 1989, earned DM 1 billion ($553 million) taking in West Berlin's trash, which included 35,000 annual tons of toxic waste.[69] West Germany paid for East German highways linking it to West Berlin, and amid the billions in German-German trade, some West German companies outsourced the manufacturing and assembly of their products to East German factories that used political prisoner labor. These were products that East Germans themselves were not able to purchase. Multinationals, too, shamefully got in on the act: in 2012, Sweden's IKEA admitted to having contracted some of its furniture assembly to East German prison labor through its then West German operation.[70] But in general, West Germany's East German interactions were designed to better East Germans' lives and to bring West and East Germans closer together. These shady East German outsourcing arrangements are somewhat akin to today's shuttered Kaesong Industrial Complex, just over the DMZ in North Korea, although North Korean workers apparently aspired to work there when it was operating. To their credit, South Korean companies have at least been up front about their Kaesong operations.

Ostpolitik vs. Nordpolitik

West German chancellor Willy Brandt's *Ostpolitik* policy is best remembered for its effective normalization of ties with East Germany. But an even bigger part of *Ostpolitik* was Bonn's acceptance of Germany's postwar borders, i.e., the relinquishing of its claims to former German territory that was now in Poland. *Ostpolitik* also entailed expanded

---

69   Debora MacKenzie, "West German Toxic Waste May No Longer Go East," *NewScientist*, January 27, 1990, https://www.newscientist.com/article/mg12517011-300-west-german-toxic-waste-may-no-longer-go-east/.

70   Wolfgang Hansson, "Ikea erkänner slavarbete i forna Östtyskland" [Ikea admits forced labor in former East Germany], *Aftonbladet*, November 16, 2012, https://www.aftonbladet.se/nyheter/a/jPm3Wo/ikea-erkanner-slavarbete-i-forna-osttyskland.

commercial ties with the Soviet Union and its Warsaw Pact allies. *Ostpolitik* was thus, a European initiative of which inner-German relations were only part. South Korean president Roh Tae-woo's late 1980s and early 1990s *Nordpolitik* was, by contrast, about establishing relations with Moscow and Beijing for the express purpose of trying to pry open North Korea. Its strategic intent was exclusively Korean in nature (not regional, as was Brandt's).

"The Class Enemy in the Living Room"[71]

East Germany was also more open in terms of access to outside media and information, another basic human right. Specifically, in 1973,[72] it gave up trying to prevent its citizens from tuning into West German television and radio; 70 percent of East Germans were able to see West German television.[73] East Germans followed JR's shooting on *Dallas*, cheered West German Bundesliga soccer, and sang along to Depeche Mode. Those parts of East Germany that didn't receive Western signals were dubbed *Tal der Ahnungslosen* (valley of the clueless).[74] West German publicly owned television stations created programs specifically aimed at East German viewers,[75] while South Korea's Moon government has sadly shut down balloon launches and loudspeakers at the DMZ. Some outside media has seeped into North Korea in recent years, but it is nothing compared to the mountain of real-time, effectively legal viewing and listening options that East Germans had.

West German publications were not available for purchase in East Germany, but Western correspondents were stationed in the East and critically reported on events there. Journalists' actions were restricted

---

71 Marlis Schaum, "West German TV: The Class Enemy in the Front Room," *Deutsche Welle,* January 7, 2009, https://www.dw.com/en/west-german-tv-the -class-enemy-in-the-front-room/a-3804892.

72 James M. Markham, "TV Brings Western Culture to East Germany," *New York Times,* February 13, 1984, https://www.nytimes.com/1984/02/13/arts/tv -brings-western-culture-to-east-germany.html.

73 Markham, "TV Brings Western Culture to East Germany."

74 Peter Hitchens, "From the Valley of the Clueless to the Valley of the Unknowing," *Daily Mail,* June 23, 2014, https://hitchensblog.mailonsunday.co.uk/2014/06/ from-the-valley-of-the-clueless-to-the-valley-of-unknowing.html.

75 Markham, "TV Brings Western Culture to East Germany."

but their stories got out,[76] allowing East Germans to learn more about what was going on in their own country by consuming Western media. East German dissidents secretly fed Western reporters scoops. Some token foreign journalists report from North Korea, but their activities are so tightly controlled that consumers of such news must carefully parse the accounts and their correlation with the actual state of affairs in the North. Either way, North Koreans themselves will never see or read reports by these foreign journalists.

The fact that West German media sometimes took its own leaders to task lent credibility to what East Germans heard about their leaders from these outlets. (Some irate East German television viewers even wrote in, asking Western media why they criticized so great and free a system as West Germany's.[77])

West German television famously played a part in how the Berlin Wall opened. It was Italian ANSA correspondent Ricardo Ehrman and West German *Bild* journalist Peter Brinkmann who pressed an unprepared East German ruling party spokesman, Günter Schabowski, at a November 9, 1989, East Berlin press conference, to incorrectly state that East Germans could now freely travel to the West, including through the Wall to West Berlin.[78] Schabowski's comments were aired back into the East, drawing thousands to the Wall, eager to try out what they had just learned from television. East German Bornholmer Straße border crossing guards, themselves confused, eventually relented and let the masses through. The rest is history.

Atheist Blessing

East Germany tolerated religion. Church grounds were supposed political safe spaces. The truth is, however, the Stasi had heavily infiltrated religious organizations, compromising many there. But these places of worship nonetheless gave dissidents a place to gather. The 1989 Monday night demonstrations that eventually brought down the regime started at Leipzig's St. Nicholas Church. There is no actual religion officially practiced in North Korea even though, before Korea's

---

76   Schaum, "West German TV: The Class Enemy in the Front Room."
77   Markham, "TV Brings Western Culture to East Germany."
78   Ewald Koenig, "The Journalist Question that Fractured the Berlin Wall," *Euractiv*, November 10, 2009, https://www.euractiv.com/section/central-europe/news/the-journalist-question-that-fractured-the-wall/.

division, Christianity was stronger in what it is today the North than in the South. Pyongyang was even called the Jerusalem of the East. Kim Il-sung, in fact, grew up in a Christian house. His grandfather was a pastor.

Unification an Afterthought

The East German events of 1989 were not about unification. The *Neues Forum* (New Forum) coalition of students, churchgoers, clergy, environmental, and peace activists, as well as discontented everyday citizens, were not out to unite Germany. Rather, they were interested in making East Germany a better place. Nobody talked about unification until *after* the Wall fell. That is when chants of *Wir Sind Das Volk* ("We Are the People," i.e., we should decide what happens in our own country) became *Wir Sind Ein Volk* ("We Are One People," i.e., one German nation).

As soon as borders opened, East Germans could at last fully experience and appreciate how much richer West Germans were. And West Germany soon realized the East's economy was in much worse shape than thought. East Germans were desperate for the hard currency Deutsche Mark. Center right Chancellor Helmut Kohl's Christian Democratic Union (CDU) was facing tough December 1990 West German reelection prospects and he knew incorporating the East in time for the vote could put his CDU party over the top, as Eastern Germans would thank him for their heavier new money (flimsy, relatively worthless East German *Ostmark* coins were made of aluminum). There was also a Western fear, with borders now open, that if Bonn didn't bring West German living standards to the East via unification that the entire Eastern population would soon end up in the West in pursuit of them. Hence, with almost no planning and unrealistic Eastern expectations, Germany reunited on October 3, 1990, only eleven months after the Berlin Wall's unforeseen fall. Contrary to many long after-the-fact South Korean observations today, German reunification was not part of any grand plan. It just happened.

Mostly peaceful revolutions were also sweeping other Eastern European communist countries at the same time, which made East Germany's transition only one part of a wider European story. But as it was with Seoul's *Nordpolitik*, anything that ever happens in North Korea will almost certainly be an exclusively Korean affair, although

Washington and Beijing would have something to say about it. And any change in Korea would likely be about unification from the start.

Lessons

West Germany's aggressive humanitarianism toward East Germans did not on its own bring down the Berlin Wall. But it helped get many of them out before the Wall fell, ensured those left behind knew more about what was actually going on in their own country (as well as in the world at large), and helped ease the eventual reunification transition. But what really cinched the deal on reunification was the Soviet Union letting ally East Germany collapse. Similarly, Korea will not unify until Beijing pulls the plug on Pyongyang and lets the North fall under its own weight, or until South Korea for some reason gives in to the North. South Koreans should be under no illusion that extending the hand of friendship to the North will bring about reunification. In the meantime, there are things that Seoul *can* do to make life more bearable for those poor souls north of the DMZ.

As West Germany did with East Germany, South Korea should put North Korean human rights front and center in its dealings with Pyongyang. Who else will speak up for North Koreans if the South does not? Seoul should make any and all aid and assistance to Pyongyang conditional on progress in North Korean human rights. This can include things like the release of political prisoners to the South and ending attempts to block the transmission of South Korean radio and television into North Korea. South Korea should also demand the North allow its citizens to access the internet. North Korea is unlikely to agree to any of these things, but South Korea must demand them all the same, and withhold aid if these demands are not met. South Korea has leverage here, as the North needs the South's money more than the South needs to give it.

Seoul should push for more North Korean human rights resolutions at the UN (instead of discouraging them) and prioritize North Koreans' well-being in its dealings with Washington and Beijing. In particular, it should ask the United States to always support any and all North Korean human rights resolutions and demand of Beijing that it end the refoulement of North Korean refugees who cross into mainland China. Wherever possible, in whichever corners of the world, South Korean officials should actively engage North Korean citizens abroad.

Seoul should again allow loudspeaker broadcasts at, and leaflet care package balloons over, the DMZ. South Korea should also try flooding North Korea with as much outside information as possible, in order to challenge the North with ideas. Seoul can call Pyongyang's bluff by welcoming Pyongyang's propaganda in the opposite direction (while being on the lookout for any coded messages therein to North Korean agents in the South)—a fair trade, as it were. West Berliners could watch East German television and none of them moved east as a result. Confident, open societies can digest and handle differing points of view even when those views are state-directed.

But sadly, much of West Germany's Cold War playbook is not directly applicable to Korea because North Korea is infinitely more closed than East Germany ever was. Because of its ideologically ultranationalist nature, North Korea cannot open to South Korea as East Germany did to West Germany. Pyongyang cannot accept the existence of another Korean state. (Meanwhile, East Berlin merely sought acknowledgement as Bonn's equal.) East Germany, until near its very end, largely took its cues and orders from Moscow, while North Korea, so long as Beijing lets it hang around, makes its own decisions and suspects any and all outsiders. Hence much of what I recommend here cannot actually happen or would not matter much even if it did. That is the bad news. But South Korea can nonetheless stand on principle so as to at least help make even a few North Koreans' lives better and to also lay down a marker for other governments as to how they should approach Pyongyang. When reunification comes, hopefully under Seoul's rule, North Koreans will know they were not forgotten when the country was divided. That is some good news.

Beijing will likely have the last word on what happens in Korea, just as Moscow did in Berlin. Korean unification under an open, free government will only happen when the Kim regime gives way, and that will only happen if enabler and guarantor Beijing cuts Pyongyang off. Sadly, Xi Jinping is no Mikhail Gorbachev. But in the meantime, South Korea should try following West Germany's example and do everything in its power to better the lives of its fellow Koreans on the other side.

11 Human Rights and Foreign Policy

Puzzles, Priorities, and Political Power

Thomas Fingar

The human rights situation in the Democratic People's Republic of Korea (DPRK) is deplorable. No one seriously challenges this judgment: the United Nations Human Rights Council's Commission of Inquiry (COI) report documents extensive and manifold violations, and even Pyongyang's closest friends shrink from defending its behavior.[1] Despite widespread recognition of the existence and magnitude of DPRK actions inconsistent with internationally recognized norms, there is little consensus on what can or should be done to ameliorate the situation. Indeed, more than seven years after publication of the COI report, even the Republic of Korea (ROK) and the United States have largely abandoned support for statements or action by the Security Council and what once was almost a "freebie" critique that all countries could endorse has again become an orphan issue championed primarily by non-governmental organizations (NGOs).[2]

---

1   See for example, Human Rights Watch, *World Report 2020: North Korea*, 2020, https://www.hrw.org/world-report/2020/country-chapters/north-korea; UN Human Rights Council, Report of the Commission of Inquiry on Human Rights in the Democratic People's Republic of Korea, A/HRC/25/63 (February 7, 2014, https://www.ohchr.org/en/hrbodies/hrc/coidprk/pages/reportofthecommissionof inquirydprk.aspx; and Tom Miles and Stephanie Nebehay, "China Rejects North Korean Crimes Report, Hits Chance of Prosecution," Reuters, March 17, 2014, http://reut.rs/1kWnlPi. China criticized the COI report's methodology but did not defend the DPRK's human rights behavior.
2   See the chapters in this volume by Joon Oh and by Peter Yeo and Ryan Kaminski. Also see Roseanne Gerin, "NGOs Call on North Korean Leader to End Human Rights Abuses," Radio Free Asia, June 17, 2018, https://www.rfa.

The lack of consensus about what to do is not surprising but the paucity and inconsistency of government attention to human rights and other dimensions of the "North Korea problem" is puzzling. It is puzzling not simply because politicians normally seize opportunities to embrace "principled" positions that do not require action on their part but also because past and current approaches have failed to manage the political, nuclear, economic, and humanitarian dimensions of the problem. Doing more of what we have done in the past—condemnation, ostracism, sanctions, tightly constrained engagement, smuggled soap operas, propaganda leaflets, etc.—is unlikely to achieve different results. If we really want to improve the human rights situation in the DPRK and ameliorate other worrisome problems, it would seem to make sense to try something different. That is easier to write than to accomplish.

Among the reasons it is difficult to address—let alone solve—human rights and other problems in the North is that they are inextricably linked and have different salience and priority for different countries and constituencies. For some, meaningful improvement of respect for human rights is a prerequisite for economic engagement; for others, denuclearization must precede economic and other forms of engagement and has such overwhelming importance that pressing for improvements in human rights must be deferred, lest engagement in that arena impede progress toward reduction of nuclear and other security dangers.[3] An obvious rejoinder to arguments calling for pursuing different objectives in sequence is to pursue all of them simultaneously, albeit not necessarily with the same urgency. However, doing so requires harmonization and integration of proposals from groups with different perceptions, priorities, and political influence.

Despite near unanimity that the human rights situation in the DPRK is bad, there is little agreement on why it is bad or whether it is

---

org/english/news/korea/ngos-call-on-north-korean-leader-to-end-human-rights
-abuses-06072018161953.html.

3   For examples illustrating different prioritization see, Bradley O. Babson, "A More Realistic Approach to the Economic Side of Nuclear Negotiations with North Korea," 38 North, September 18, 2019, https://www.38north.org/2019/09/bbabson091819/; and Kim Tae-Woo, "Human Rights in North Korea: The Real Key to Denuclearization," *The Diplomat*, July 25, 2016, https://thediplomat.com/2016/07/human-rights-in-north-korea-the-real-key-to-denuclearization/.

worsening or improving.[4] Many analysts make an essentialist argument that the human rights situation is bad because the regime is bad. Others assert or imply a more instrumentalist explanation to the effect that the regime must repress and exploit its people in order to retain power and/or pursue nuclear weapons and other objectives. Each of these explanations has clear implications. Logically, if violation of human rights is an essential attribute of the regime, the only way to improve respect for those rights is to weaken and ultimately dismantle the regime. If rights are violated to facilitate development of nuclear weapons, then denuclearization should facilitate improvement of human rights.[5] How one conceptualizes priorities and causal relationships among categories of issues shapes policy options and strategies to achieve specific goals.

Most characterizations of human rights in the North are long on description and outrage but short on analysis of why the regime employs the methods that it does. Given the amount of effort and expense devoted to blocking access to information and entertainment from abroad, restricting movement, and incarcerating entire families for the attempt of a single member to exercise universal rights, it seems appropriate to ask why the DPRK does each and all of the repressive things that it does (see chapters 6 and 7). Does it really consider all of them to be critical to survival of the regime, or are some deemed less important and therefore better candidates for improvement if the right incentives or pressures are utilized? Limited progress toward respecting the rights of children, women, and people with disabilities suggests that this might be the case.[6]

Better understanding of motivation requires empirical research that is almost unimaginable under current conditions. At minimum it would seem imperative to develop hypotheses and more nuanced explanations about why Pyongyang does what it does, if we are to identify relatively more promising areas in which to seek engagement with the

---

4   See, for example, "Five Years of Kim Jong-un: Are Human Rights Getting Worse?" NK News, December 23, 2016, https://www.nknews.org/2016/12/five-years-of-kim-jong-un-are-human-rights-getting-worse/.
5   Examples of implied directional linkages include Jamie Metzl, "Doomsday: The Coming Collapse of North Korea," National Interest, June 14, 2015, https://nationalinterest.org/feature/doomsday-the-coming-collapse-north-korea-13107; and Joseph A. Bosco, "The North Korea Regime Change Debate," The Diplomat, January 6, 2015, https://thediplomat.com/2015/01/the-north-korea-regime-change-debate/.
6   Human Rights Watch, World Report 2020: North Korea.

regime or ones that can be worked in the ROK-DPRK relationship or by subcomponents of the United Nations. Increased information and enhanced understanding would be useful but are insufficient for development and implementation of more effective human rights policies for the DPRK. Other requisite conditions include an understanding of how improving human rights in North Korea and/or other countries fits into the larger matrix of foreign policy concerns and objectives. The remainder of this chapter examines, albeit briefly, both this question and competing visions of why and how to address human rights concerns.

Human Rights and Foreign Policy

Human rights objectives and policies can be treated as discrete subjects for analytical and other purposes but they are inextricably enmeshed in, facilitated, and constrained by other goals and dimensions of a nation's foreign policy. In any political system, myriad groups, constituencies, and bureaucratic organizations view developments through self-interested lenses and endeavor to protect or advance their own interests in the policymaking process. Many—probably most—players consider protection of human rights to be a desirable or important goal and responsibility of a nation's foreign policy. A much smaller subset considers human rights in general and violations of human rights in North Korea in particular to be the most important objective or responsibility. Most of the time most players in most systems accord higher priority to other objectives. This does not make them more selfish or less virtuous. But it does mean that admonitions and strategies to address human rights problems must compete with many other policy advocates and objectives for attention, priority, and resources.

Foreign policy is always an agglomeration of objectives and strategies to achieve those objectives. In theory, individual goals have been prioritized and harmonized to facilitate achievement of all of them. In reality, policy results from at times intense competition among players with disparate skill, power, and access; tradeoffs and compromises; and serendipitous developments in domestic and external arenas. The competition for priority occurs within overarching frameworks defined by perceptions of the international situation, national interests, and the platforms and proclivities of the administration in power. Thus, for example, foreign policy during the Carter administration was shaped by the Cold War, stagflation, and the president's personal commitment to human rights.[7]

The making of foreign policy is messy, sometimes unsavory, and produces results more like a collage than a da Vinci sculpture. Any foreign policy consists of many strands and specific objectives but for purposes of this chapter, I will simplify by dividing objectives and considerations into just three bins or categories: peace and security, economic goals, and humanitarian considerations. All are important and their relative priority has been quite consistent over time and from one nation to another. The de facto ranking accords highest priority to national security as a necessary prerequisite for achievement of economic goals and protecting the safety and well-being of people inside and outside the country. As both cause and consequence of this de facto ranking, bureaucratic agencies, legislative committees, defense contractors, and other players in the national security enterprise enjoy relatively greater access and influence in the policymaking process than do most other interests. Similarly, economic goals (prosperity, trade, opportunities for national firms) generally have larger, more diverse, and more powerful constituencies than do humanitarian considerations (including human rights). One can applaud or decry this situation, but one must also recognize that it constrains and shapes policy alternatives.

The normal ranking of foreign policy objectives does not mean that they must be pursued sequentially or that economic and humanitarian goals must be deferred or downplayed until security objectives have been achieved. In the case of North Korea, the priority accorded to avoidance of war and denuclearization does not dictate silence or inactivity to reduce violations of human rights. Nor does it preclude the use of positive economic incentives to enhance prospects for both denuclearization and interactions conducive to expansion of human rights. The current situation in which economic sanctions ("maximum pressure") are the instrument of choice to persuade Pyongyang to surrender its nuclear weapons is not the only option available. The fact that all strands of foreign policy are interconnected and, in both theory and reality, can be intertwined in ways that facilitate pursuit of multiple goals simultaneously creates opportunities for alternative approaches. The chapters by Victor Cha and Tae-Ung Baik illustrate possible alternative

---

7   See, for example, Stuart Eizenstat, *President Carter: The White House Years* (New York: St. Martins, 2018).

ways to pursue multiple objectives. Nations, like people, can walk and chew gum at the same time.

The discussion thus far has focused on priorities and process dimensions of foreign policymaking, but they are not the only shaping factors. Other factors include ambiguities regarding responsibility for enforcement of human rights, fundamental principles of international relations, and the advantages of/need for collective actions involving multiple states and international institutions. All states that are members of the United Nations have acknowledged responsibility to promote and encourage respect for human rights.[8] Most, but not all (and specifically not the DPRK), have also signed the Universal Declaration of Human Rights, which enumerates in greater detail the rights to be protected.[9] Responsibility for enforcing these commitments in member states normally is left to the contracting parties themselves. The only partial exception to this is the list of enumerated rights covered by the Responsibility to Protect (R2P) commitment endorsed by all UN members at the 2005 World Summit. The R2P commitment specifies the obligation of all states to prevent genocide, war crimes, ethnic cleansing, and crimes against humanity within their territory, and obligates the international community to act if an individual country is unwilling or unable to prevent them.[10]

Assigning responsibility for protection of human rights in cases other than those covered by R2P to member states is consistent with and a consequence of the concept of state sovereignty that has shaped international relations and international law since the Peace of Westphalia was concluded in 1648. Until quite recently, state sovereignty was defined to mean that the sovereign (i.e., the government) of a country had absolute authority to manage affairs within the boundaries of the state. That idea has been challenged and eroded in the decades since

---

8   Charter of the United Nations, chapter 1, article 1, https://www.un.org/en/about-us/un-charter/full-text.

9   The DPRK has, however, acceded to the International Covenant on Civil and Political Rights, which embraces the Universal Declaration of Human Rights. See UN Office of the High Commissioner for Human Rights, "International Covenant on Civil and Political Rights," https://www.ohchr.org/EN/ProfessionalInterest/Pages/CCPR.aspx.

10   See UN Office on Genocide Prevention and the Responsibility to Protect, "Responsibility to Protect," https://www.un.org/en/genocideprevention/about-responsibility-to-protect.shtml.

World War II, but it is still nearly sacrosanct.[11] Many, perhaps most, nations view diminution of state sovereignty as a slippery slope and are reluctant to infringe on the authority of other governments for fear that doing so will increase their own vulnerability to external pressure and interference.[12]

Reluctance to step onto that slippery slope may explain, in part, why widespread acknowledgement of DPRK human rights violations has not resulted in sustained individual or collective state action to do anything about them.[13] That is a more persuasive explanation than assumptions or assertions that nations unwilling to support forceful action have affinity or sympathy for the regime in Pyongyang.[14] One could argue that the reticence of others to "do the right thing" should not prevent countries, like the United States and the Republic of Korea, that espouse the importance and universality of human rights from doing more to punish and alleviate violations of human rights in the DPRK and elsewhere (see chapter 4 in this volume). Such "do the right thing" and "go it alone" arguments appeal to self-image and downplay vulnerability to charges of hypocrisy, but ignore the fact that all actions have consequences and all nations pursue numerous objectives involving multiple countries. Leading by example to induce other nations to follow works best when potential followers judge that it is in their own interest to join the would-be leader. This involves sometimes difficult cost-benefit calculations that weigh the potential for punishment or benefits of acting in comparison to sitting on the sidelines. Prospective leaders must also calculate the likelihood that their calls to action will be ignored by many or key countries whose cooperation is needed on other issues. Such calculations help to explain the inaction of both

---

11   See, for example, Stephen D. Krasner, *Power, the State, and Sovereignty: Essays on International Relations* (Abingdon, UK: Routledge, 2009).

12   See, for example, Jeremy Rabkin, *Why Sovereignty Matters* (Washington, DC: AEI Press, 1998).

13   It is useful to distinguish between states acting individually and acting with the "cover" of membership in the United Nations. Endorsing or acquiescing to UNCHR positions, for example, provides a degree of "arms-length" insulation to nervous member states.

14   See, for example, David Albright, Sarah Burkhard, Allison Lach, and Andrea Stricker, *Countries Involved in Violating UNSC Resolutions on North Korea* (Washington, DC: Institute for Science and International Security, December 5, 2017), https://isis-online.org/uploads/isis-reports/documents/Countries_Involved _in_Violating_NK_UNSC_Resolutions_5Dec2017_Final.pdf.

prospective leaders and followers in an international effort to address human rights problems in North Korea.

Clarification of Objectives

Even a cursory review of calls for action to address human rights problems in the DPRK reveals confusion and contradiction with regard to the putative objectives of such action. Saying this is not to demean the proposals or their advocates. But if we are to devise an effective strategy to address and improve the deplorable human rights situation in the North, we need much greater clarity about the objectives. For example, should the primary objective be to improve the lot of particular categories of people (e.g., women, children, the disabled), alleviate the effects of specific infringements (e.g., on speech, travel, access to information), or to achieve maximum and comprehensive elimination of all restrictions at more or less the same time? Or is the goal to use criticism of human rights and anticipated consequences of increasing access to information or expanding opportunities for travel or religious freedom to undermine and ultimately remove the repressive regime? Stated another way, is improving human rights the primary objective or a mechanism to achieve regime change?

Such questions are not trivial because without clarity about what is to be achieved, it is difficult to formulate effective strategies and policies to accomplish desired objectives. It is also difficult to marshal support at home or abroad without a clear statement of objectives and rationale for pursing them in a particular way. If others do not understand what an advocate wishes to accomplish, they will assume that he/she has not thought through the requirements and possible consequences, or is being disingenuous and hiding the true purpose. Before legislators, other governments, or the staffs of multinational organizations are willing to sign on to a proposal, they want—and need—to be clear about what it is, why it might work, and what the possible downsides would be if things do not go according to plan.

I can illustrate the point I wish to make with a non–human rights DPRK example. In 1993, the Clinton administration had almost decided to begin negotiations with Pyongyang to explore the regime's willingness to halt work on its nuclear weapons program in exchange for a less confrontational relationship with the United States. It was both prudent and ultimately necessary to obtain Congressional support for such an effort. For partisan reasons, most Republicans were opposed to any such initiative, but others, and many Democrats, were reluctant to endorse an undertaking they thought was doomed to fail. The short version of this story is that they thought the objective was to negotiate an immediate end to the North's nuclear program. Chair of the National Intelligence Council Joe Nye and I explained that the purpose of the proposed talks was to determine whether Pyongyang was serious about discussing proposals that it had floated. This would enable the administration to make an informed judgment about whether and how to proceed. After we clarified the objective, a key senator said, "Oh, if that is the purpose, we can endorse it." The example may not be entirely apt but it illustrates, I hope, the need for clarity of purpose and how the proposed approach would achieve that objective.[15]

Clarity of purpose is necessary not only to build consensus among groups with different priorities and preferred approaches and, later, to seek the cooperation of other national actors; it is also necessary to integrate the approach into the broader array of foreign policy objectives. Few policy initiatives can win approval as stand-alone undertakings. They must be integrated with other objectives and undertakings to capture possible synergies and avoid unwanted interference with higher priority goals. In addition, the proposed initiative and its objectives and instruments must also be "sold" to skeptical DPRK officials. If they judge that the "real" intent is to undermine the regime, they will respond accordingly.

There is good reason for North Korean officials to be suspicious of any human rights–related initiative from the ROK, the United States, or any party thought to be acting on behalf of South Korea and the United States. The regime has a long memory and a real or metaphorical tally sheet of past efforts to use revelations about and denunciation of human rights abuses to blacken the image of the DPRK and its leaders. The same is likely true of efforts to smuggle pamphlets, CDs, and thumb drives containing proscribed material. I am not defending the way the regime perceives or characterizes such efforts; my purpose is simply to note that measures outsiders conceive as modest ways to provide information or entertainment to a deprived citizenry can look very different to the regime. Rather than opening the way for substantive

---

15 See Thomas Fingar, *Reducing Uncertainty: Intelligence Analysis and National Security* (Stanford, CA: Stanford University Press, 2011), 72–73.

dialog about conditions and how to improve them, such measures—or, more accurately, the way they are perceived—can be an obstacle to meaningful improvements.

All past and prospective actions to address human rights problems in the DPRK can be arrayed on a spectrum that ranges from "feel-good" activities recognized as having little real impact, to modest pragmatic proposals designed to begin dialog or address very specific problems. Feel-good initiatives such as propaganda balloons, loud music, and condemnatory resolutions by national legislatures may anger the regime and fool those who undertake them into believing they have done something meaningful, but they demonstrably have not done much, if anything, to improve conditions in the North. Indeed, some activities on the feel-good side of the spectrum, such as smuggled South Korean entertainment programs, arguably have put already repressed people at greater risk of punishment and even more egregious violations of basic rights (see chapter 7 by Martyn Williams). Putting ordinary North Korean people at greater risk is a high price to pay for feel-good actions.

Lack of consensus about the goals of human rights initiatives is compounded by the absence of an agreed strategy that can endure from one administration to another. This is true in the United States (where the promising initial successes of the Clinton administration were immediately discarded when George W. Bush took office, for example).[16] It is even more true in the ROK, where conservatives and progressives have very different views on how to address problems in the North.[17] Given the leading roles that these two countries have played—and according to some should and must play—their own policy inconsistencies make other governments reluctant to commit to policies toward the DPRK that could soon be abandoned or reversed by their principal advocates (see chapters 3 and 4). That is particularly the case for governments that would commit to the policies more to preserve or bolster their relationship with the United States or ROK than to satisfy demands

---

16   See, for example, Don Oberdorfer and Robert Carlin, *The Two Koreas, Third Edition* (New York: Basic Books, 2014); and John Feffer, "Bush Policy Undermines Progress on Korean Peninsula," Institute for Policy Studies, October 4, 2005, https://ips-dc.org/bush_policy_undermines_progress_on_korean_peninsula/.

17   See, for example, Danielle L. Chubb, *Contentious Activism and Inter-Korean Relations* (New York: Columbia University Press, 2014); and Choe Sang-Hun, "South Korea Elects Moon Jae-In, Who Backs Talks with North, as President," *New York Times*, May 9, 2017, https://www.nytimes.com/2017/05/09/world/asia/south-korea-election-president-moon-jae-in.html.

from their own constituents to take a stand on DPRK abuses. For most governments, other considerations have greater salience than human rights in North Korea.

Competing Approaches

Inconsistency with respect to goals and approaches to achieving them diminishes the efficacy of any approach, confuses Pyongyang, and/or reinforces conviction that any approach is likely to be transitory and can or should be ignored. Inconsistency also impedes collective action by the international community. This argues for greater consistency and policy stability over time, but policy content is as important as durability. Lessons from North Korea and human rights–related inter-actions with other countries indicate clearly that the goals and instru-ments of the policies employed have different efficacy.

Policies toward "problem" regimes, including regimes in countries with serious human rights problems, range from complete eschewal of contacts to broad engagement. Policies that fall at or near the eschewal end of the spectrum often include conditions that the target country must satisfy in order to qualify for general or specific forms of political, economic, or people-to-people engagement. In the case of U.S. policy toward North Korea, for example, denuclearization has often, but not always, been characterized as a prerequisite for greater economic en-gagement.[18] Some expand the list to include progress on human rights as a condition for easing economic sanctions.[19] Still others characterize the DPRK (and other regimes) as "evil" or "rogue" and unworthy of engagement with "normal" or "civilized" nations.[20]

---

18   See, for example, Stephen Biegun, "U.S. Special Envoy for North Korea Ste-phen Biegun Delivers First Public Address on U.S.-DPRK Diplomacy at a Shoren-stein APARC Event," Freeman Spogli Institute for International Studies, Janu-ary 31, 2019, https://fsi.stanford.edu/news/us-special-envoy-north-korea-stephen-biegun-delivers-first-public-address-us-dprk-diplomacy.

19   Holly McKay, "U.S. Must Address North Korea's Abhorrent Human Rights Record at Trump-Kim Summit, Report Urges," Fox News, February 22, 2019, https://www.foxnews.com/world/us-must-address-north-koreas-abhorrent-human-rights-record-at-trump-kim-summit-report-says.

20   See Walter C. Clemens, Jr., "Can-Should-Must We Negotiate with Evil?" *Pa-cific Focus* 26, no. 3 (December 2011), https://www.law.upenn.edu/live/files/5127-clemens-walter---negotiate-with-evilpdf; and Michael Rubin, *Dancing with the Devil: The Perils of Engaging Rogue Regimes* (New York: Encounter Books, 2014).

Some such approaches are more extreme than others, but as a group they call for major changes in the behavior of a nation before it can be a legitimate economic partner with access to educational, healthcare, or other benefits of people-to-people interchange. Approaches clustered toward the other end of the spectrum generally call for broad or focused engagement as a useful or necessary step to achieve security, humanitarian, or other objectives. The first approach treats engagement as a reward for better behavior (or, as some would say, preemptive capitulation), the second as an inducement or instrument to achieve higher priority goals.[21] Each category—and less extreme variants nearer the middle of the spectrum—has a defensible logic and should not be dismissed out of hand. However, many real-world examples provide empirical evidence useful to assess their efficacy.

Three cases are sufficient to demonstrate the ineffectiveness of eschewal or extreme nonengagement. For varying but extended periods, U.S. policy has attempted to force change in North Korea, Cuba, and China by constraining development and blocking access to American markets, technology, capital, and diplomatic recognition. Variants of this policy have been pursued with the DPRK since the Korean War, with Cuba since 1960, and with China from 1950 until the 1970s. Suffice it to say that DPRK and Cuban behavior on human rights and other matters the policy was supposed to change is not significantly better (from an American perspective) than it was when the policies were adopted. Perhaps the policies just need a little more time to prove their efficacy, but maybe it is time to admit that they have failed.[22]

China provides an example that facilitates comparison between the efficacy of eschewal and of engagement. During the period of "containment" and non-engagement, the People's Republic subjected its people to the human rights outrages and economic disasters of the Great Leap Forward (1958–62) and the Cultural Revolution (1966–76). During the same period, China developed and deployed nuclear weapons. The

---

21   See, for example, Frank Jannuzi, "Engage, Don't Just 'Name and Shame,'" 38 North, March 26, 2014, https://www.38north.org/2014/03/fjannuzio32614/; and Chad O'Carroll, "Engage or Isolate? How the World Should Deal with North Korea, according to Its Citizens," *The Guardian*, April 25, 2014, https://www.the guardian.com/world/2014/apr/25/how-the-world-should-deal-with-north-korea.
22   See, for example, Rick Zhong, "Harm and Inefficacy: The U.S. Sanctions on Cuba," *Brown Political Review*, May 22, 2020, https://brownpoliticalreview .org/2020/05/harm-and-inefficacy-the-u-s-sanctions-on-cuba/.

decades since Nixon and Mao began the process of "normalization" in 1972, and especially since engagement began in earnest in 1979, life for most Chinese has become much better and China is far more constrained by participation in the rules-based liberal order than it was when pursuing a policy of extreme autarky. China has backslid on a number of dimensions in the past decade, including respect for civil and human rights, but the situation is far better today than during the period of self-imposed and externally imposed isolation.

Examples of positive change that included greater respect for and protection of human rights that were probably encouraged and facilitated by sustained engagement with the United States include, in addition to China, the ROK and Taiwan. In the 1970s and earlier, South Korea and Taiwan were essentially one-party autocracies that made liberal use of their militaries to suppress dissent and in other ways infringe universal rights. Today both are vibrant democracies with "freedom scores" that bracket the United States (ROK 83, USA 86, Taiwan 93). By comparison, the freedom scores for North Korea and Cuba are 3 and 14.[23] Neither the isolation nor engagement policies were undertaken primarily to address human rights problems, and the scores awarded by Freedom House provide only a rough measure of relative human rights performance, but the differences are too great to be ignored.

The case of U.S. engagement with China also offers an instructive example of how foreign policy is shaped by the priorities and political influence of different interest groups. When Beijing used military force to disperse the demonstrators who had occupied Tiananmen Square in 1989, publics across the developed and democratic world responded with moral outrage and demands for a high-profile response. The George H. W. Bush administration imposed sanctions immediately but also sought to preserve ties that could facilitate rehabilitation of the bilateral relationship when conditions allowed.

During the 1992 presidential campaign, Bill Clinton condemned Bush's coddling of the "butchers of Beijing." Congress, which often styles itself the conscience of the nation (in contrast to the executive branch, which is depicted as often pursuing American interests in ways that conflict with our values), twice blocked renewal of most favored nation trade status (now called permanent normal trade relations), but

---

23 *Freedom in the World 2020* (Washington, DC: Freedom House, 2020).

the legislation was vetoed by President Bush.[24] Clinton endorsed and signed similar legislation after he became president, no doubt because he agreed with its sentiment and because it contained a provision enabling him to waive the restriction if he determined that China had made progress in terms of respect for human rights.[25] Bush and Clinton were both appalled by the killing of student-led demonstrators, but both were also aware that the American business community was determined to protect and expand commercial undertakings in and with China. This was neither the first nor the last time that political pressure from the business community, which is also the principal funder of political campaigns in the United States, proved more influential than moral outrage and pressure from individuals and NGOs.

Foreign policy decisions in the United States (and in most countries) are shaped by competition among multiple groups with different skill, will, and political power. The example given above is by no means unique. At different times and for different reasons, calls for punitive actions to protest Israeli treatment of Palestinians, discriminatory treatment of Blacks and other non-whites by the South African government under Apartheid, gender and religious discrimination in Saudi Arabia, and the actions of right-wing and military regimes in Chile, Argentina, and other Latin American countries were less influential in shaping U.S. policy than were the views and pressure from powerful interest groups.[26] Many lessons can be drawn from these and

---

24   Congress has taken more critical—if still largely ineffective—positions on DPRK human rights issues than has the executive branch under various presidents. Examples include House passage of the North Korean Human Rights Act in 2017 by a vote of 416 to 0; and hearings on DPRK human rights in both the Senate and the House. See, for example, Emma Chanlett-Avery, *Congress and U.S. Policy on North Korean Human Rights and Refugees: Recent Legislation and Implementation*, Congressional Research Service RS22973, January 30, 2009, https://crsreports.congress.gov/product/pdf/RS/RS22973/5; and Victor Cha, "North Korean Human Rights Reorganization Act," George W. Bush Presidential Center, July 23, 2018, https://www.bushcenter.org/publications/articles/2018/07/reauthorization-human-rights-act.html.

25   See, for example, James Mann, *About Face: A History of America's Curious Relationship with China from Nixon to Clinton* (New York: Vintage, 2000).

26   Illustrative examples include John J. Mersheimer and Stephen M. Walt, *The Israel Lobby and U.S. Foreign Policy* (New York: Farrar, Straus, and Giroux, 2007); Alex Thomson, *U.S. Foreign Policy towards Apartheid South Africa, 1948–1994: Conflict of Interests* (New York: Palgrave Macmillan, 2008); Bruce Reidel, *Kings and Presidents: Saudi Arabia and the United States since FDR, Updated Edition* (Washington, DC: Brookings, 2019); and David F. Schmitz, *Thank God They're on*

other case studies but the one I wish to note here is that human rights, almost regardless of how outrageous the behavior of the repressive government, almost always carries less weight in the policymaking process than do many other objectives. A second is that efforts to improve the conditions of victims and address unacceptable policies of other governments are more effective when they are integrated with, rather than treated as separate from and morally superior to, other interests and objectives.

U.S. and ROK Roles and Responsibilities

As is noted by other contributors to this book (see especially chapters 2–4), the ROK and the United States have played leading roles in recurring efforts to illuminate, condemn, and address human rights violations in the DPRK. That is a demonstrable fact, as is the collapse of many such efforts when either or both have demurred from playing such a role.[27] The special roles that Seoul and Washington have played in forcing other nations to grapple with this issue are unsurprising but raise a number of puzzling questions about international responsibility for violation of universal rights. For example, since all UN member states have acknowledged such rights to be universal, why do other countries not step forward when the ROK or the United States steps back? Why is there an operative assumption that South Korea has special responsibility for addressing human rights problems in the North? I am not criticizing the special roles assumed by or attributed to the ROK and the United States but think it worth noting that the governments of both, and of other nations, seem to accept—and certainly do not challenge—the idea that it is appropriate for them to adjust the importance ascribed to human rights in the North on the basis of their own domestic and other international objectives. Violations of human rights may be unacceptable at all times and wherever they occur, but international practice does not demonstrate the same level of displeasure, even from the countries that have taken leading roles.

Our Side: The United States and Right-Wing Dictatorships, 1921–1965 (Chapel Hill, NC: University of North Carolina Press, 1999).

27 See Colum Lynch and Robbie Gramer, "Desperate to Save Diplomacy, White House Blocks UN Meeting on North Korean Atrocities," *Foreign Policy*, December 9, 2019, https://foreignpolicy.com/2019/12/09/white-house-blocks-un -meeting-north-korea-atrocities-trump-kim/.

Assuming that South Koreans have greater empathy for the plight of fellow Koreans, many of them relatives, living in the North than do people of other nationalities is understandable. But general acceptance of Seoul's "right" to ratchet attention to DPRK violations up and down in response to shifting priorities and policy strategies suggests that sovereignty, especially when exercised by a democratically elected government, trumps obligations to enforce universal rights. I write this as an empirical observation, not as a normative judgment about whether this should or should not be the case. But many serious and well-meaning people and NGOs do not agree that human rights violations in the DPRK or elsewhere should be subordinated to any other policy objectives (see chapter 5).

The role—and, for some, the responsibility—of the United States is different in at least two respects. One is that despite the fact that many Korean Americans share some of the sentiments and objectives of Koreans in the ROK, the vast majority of Americans do not. The plight of people in the North is—or should be—of concern to all Americans, but the intensity and priority of that concern tends to be lower for those who are not of Korean descent. However, widely shared notions of American exceptionalism and belief that the United States can and should be an exemplar and champion of American values and universal rights often impel Washington to take principled stands despite serious blemishes on our own human rights record. As the current—and long-overdue—demonstrations and demands to end racism and social injustice in the United States underscore, the U.S. claim to hold the moral high ground has always been hypocritical.

The self-declared responsibility to lead has been tarnished by recent developments, but the willingness of others to follow the U.S. lead on human rights and many other issues has been based less on acceptance of arrogant U.S. claims than on recognition that Washington has often been in a better position to lead than any other country. As a Chinese interlocutor put it a few years ago, the world needs leadership, and only the United States has the will and thick skin necessary to provide that leadership. Partly it is the U.S. ability to do the necessary homework, and partly it is Washington's willingness to pay the costs, but the U.S. thick skin is even more important. The United States can afford to propose ideas that are rejected. Most countries do not have the credibility to have ideas taken seriously and most leaders, including China's leaders, cannot afford to have proposals rejected by other nations. A failed attempt to lead on an important issue could be politically fatal for the regime and the individual leader. This analysis is flawed but, I believe, basically correct. The United States has often played a leading role because it can and because, on many issues, others want the promised outcome but not the responsibility for achieving it.

Those concerned about human rights violations in the DPRK, including some contributors to this volume, have called for the United States to revitalize the effort that it once led. Some go further and argue that it is a mistake to defer action to improve human rights in hope that restraint would improve prospects for denuclearization, because doing so prolongs the dire plight of the North Korean people and because Pyongyang will "never" surrender all of its nuclear weapons. Others argue that the United States can and should pursue both objectives simultaneously.[28] I will return to the question of whether and how denuclearization and human rights objectives should be pursued in the final section of this chapter but first must underscore that reassertion of U.S. leadership on human rights will be more difficult than in the past because our credentials are now badly tarnished. It will also be less likely because recent developments and the need to devote greater attention to domestic problems (social justice, the economy, infrastructure, healthcare, etc.) will use up government bandwidth that might otherwise have gone into addressing problems on the Korean Peninsula.

Will Seoul step forward when Washington remains reluctant to do so? Perhaps it will and perhaps it should. But what Seoul and Washington are willing and able to do will be influenced by the concerns of both about their bilateral relationship and the relations of each with China and Japan.[29] I raise this to make the simple but important point that human rights policy, denuclearization, and many other foreign policy concerns of both nations are enmeshed in larger sets of interconnected issues and embedded in layers of bureaucracy and prioritized

---

28   See, for example, the chapter by Victor Cha in this volume; and Victor Cha, "On the Eve of the Summit: Options for U.S. Diplomacy on North Korea," Testimony before the House Committee on Foreign Affairs, Subcommittee on Asia, the Pacific, and Proliferation, February 26, 2019, https://csis-website-prod.s3.amazonaws.com/s3fs-public/congressional_testimony/190225_Cha_Testimony.pdf.

29   See, for example, Nam Hoon Cho, Kuyuon Chung, Roberta Cohen, Patrick M. Cronin, Yong-sup Han, Bruce Klinger, Kongdan Oh, Andrew Injoo Park, and Hun Joo Park, *The Future of the U.S.-ROK Alliance* (Seattle, WA: National Bureau of Asian Research, 2017); and Clint Work, "Alternative Futures for the U.S.-ROK Alliance: Will Things Fall Apart?" 38 North, May 2020, https://www.38north.org/wp-content/uploads/pdf/2020-0507_Work-Clint_Alternative-Futures-for-the-US-ROK-Alliance.pdf.

objectives. Successful efforts to elevate the relative priority of human rights policy in the United States, South Korea, or other countries will require persistence, skill, and big-picture thinking.

A final question that must be posed, even if it cannot be answered, is whether sustained and significant international action to address human rights violations in the DPRK is possible without U.S.-ROK coordination and leadership. My short answer is, probably not. The United Nations is a venue through which nation-states can pursue their own objectives, but it is seldom, if ever, an autonomous actor. History indicates that although a number of other countries feel strongly about the situation in the North, none has been willing to invest the time, effort, and political capital to secure UN endorsement for narrowly focused human rights actions. To the extent that U.S. and ROK foreign policies have subordinated human rights in the North to other objectives and the United States has lost the will and moral authority to take the lead, human rights in the DPRK will remain an orphan issue that all will lament but no one will adopt.

Lessons and Implications: What Is to Be Done?

As noted in the opening sentence of this chapter, the human rights situation in the DPRK is deplorable. This is widely recognized and almost as widely condemned. The scope and magnitude of repression in the North is arguably greater than anywhere else on the planet because everyone, with the exception of a small elite, is a victim. But awareness, condemnation, and lamentation have had little discernable effect on the situation. Many policy responses have been proposed and some have been attempted. Precise measurement of their relative efficacy is impossible, but it seems fair to say that their individual and cumulative impact has been small and might be more negative than positive.

This is a harsh and dismaying judgment, but if we are to find more effective ways to address this very real problem, we must begin with an honest appraisal of where we are, how we got here, what we have tried, and what can be learned from past attempts. The chapters in this volume begin to do this. Their purpose is not to bemoan or belittle; it is to derive insights and lessons for what must be a continuing—and hopefully more efficacious—effort to improve the lot of the North Korean people. This chapter has endeavored to step back from a narrow focus on policies toward the DPRK human rights situation in order to illuminate how such policies fit into a larger foreign policy matrix. The remaining paragraphs will explore the implications of previously summarized findings for insights that might help to develop and implement more effective policies.

One starting point is to acknowledge—and work with—the reality of differential political power. As noted, more or less everyone would like to see improvement in the human rights situation in the DPRK, but few assign higher priority to that objective than to all others. As importantly, the human rights constituency (composed primarily of passionate individuals and narrowly focused NGOs) is a legitimate but weak player in the foreign policy arena. Other players/constituencies (e.g., national security interests, businesses and business associations, opponents of nuclear proliferation, etc.) have larger numbers, better access, and more political and bureaucratic heft. One can lament this situation and contend that moral issues should trump concerns about nuclear weapons or corporate profits, but doing so is unlikely to alter the balance of power. Even during the administration of Jimmy Carter, who did more to elevate the status of human rights concerns than any predecessor or successor, that balance shifted only marginally.[30] The implication for those wishing to secure more effective policies to address human rights problems in North Korea is clear. Attempts that present human rights considerations or policy options as more important than the goals of more powerful players are doomed to fail. If they are to have a greater chance of adoption, they must be conceived and presented as correlates of or contributing to achievement of higher priority goals. Doing so is not moral capitulation; it is smart politics.

If or to the extent that this analysis is correct, there are clear implications for choices between feel-good and more effective alternatives. Simply stated, it will be difficult to win support for proposals with the potential to impede achievement of higher priority goals if they are judged to be more likely to annoy or anger DPRK leaders than to achieve concrete improvement of human rights. An obvious corollary is to avoid overselling or overpromising.

Another lesson is that attempts to discredit, ignore, or isolate the regime have not worked. Suffice it to say that the regime in Pyongyang cannot be shamed into improving its human rights practices. Detailing and denouncing abuses is not going to cause remorse in the ruling

---

30   Itai Nartzizenfeld Sneh, *The Future Almost Arrived: How Jimmy Carter Failed to Change U.S. Foreign Policy* (New York: Peter Lang, 2008).

family. Similarly, refusing to meet with senior representatives of the regime, including Kim Jong-un, because meeting with them would give them "face" internally or externally is a sure recipe for stasis. It also is arrogant and unsupported by what we know about the North. There is simply no evidence that regime legitimacy is shaky in ways that can be exacerbated or ameliorated by meetings with foreign officials. And what relevant foreign audience might change its judgment about the regime and its human rights policies because one or another foreign leader was willing to meet? This argument against engagement is no more credible than is the argument that Pyongyang can be shamed into better behavior.

Yet another implication of this analysis is that demanding improved behavior on human rights as a precondition for engagement probably will fail, because it assumes the regime wants or needs engagement so badly that it would end repressive behaviors that it apparently thinks have value worthy of the real and opportunity costs of maintaining them. As noted earlier, we do not know enough about why the regime represses human rights in the way that it does for us to make informed judgments about what pressures or inducements would cause Pyongyang to change its behavior.

My final observation or implication is that any proposals seeking to integrate negotiations and tradeoffs on human rights into broader foreign policies must clarify whether the goal is to work with or against the regime. In other words, is it to achieve human rights, denuclearization, and/or some other combination of objectives even though doing so could, and probably would, increase regime legitimacy and prolong its existence, or is it to erode legitimacy and capacity to satisfy the needs and aspirations of the people in order to speed its demise? This is not a trivial question because if policy advocates do not know or cannot explain what they want to achieve and cannot demonstrate that they have thought through the costs, risks, and potential benefits of proposed actions, they will find it very difficult to marshal the support needed to make human rights part of the overall policy package. Absent evidence and persuasive arguments to the contrary, Pyongyang will assume that any initiative from the ROK, the United States, or elsewhere is intended to weaken the regime.

Index

f denotes figure; *t* denotes table

North Korea: access to information in, 13–16; awareness of human rights situation in, 46–47; as boasting of its supposed independence, 190; censorship in, 75; changing information environment in, 103–22; East Germany as compared to, 187–88; economic changes in, 153; economic growth in, 177; elite loyalty in, 7–8; emergence of defector-activists, 78; "freedom scores" of, 217; humanitarian crises in, 145; ideology of, 203; impacts of famine in, 105, 158, 177; information control in, 104, 105; information wall around, 81, 82; as more closed than East Germany ever was, 203; no actual religion as practiced in, 200–201; nuclear development in, 83–84; one case of bilateral human rights dialogue with, 47–48; as one of world's worst human rights abusers, 5; as one of worst human rights disasters in modern era, 158; as only country that has attempted to withdraw from international covenant on human rights, 10; percentage of households with computers, 82; percentage of households with Notel, 82; political prison camps in, 48, 69; politics of human rights issues in, 80; as precarious house of cards, 8; punishments in, 7; refugees from, 164, 164*t*; retrograde ideology of, 189; special economic zones (SEZs) in, 153; system of rewards in, 7; treatment of dissidents in, 195. *See also* Democratic People's Republic of Korea (DPRK)
North Korea Intellectuals Solidarity, 100*t*

North Korean Criminal Code, as response to influx of foreign media, 124–25
North Korean Human Rights Act (NKHRA), 16, 56–57, 60–61, 84, 94, 161–62, 164, 167, 170
North Korean Human Rights Documentation Office, 56
North Korean Human Rights Foundation, 56, 94, 166, 167
North Korean Human Rights Report, 94
North Korean TV, 108
North Korea Reform Radio, 89
North Korea Sanctions and Policy Enhancement Act (2016) (NKSPEA), 171
North Korea Strategy Center (NKSC), 99*t*
Notel, as means of information transfer, 82, 84, 89*t*, 92, 109, 113
Now Action & Unity for Human Rights (NAUH), 100*t*
nuclear crisis, origins of and need for change, 151–54
nuclear development: grim environment of in North Korea, 83–84; origins of, 151
nuclear issue: Beijing's proposal for resolving, 153; Biden administration's understanding of, 152; as toughest stumbling block in order for two Koreas to get back on road to cooperation and future reunification, 58
Nye, Joe, 213

Obama, Barack, 61, 71
Office of the UN High Commissioner for Human Rights (OHCHR), 26, 32, 46n2, 70, 71, 160, 161
Open North Korea Radio, 89, 90*f*
Optional Protocol on the Rights of the Child (UN), 11

The authorized representative in the EU for product safety and compliance is:
Mare Nostrum Group
B.V Doelen 72
4831 GR Breda
The Netherlands

www.ingramcontent.com/pod-product-compliance
Lightning Source LLC
Chambersburg PA
CBHW071851270326
41929CB00013B/2192